AFRICAN ISSUES

Women & Peacebuilding in Africa

T0375005

AFRICAN ISSUES

AFRICAN ISSUES

Women & Peacebuilding in Africa

Edited by

Ladan Affi, Liv Tønnessen & Aili Mari Tripp

JAMES CURREY

James Currey
is an imprint of
Boydell & Brewer Ltd
PO Box 9, Woodbridge
Suffolk IP12 3DF (GB)
www.jamescurrey.com
and of
Boydell & Brewer Inc.
668 Mt Hope Avenue
Rochester, NY 14620-2731 (US)
www.boydellandbrewer.com

British Library Cataloguing in Publication Data
A catalogue record for this book is available from the British Library

ISBN 978-1-84701-281-4 (James Currey paperback)
ISBN 978-1-84701-282-1 (James Currey hardback)

The publisher has no responsibility for the continued existence or accuracy of
URLs for external or third-party internet websites referred to in this book, and does not
guarantee that any content on such websites is, or will remain, accurate or appropriate.

This publication is printed on acid-free paper

Printed and bound in Great Britain by
TJ Books Ltd, Padstow, Cornwall

CONTENTS

ILLUSTRATIONS

NOTES ON CONTRIBUTORS

Ladan Affi is a political scientist who received her PhD from the University of Wisconsin-Madison. She has taught and researched at several universities in the US, Djibouti, Qatar, and the United Arab Emirates, where she is now based. She is currently an Assistant Professor at Zayed University. She has carried out extensive research there and published in the area of gender and politics in Somalia, piracy off the Horn of Africa, the role of diaspora in Somalia's development, and conflict and governance within fragile states.

Hauwa Abdu Biu is a Professor of Curriculum and Instruction and Dean of the Faculty of Education in the Department of Education, University of Maiduguri, Borno State in Nigeria. She obtained her B.Sc.Ed. and M.Ed. from the University of Maiduguri and a doctorate from Kenyatta University, Kenya. Professor Biu's research focuses on gender issues, with an emphasis on bridge-building between communities (peace negotiation and mediation), training of trainers on gender issues, capacity-building, and conflict resolution and participatory rural appraisal. A women's rights activist, Hauwa Biu is the Borno State coordinator of BAOBAB for Women's Human Rights, and has been active in the campaign to BringBackOurGirls, liaising with the Chibok community, among others.

Samia El-Nagar worked as a part-time lecturer at the Regional Institute for Gender, Diversity Peace and Rights (RIGDPR) at the Ahfad University for Women from 1996 to 2019. Before that she was a Lecturer at the University of Khartoum. Presently she is working on a project 'Assisting Regional Universities in Sudan and South Sudan'. Between 2011 and 2014 she was lead researcher in a collaborative project with Chr. Michelsen Institute (CMI), Norway, and the Regional Institute of Gender, Diversity, Peace and Rights (RIGDPR), Ahfad University, on 'Gender Justice and Violence against Women'. El-Nagar has published extensively on women and conflict in Sudan, gender quotas, women's rights reform in Sudan, and the women's movement in Sudan. She serves on the Advisory Board of Babiker Badri Scientific Association for Women's Studies, which focuses on reproductive rights. A Sudanese national, she is active in MANSAM, a women's organisation established in the wake of the Sudanese revolution in 2019.

Ayesha Imam is a Nigerian researcher, women's rights activist, and consultant. She has published widely for policy, academic, and activist uses, including *The Devil is in the Details: At the Nexus of Development, Women's Rights, and Religious Fundamentalisms* (AWID 2016), *Women in Search of Citizenship: Experiences from West Africa* (KIT 2013), *Warning Signs of Fundamentalisms* (2004), writing for and co-editing *Knowing Our Rights: Women, Family, Laws and Customs in the Muslim World* (Women Living Under Muslim Laws, 2003, 2006, French edition 2014), and *Engendering African Social Sciences* (CODESRIA, 1994, 1996, French edition 2004). She has worked with and for a range of organisations, including those on women's rights, international NGOs, official aid, and UN agencies on women's rights (including in customary, religious, and secular rights regimes), gender-sensitive research and programming, democracy, sustainable development, organisational support, and training. She is a member of Development Alternatives with Women for a New Era (DAWN)'s Executive Committee. She was the founding Executive Director of BAOBAB for Women's Human Rights (which initiated and led the anti-stoning sentence campaigns in Nigeria), a founding member of the African Feminist Forum, active in the international solidarity network Women Living Under Muslim Laws and on the Board of Greenpeace International (Chair since 2017).

Helen Kezie-Nwoha is the Executive Director of Women's International Peace Centre (formerly ISIS-Wicce). With an academic background in gender and international development and over 16 years of experience working on women's rights, gender, peacebuilding and conflict resolution, and governance, she provides leadership in resource mobilisation, institutional visioning, and management. She has led regional and international training and research programmes and advocacy on peace and security in Africa (Liberia, South Sudan, Uganda, Democratic Republic of Congo, Sierra Leone, and Burundi) and Asia. She has also provided technical support for peace mediation engagements by women activists in Burundi and Democratic Republic of Congo. Helen has co-authored the following publications: *Making Gender-Just Remedy and Reparation Possible: Upholding the Rights of Women and Girls in the Greater North of Uganda* (Isis-WICCE, Feinstein International Center, Tufts University, 2013) and *Women's Participation in Post Conflict Reconstruction: The Case of Burundi, Liberia and Sierra Leone* (Isis-WICCE, 2013); *Policy Brief on Gaps between Policy and the Reproductive Health Needs of Women* (Isis-WICCE, 2011); *Policy Brief on Addressing Women's Post Conflict Needs in Uganda* (Isis-WICCE, 2012); Kezie-Nwoha, H. and Brown, J., *Technical Brief: Africa Transformation – Examining Gender Norms and Transforming Lives* (Department for International Development, 2009).

Liv Tønnessen is a Research Director at the Chr. Michelsen Institute (CMI) in Bergen, Norway. She is a political scientist researching women, politics, and Islam in the Middle East and Northern Africa, with long-term stays in Sudan, Lebanon, and Syria. Specialising in Sudanese politics for more than a decade, Tønnessen has conducted extensive fieldwork in the country and lectured at Ahfad University for Women. A Norwegian, Tønnessen is currently involved in the research projects 'Political determinants of sexual and reproductive health: Criminalisation, health impacts and game changers', 'Women and Peacebuilding in Africa', and assisting regional universities in Sudan. Tønnessen has published extensively, her most recent publications being, co-authored with Ragnhild Muriaas and Vibeke Wang, 'Counter-mobilization against child marriage reform in Africa', *Political Studies* (2018), co-authored with Samia al-Nagar, 'The politicization of abortion and Hippocratic disobedience in Islamist Sudan', *Health and Human Rights Journal* (2019), and 'Women at work in Sudan: Marital privilege or constitutional right' *Social Politics* (2019). She is a founding member of the Norwegian Center for Humanitarian Studies, and she serves on the steering committee for the Center on Law and Social Transformation.

Aili Mari Tripp is Wangari Maathai Professor of Political Science and Gender and Women's Studies at the University of Wisconsin-Madison. Tripp's research has focused in recent years on women and politics in Africa, the gendered nature of peacebuilding, women's movements in Africa, and transnational feminism. Her current research involves a comparative study of women and legal reform in North Africa. Her most recent book is *Seeking Legitimacy: Why Arab Autocracies Adopt Women's Rights* (Cambridge University Press, 2019). She is the author of several award-winning books, including *Women and Power in Postconflict Africa* (Cambridge University Press, 2015), *Museveni's Uganda: Paradoxes of Power in a Hybrid Regime* (Lynne Rienner 2010), co-authored with Isabel Casimiro, Joy Kwesiga, and Alice Mungwa, *African Women's Movements: Transforming Political Landscapes* (Cambridge University Press, 2009), and *Women and Politics in Uganda* (James Currey, 2000). She has also co-edited (with Balghis Badri) *Women's Activism in Africa* (Zed Publishers, 2017), (with Myra Marx Ferree and Christina Ewig) *Gender, Violence, and Human Security: Critical Feminist Perspectives* (New York University Press, 2013), (with Myra Marx Ferree) *Global Feminism: Transnational Women's Activism* (New York University Press, 2006), *Organizing, and Human Rights* and (with Joy Kwesiga) *The Women's Movement in Uganda: History, Challenges and Prospects* (University of Wisconsin Press, James Currey and Fountain Press, 2002).

Juliet Were has been the Program Manager at the Women's International Peace Centre (formerly ISIS-Wicce) since 2016. She is responsible for strategic programme planning, design, implementation, and monitoring, and evaluation in line with programme quality procedures. Before this, she was the organisation's Research, Monitoring, and Evaluation Coordinator. She has led the conceptualisation and coordinated studies and programmes in Africa (Uganda, South Sudan, Democratic Republic of Congo, Liberia, Sierra Leone, Burundi) and Asia (Nepal and Kashmir) on governance, peace and security, women's health, and related development issues. She has co-authored a number of publications, including *Women's Experiences During the Armed Conflict in Southern Sudan, 1983–2005* (Isis-WICCE research report in collaboration with Central Equatorial State, Juba and Totto Chan Trauma Centre, 2007) and *Unveiling Justice: Rape Survivors Speak out; A Report on Access to Justice for Rape Survivors in Nepal* (Women's Rehabilitation Centre, Nepal 2011).

Maina Yahi was born in Maiduguri in 1983 and is a resident of Chibok local government of Borno State. He obtained his BSc Education (business) and MSc in marketing from the University of Maiduguri, in Borno State, Nigeria. Yahi is involved in humanitarian work; he has worked with BAOBAB for Women's Human Rights, and the United Nations' World Food Programme.

ACKNOWLEDGEMENT

This manuscript was produced with the generous support of the Carnegie Corporation of New York, the Norwegian Foreign Ministry, the Center for Research on Gender and Women at the University of Wisconsin, the Christian Michaelson Institute in Norway, and the Women's International Peace Centre (formerly Isis-WICCE) in Uganda. Many thanks to Kaden Paulson-Smith for their assistance in finalising the manuscript.

ABBREVIATIONS

ARCSS	Agreement on the Resolution of the Conflict in South Sudan
CEDAW	Convention on the Elimination of All Forms of Discrimination Against Women
DDR	Disarmament, demobilisation, and reintegration
FFC	Forces for Freedom and Change (Sudan)
FIS	Islamic Salvation Front (Algeria)
FLN	National Liberation Front (Algeria)
ICC	International Criminal Court
IDP	Internally displaced people
IGAD	Intergovernmental Authority on Development
INGO	International nongovernmental organisation
MENA	Middle East and North Africa
MNSM	Civil and Political Sudanese Coalition
NGO	Nongovernmental organisation
OECD	Organisation for Economic Co-operation and Development
PCVE	Preventing and Countering Violent Extremism
SAVE	Struggle against violent extremism
TMC	Transitional military council (Sudan)
UN	United Nations
UNDP	United Nations Development Programme
UNMISS	UN Mission in South Sudan
UNOCHA	United Nations Office for the Coordination of Humanitarian Affairs
UNOHCR	UN Office of the High Commissioner for Human Rights
UNSC	United Nations Security Council
UNSCR	United Nations Security Council Resolution
WPC	Women Peace Committees (South Sudan)

TUNISIA

MOROCCO

ALGERIA

LIBYA

EGYPT

WESTERN
SAHARA

CAPE VERDE

MAURITANIA

MALI

NIGER

CHAD

SUDAN

ERITREA

DJIBOUTI

SENEGAL

GAMBIA

GUINEA-
BISSAU

GUINEA

BURKINA
FASO

BENIN

CÔTE
D'IVOIRE

TOGO

GHANA

NIGERIA

CENTRAL AFRICAN
REPUBLIC

SOUTH
SUDAN

ETHIOPIA

SIERRA
LEONE

LIBERIA

CAMEROON

SOMALIA

EQUATORIAL
GUINEA

UGANDA

KENYA

GABON

CONGO

RWANDA

SEYCHELLES

DEMOCRATIC REPUBLIC
OF CONGO

BURUNDI

TANZANIA

ZANZIBAR

COMOROS

ANGOLA

ZAMBIA

MALAWI

MADAGASCAR

MAURITIUS

ZIMBABWE

MOZAMBIQUE

REUNION

NAMIBIA

BOTSWANA

SWAZILAND

SOUTH
AFRICA

LESOTHO

1000 km
500 miles

1

Introduction

The Gendering of Peacebuilding in Africa

AILI MARI TRIPP

In October 2000, Namibia, which held the presidency of the United Nations Security Council at the time, brought a seminal resolution to the floor of the Council. After considerable pushback from Security Council members, the resolution, UNSCR 1325, was finally passed. It was to redefine women's role in peacebuilding (Ileke and Imene-Chanduru 2020). It recognised the importance of women's participation and the inclusion of gender perspectives in peace negotiations, humanitarian activities, peacekeeping operations, and postconflict peacebuilding and governance. Twenty years after the passage of UNSCR 1325, there is widespread recognition that although some gains have been made, there is still a long way to go to fully implement this resolution and to do so in a way that more fully accounts for the many ways both men and women are treated in peacebuilding. This has particular bearing on Africa because some of the deadliest conflicts can be found on the continent, in the areas affected by Boko Haram, the Sahel, South Sudan, and Somalia.

Peacebuilding is commonly understood to involve measures aimed at reducing the risk of return to conflict by strengthening national capacity for conflict management and laying the foundation for durable peace and development. Traditionally, peacebuilding has included support for conflict prevention through the protection of civilians; peacemaking through the use of diplomacy, negotiations, and community strategies; peacekeeping through external interventions supported by the UN or regional peacekeepers; and disarmament, demobilisation, and reintegration (DDR) programmes; along with security sector reform. And finally, peacebuilding has included transitional justice mechanisms that focus on inclusive dialogue, reconciliation and truth processes, and strengthening the rule of law.

Many of these liberal peacebuilding strategies have been seen as problematic because they have focused almost exclusively on formal statebuilding and technocratic solutions, the professionalisation of personnel, standardisation of operating procedures, and honing best practices focused on the state. These types of strategies have been carried out to the exclusion of grassroots activities (Mac Ginty and Firchow 2016). Critics of peacebuilding and statebuilding have argued that these strategies, as they have been implemented, have not always delivered results and that they are an extension of Western ideology, promoting a free market economy and creating countries dependent on Western aid (Bindi and Tufekci 2018). Although most of the attention has focused on formal and national processes, increasingly, informal peace processes are seen as seeking to influence formal processes, but also activities aimed at grassroots solutions, issues of survival, and equal rights (United Nations 2002). However, in spite of this recognition, much of the focus still remains on formal and national processes.

A key challenge to conventional peacebuilding has been the difficulty of incorporating gender perspectives. Gender was formally included in discussions of peacebuilding after 2000, when the UNSC passed Resolution 1325 on women, peace, and security, stating the importance of women's participation and the inclusion of gender perspectives in peace negotiations, humanitarian activities, peacekeeping operations, and postconflict peacebuilding and governance. Subsequent resolutions strengthened this original resolution. However, there is still a long way to go to fully implement this resolution and to implement it in a way that more fully accounts for the many ways both men and women are treated in peacebuilding.

This book is concerned with what is at stake in continuing exclusions of women from the negotiating table and postconflict governance structures, and from not having women's concerns accounted for in legislation and transitional justice processes. But it also shows the difference women's informal peacebuilding activities make, the importance of women's representation in postconflict governance structures, and the importance of women's demands for legal reform in pushing back against, in particular, conservative Islamist forces that today dominate much of the armed conflict we see in many parts of Africa.

This book aims to show how the failure to recognise women's many contributions becomes a major cost to peacebuilding efforts. Through a focus on the gendered nature of peacebuilding in five African countries – Algeria, Nigeria, Somalia, South Sudan, and Sudan – it demonstrates the resourcefulness of women; how they create spaces within patriarchal structures to relieve the immediate effects of conflict on women in their communities; how they constantly redefine what is necessary for sustainable peace; and their consistent struggle for a seat at peace tables and in leadership in general.

Centring the experiences of women working on the frontlines of conflict and peacebuilding, the book builds on original field research from five African countries that have experienced different forms of conflict, ranging from civil wars in the cases of Algeria, Somalia, Sudan, and South Sudan; conflict and ineffective governance driven by the presence of terrorist organisations in the cases of Nigeria and Somalia; and the forced implementation of extremist Islamist agendas specifically directed at women in the cases of Sudan and Algeria. African researchers and women's rights activists have been the driving forces behind this research exploring largely understudied contexts. The book focuses on three themes: 1) women's exclusion from formal peacebuilding processes in postconflict governance, but also women's continuous struggle for a seat at the table; 2) women's informal peacebuilding, demonstrating the ingenuity of women and how they create spaces within patriarchal structures; and 3) women stemming the tide of Islamist extremism through multiple avenues, including legal contestation and everyday resistance.

While there is extensive literature that shows how conflict is gendered, this introductory chapter and the book more generally argue that peacebuilding is also gendered. It is gendered in the imbalance of women represented in peacekeeping forces and peace talks; in the issues incorporated in or left out of peace accords; in the way in which women's experiences are included in transitional justice mechanisms; in the way women and men are treated in disarmament, demobilisation, and reintegration processes; and in the extent to which women are included in postconflict governance structures. The consequences of these 'oversights' are serious. Studies have shown that not including women in peace talks can prolong the conflict or contribute to reigniting a conflict (Krause, Krause, and Bränfors 2018). It means that women's concerns, which impact not only women's welfare but the entire household, are not adequately attended to, and it means that women are relegated to informal peacebuilding activities and to the margins.

Given these patterns, it is astonishing to note that the literature on peacebuilding in Africa and more generally has virtually ignored the role of women in peacebuilding (Chetail 2009; Curtis and Dzinesa 2012; Newman and Richmond 2009). Few look at women's peacebuilding activities and their demands, even though these activities can be quite extensive and a potential resource for national peacebuilding efforts. Even the burgeoning literature on local-level, indigenous, and informal peacebuilding strategies largely ignores the role of women (see, for example, Mac Ginty and Firchow 2016; Luckham 2017; Lee and Özerdem 2015; Randazzo 2016; Leonardsson and Rudd 2015).

By the same token, most of the feminist security studies literature has problematised the gendered nature of the way in which security is understood. In the area of peacebuilding, it has engaged in critiques of international norms and practices regarding international treaties and peacekeeping efforts. However, little attention has been paid to what women themselves have actually done on the ground to build peace, especially informal strategies, and women's efforts to fight exclusion in peacebuilding. Perhaps this is because of the essentialist (considering women only in their 'natural' roles as women or mothers) ways in which women and peacebuilding have sometimes been framed and a fear that this will lead to further stereotyping women and men and pigeonholing women into restricted roles.

The case studies in this book show how peacebuilding is gendered in some important ways and why that matters in developing meaningful and sustainable approaches to peacebuilding. It shows how even in the best of circumstances, women are all too often excluded from formal peacemaking and peacebuilding processes, are relegated to working from the sidelines as observers, or are limited to informal peacebuilding strategies. As important as these informal strategies are, they are often devalued, and women peacebuilders remain marginalised and often unnoticed by the powers that be. Yet there is enormous potential in these strategies as women often strive to build bridges across political, ethnic, religious, clan, and other differences and address sources of conflict both at the national and local levels. These alliances arise out of common concerns women have around violence, land, access to resources, and protection of their families and communities. They also often arise out of necessary quotidian concerns that give them particular urgency. And these strategies often take peacebuilding as a process and not something that has an end point like peace talks or peace accords.

This chapter looks at how peacebuilding is gendered. It first looks at how feminist theory has regarded the gendering of violence and feminist approaches to peacebuilding. It then looks at women's exclusions from formal peace processes and how women's organisations have nevertheless sought to influence those processes, largely through grassroots pressure and informal strategies. It then shows how and why women's organisations were often orientated towards building bridges across difference. Finally, the chapter concludes by examining the extent to which women activists have engaged in initiatives involving regional and international organisations in order to put pressure on governments through the international arena. Women's multilevel strategies involving institutions at the local, national, regional, and international levels have complemented each other in important ways, while reflecting varied goals and opportunities.

How Violence Constitutes Gender and is Constituted by Gender

Building on the work of Judith Butler, Laura Shepherd (2008) argues that changing and dynamic understandings of gender are reproduced, reified, and reconstituted through violence and insecurity. Gender is a power relationship and it is therefore implicated in violence, which is gendered. She sees gender as a way of ordering society. At the same time violence recreates gender relations in a dynamic way. Gender myths help maintain that hierarchical ordering of society. Culture and history influence how gender is performed, reproduced, and constituted through violence over time. Thus, simply addressing the problem of violence against women does nothing to change the gendered order that is produced through violence. It means that action merely directed at providing shelters, counselling, and treating 'victims' is inadequate because it does not tackle the broader issue of how security is conceptualised in the first place and the underlying problem of power imbalances that give rise to violence.

Feminist scholars have argued that state foreign policies are influenced by masculinity, heterosexism, and the gendered nature of militarism (Peterson and Runyan 1999). As Rigual (2018) explains, violence is linked to gender relations through hierarchical masculinist social arrangements in which men exercise power and dominate women through a variety of governmental, societal, economic, religious, and cultural institutions, as well as through violence and 'the social construction of masculinities and femininities which support a militarized state'.

One of the ways in which discourses of security function is to place the state as the boundary between the domestic and international spheres to protect internal and external sovereignty, with the assumption that the state acts in the best interests of its citizens.

Feminist security scholars have examined the relationship between masculinity and war: men are regarded as fighters, and when they are seen as peacemakers, they are seen as 'protectors of vulnerable women', as is amply evident in UN documents (Enloe 2002). However, in many contexts women are fighters. In Sierra Leone and Liberia, for example, about 20–30 per cent of the fighters were women, yet in these same conflicts, women featured prominently as peacemakers as well. Not fully accounting for this meant that DDR programmes did not adequately respond to the needs of women fighters after the war, particularly those who were not involved in combat roles, but were nevertheless involved with the militia. Generally, when we do hear about women in conflict in the media and in the literature of international and national policymakers, donors, development practitioners, military strategists, and even some of the Women, Peace, and Security community, they are still often framed as victims, survivors, mothers, and other reductionist tropes. Take, for example, African peace accords, 28 of which since 1990 draw on the language of 'vulnerability' to talk about women, children, and other groups. According to the Sun City Accords for the Democratic Republic of Congo, 'NOTING that the armed conflict has increased discrimination against women thus violating the universal principle of equal rights and respect for human dignity, rendering women more vulnerable' (UN 2003, 48). Thus, the performance of gender is expressed through the performance of security and vice versa.

Feminist Perspectives on Peacebuilding

Just as war is gendered, so is peacebuilding. Feminist security scholars have critiqued the essentialist link that is so often drawn between women and peace. One of the most common popular frames has to do with the perception that women have a natural affinity to peacemaking and are reluctant to endorse violence to resolve conflicts. Women's role as peacebuilders is often mythologised in ways that are essentialising. Simplistic assumptions suggest that women, often because of innate qualities, are key to peace. While the critique of these tropes is not new, the persistence of such frames continues to capture the popular imagination, without fully accounting for women's roles in promoting and participating in war or men's roles in promoting peace. Such assumptions drive the financing of peacebuilding by donors and determine which policy strategies gain traction for women's rights actors. Thus, feminist security studies has been wary of such associations between women and peacemaking, in part, because it can easily fall back on essentialised notions of women's innate capability or desire to be peacemakers.

To the extent that gender has been examined in relation to peacebuilding, it has generally been in the context of looking at how male peacekeepers enact masculinity (Higate and Henry 2004); the treatment of nonconforming gender and sexuality in the military; and the gendered basis of the 'combatant/non-combatant' distinction and its discriminatory operation in conflict management and peacekeeping (Kinsella 2004). Women are treated primarily as victims rather than as combatants, while men are seen mainly as fighters rather than as civilians, thus reifying gender binaries. Some look at gendered experiences of peacebuilding within community initiatives and at 'everyday violence' (Rigual 2018).

An extensive feminist literature examines the causes of violence and how to create peace, in which generally the goals have been to transform existing patriarchal structures of domination, which are seen as promoting violence, and paying attention to women's security needs while seeking peace through nonviolent means. Some have focused on how to reform institutions like UNSCR 1325 through gender mainstreaming, while others have been sceptical of the entire peacebuilding agenda because of the limitations of UNSCR 1325. Few of these approaches look at the peacebuilding activities of women themselves and what women want in specific contexts, as we do in this book. Generally speaking, there has not been as robust a discussion on the gendering of peacebuilding in the feminist literature as there has been on conflict.

One of the reasons for this, as mentioned earlier, is that one of the most common tropes in popular discourse worldwide draws on connections between women's peacemaking and what many consider their essentialised roles as women or mothers. There are, nevertheless, a variety of ways in which some feminists have explained women's peacemaking roles. To be sure, some see motherhood as a basis for women's engagement in peace activism (Naples 1998; Rupp 1997). For others, the gender division that they claim links men to the use of force and women to an affinity with peacemaking in international conflicts is reduced to sex-specific physiological differences, such as reproductive ability (Daly 1984). For Sara Ruddick (1995), it is not so much a biological imperative but, rather, the act of mothering (by men or women) that lies at the basis of the connection between women and peace, because it makes people more caring and empathetic of others.

Some feminists have argued that women use motherhood strategically to give their movements greater leverage and credibility and to broaden their base of support (Swerdlow 1993; Taylor 1997). There is often a stereotypical belief in society that women are less threatening than men, thus allowing women greater room to manoeuvre in public spheres than men during war and emboldening them to transform their private suffering into public protest. This sometimes allows women to protest relatively unscathed in contexts where men protesters might invite greater retribution (Sharoni 2001, 92–93). During the *hirak* protest movement in Algeria against the government (2019–20), it was often noted by observers and protesters themselves that the large presence of women had the effect of keeping the protests from becoming violent, subduing both the military and the men protesters. Some scholars have noted that wars break down the public and private spheres as homes become locations of raids by soldiers and sites of destruction, thus pushing women into public action (Aretxaga 1997, 54, 69).

Variants of the maternal peace argument have come under criticism by those who find that it is not supported empirically. For example, mothers' and fathers' attitudes towards militarism and war in the United States do not differ significantly from those of non-mothers and non-fathers (Conover and Sapiro 1993, 1087). Others, however, criticise the conflation of women and motherhood with the idea that women are by nature peaceful. They point out the many ways in which motherhood has been used to serve racist practices and militarised nationalism – for example, in Nazi Germany (Koontz 1997). Some women have been willing accomplices in nationalist or ethnic propaganda campaigns, idealising women and mothers of a particular group in ways that may serve to foment conflict with other groups (Waller and Rycenga 2001). Motherhood, according to Cynthia Cockburn (2004), thus skirts dangerously close to patriarchal definitions of women's roles that can be coopted by nationalisms. Women and mothers thus have historically played and continue to play significant roles in promoting wars and even in participating in war as fighters.

Yet another line of argumentation draws on the actual experiences of women in peacebuilding. For example, Women in Black in Kosovo in the 1990s mobilised to demand effective international peacekeeping. Because women had not been subjected to male socialisation and narrow constructions of masculinity, they were freer to pursue nonviolent strategies in this context (Cockburn 2004, 38). In Africa, some have argued that patriarchal gender relations are transformed in the context of war as women assume men's tasks and gain access to new public spaces. The absence of male household members may give women the space that they might not otherwise have to participate in civil society organisations and in peace initiatives (Tripp 2015). Some have argued that this is often accompanied by a backlash in the postconflict context, where women are pushed back into their former roles after the conflict subsides (Meintjes 2001, 72; Turshen 2001, 80).

The chapters in this volume show that peacebuilding at different stages during and after conflict is gendered in the same way that Shepherd (2008) and others have argued that war is gendered. Like violence, it creates and reifies existing gendered power relationships. We diverge from the essentialist interpretations of the link between women and peacebuilding as something innate or natural to women, by recognising that these are constructed activities that are forged out of common experiences. Because women are so often relegated to the frontline of survival when it comes to caring for their households, they are forced to confront common issues and realities, which they act on.

How Peacebuilding is Gendered

The central argument of this chapter is that peacebuilding is gendered and that it reinforces or recreates gender. It is a reflection of a set of power relations that are gendered, but it is also shaped by class, ethnicity, race, and other differences. As in conflict, women and men are constrained by socialisation and social expectations of their roles. Women are marginalised from certain aspects of peacebuilding, and when formal avenues are closed, they may pursue informal means. There are, however, some moments when women can play larger public roles than men because they are less likely to be targeted as potential militia. Essentialist understandings of gender often shape what types of peacebuilding activities are open to men and women, further gendering peacebuilding.

A number of key features have characterised women's peace mobilisation at all levels in the post-Cold War era in Africa, but also elsewhere. Although women's organisations have often tried to participate in formal peace negotiations and disarmament processes, they have been largely excluded, with their contributions to peacemaking unrecognised, even after the passage of UNSCR 1325. The focus on warlords, on rebel militia, and on government priorities sidelines the interests of half the population, who despite fierce efforts to be represented are rarely given more than a few seats at the negotiating table or, more commonly, have very little direct input into the outcome. Moreover, formal peace processes dominate the scholarship, media reports, and the attention of policymakers, thus pushing women's local and informal contributions out of the picture. These local contributions have not received the recognition they deserve because of their quotidian nature: they are not out of the ordinary, nor do they always directly impact the national-level peace negotiations. Yet they are every bit as important in impacting the daily lives of communities and families.

Women's presence in formal processes is minimal. The number of women peacekeepers has historically been low: only 20 women served as UN peacekeepers between 1957 and 1989 (Karim and Henry 2018). After UNSCR 1325 was adopted in 2000 acknowledging the unique impact of conflict on women, the numbers increased: by 2019 women made up only 4.7 per cent of military personnel and 10.8 per cent of police personnel in UN Peacekeeping missions. The 2028 target for women serving in military contingents is 15 per cent, and 25 per cent for military observers and staff officers.[1] About 35 per cent of heads of UN peacekeeping and special political missions and 48 per cent of their deputy heads are women.

Women and women's rights have been largely excluded from peace negotiations in all parts of the world even after the passage of UNSCR 1325 in 2000, which was intended to remedy this by calling 'on all actors involved, when negotiating and implementing peace agreements, to adopt a gender perspective'. Nevertheless, peace agreements have incorporated women's rights language as a result of domestic and international pressures. This is evident in Africa, as references to women's rights between 2000 and 2012 tripled in all peace agreements from 12 per cent to 34 per cent and more than doubled in all comprehensive peace agreements from 33 per cent to 78 per cent compared with the previous decade, based on data from the UN Peacemaker.[2]

According to the University of Edinburgh Peace Agreements Database (Bell et al. 2019), between 1990 and 2019, 30 per cent (164 out of 554) of the various peace agreements in Africa (excluding North Africa) had references to women, gender, or sexual violence. This helped set the stage for the later incorporation of women's rights into constitutions and legislation, as well as for women's presence in key governmental, legislative, and transitional institutions. The percentage of references to gender in African peace agreements was far greater than in other regions of the world (Table 1.1). A similar pattern emerges when it comes to women's rights in constitutional reforms, in which African constitutions have a higher number of provisions per constitution than any other part of the world (UN Women 2019). This is especially visible in postconflict constitutions. These reforms are particularly evident in clauses pertaining to gender equality, anti-discrimination, customary law, violence against women, quotas, and citizenship rights (Paulson-Smith and Tripp *forthcoming*). The relatively large number of women's rights peacekeeping provisions in Africa can probably be attributed to

---

[1] https://peacekeeping.un.org/en/women-peacekeeping (accessed 18 May 2021).
[2] https://peacemaker.un.org/ (accessed 18 May 2021).

Table 1.1. References to Women's Rights in Peace Agreements by Region.

Region	Agreements referencing women, gender, or sexual violence	
	Percentage	Number of references in agreements
Africa	30	164/554
Middle East and North Africa	15	39/262
Latin America	21	40/195
Europe and Eurasia	11	44/410
Asia and Pacific	20	72/377
World (excluding Africa)	16	195/1244

Source: http://peaceagreements.org (accessed 20 May 2020)

the extent to which there has been mobilisation by women's movements in affected countries around these concerns both locally and regionally. The West Africa Network for Peacebuilding (WANEP), Federation of African Women's Peace Networks (FERFAP), Mano River Union Women Peace Network (MARWOPNET), Femmes Afrique Solidarité (FAS), and Women's International Peace Centre (WIPC) have been among the many active regional movements collaborating around women's rights in contexts of conflict. The African Women Leaders Network is among the many organisations that have been advancing women's leadership in Africa. There is a lot of coordination among African participants in various UN activities relating to peacebuilding. Representing 54 countries that tend to support one another, and with many countries having experienced conflict, African countries form a large bloc in international forums. African women have also been relatively well represented in international bodies and they take advantage of these connections. Moreover, with little to lose, they are fairly dynamic in promoting their goals.

Most women's rights provisions in the African peace agreements relate to political participation, which is seen as key to having a voice in decisions affecting women – in particular, the adoption of quotas for women in decision-making bodies (Table 1.2). The second most important area has to do with development and the need for women to acquire the means to support their households as a result of the disruptions of conflict. The third area of importance relates to violence against women, another common concern heightened by conflict.

Table 1.2. Subject of Women's Rights References in African Peace Agreements.

Area of concern	Number of references in African peace accords
Political participation	75
Development	66
Violence against women	56
Equality and anti-discrimination	42
Institutional reform	39
New institutions	38
International law	35
Implementation	35
Transitional justice	29
Particular groups of women: mothers, child mothers, IDPs, refugees, widows, disabled, women and young girls who have been raped, and women and girls who have contracted serious illnesses and unwanted pregnancies.	19

Source: http://peaceagreements.org (accessed 20 May 2020).

In terms of women's representation in peace negotiations, the numbers are low. There has been little change in women's engagement in this area. In 2018, out of six ongoing peace processes, women were included in 14 out of 19 delegations.[3] According to the Council on Foreign Relations, between 1992 and 2018 women made up 13 per cent of the negotiators, 3 per cent of the mediators, and only 4 per cent of the signatories in major peace processes.[4] A 2019 study similarly found that women were signatories in only 13 of 130 peace agreements from 1990 to 2014, and the numbers have not increased since 2000 when UNSCR 1325 was passed (Krause, Krause, and Bränfors 2018). Only three women have served as chief mediators at the international level: Miriam Coronel Ferrer of the Philippines, Tzipi Livni of Israel, and Mary Robinson of Ireland. Only Ferrer signed a final peace accord as chief mediator. Often when women have been brought on to delegations it has been a result of advocacy on the part of UNIFEM and its successor organisation, UN Women. In

[3] https://www.unwomen.org/en/what-we-do/peace-and-security/facts-and-figures (accessed on 18 May 2021).
[4] *Women's Participation in Peace Processes*, https://www.cfr.org/womens-participation-in-peace-processes/ (accessed on 23 October 2019).

some cases, because of exclusions, women have played a role behind the scenes, as Betty Bigombe did both before and during the Juba peace talks (2006–07), at her own expense. Not only do women generally not have significant formal roles in the peace talks, they have also experienced difficulty gaining consultative access to the negotiations, which would provide women's organisations with a formal mechanism with which to influence and observe the proceedings.

Scholarship has shown that civil society, including women's organisations, can make a difference in enhancing peace outcomes when it is included in peace talks. Civil society is often seen as bringing added legitimacy to the negotiation process. Since the Cold War, 34 per cent of peace negotiations have included at least one civil society actor. When civil society actors are included in peace agreements, the risk of peace failing is reduced by 64 per cent, regardless of regime type (Nilsson 2012). Another study similarly found that between 1998 and 2011, peace agreements that had women signatories were linked to durable peace and a higher rate of implementation of the peace agreement (Krause, Krause, and Bränfors 2018). However, with the adoption of UNSCR 1325, the number of references to women's rights in peace accords increased from 19 per cent (1995–99) before the resolution to 35 per cent (2005–19), according to data from the University of Edinburgh Peace Agreements Database (Table 1.3). A case in point is South Sudan: women were completely left out of the Comprehensive Peace Agreement process in South Sudan in 2005, and as a result the agreement focused only on stopping the war, leaving all other parties, civil society organisations, and women's associations out of the negotiation process. The agreement did not even mention gender inequality as a factor contributing to insecurity, leaving women completely outside of considerations of justice. The country has subsequently experienced continued and recurring conflict.

When women are brought into peace processes, the likelihood of the success of the agreement is enhanced. This was shown to be the case in 40 peace processes since the end of the Cold War where women's engagement was positively correlated with greater implementation of the process and had a positive impact on the sustainability of peace (Paffenholz et al. 2016). In spite of the positive benefits of including civil society actors, at the most basic level, women's organisations have found it difficult to get women represented in peace negotiations. While there has been no significant change with respect to women being included as chief mediators, negotiators, or signatories, in recent years there has been an increase in the number and frequency of women's informal representation through consultations between mediation teams and women's organisations.

Overall progress towards increasing women's formal roles has been slow even since the adoption of UNSCR 1325. These exclusions are even more egregious when one considers that often women's organisations have been among the few local actors independently seeking cooperation

Table 1.3. Gender-related Provisions in African Peace Agreements.

	1990–94	1995–99	2000–4	2005–9	2010–14	2015–19
Gender-related provisions	18/85 (21%)	11/59 (19%)	26/93 (28%)	42/119 (35%)	41/116 (35%)	28/83 (34%)

Source: http://peaceagreements.org (accessed 20 May 2020)

across political, ethnic, religious, and/or other differences that had contributed to conflict, yet combatant and government forces are often the only ones deemed relevant to bring to the negotiating table.

Women's organisations have sought a variety of strategies to influence talks and advance a women's rights agenda in peace negotiations, often with mixed results. They have sought observer status for women when they failed to become negotiators. But being in a non-speaker observer role means that they have limited influence; for this reason, UNSCR 2242 (2015) calls for women's representation in all peace negotiations, not simply as observers. Women's organisations and leaders sometimes work behind the scenes through informal initiatives. But, in general, apart from those who have held official roles as representatives of their political parties, women's organisations have had to lobby for a role for women through ad hoc pressure as well as collective mobilisation. In many cases, UNIFEM, and later UN Women, provided important support for such efforts. More often than not, women's organisations have sought to influence negotiations from the outside. Some have held parallel peace conferences, rallies, and other events to draw attention to women's demands and exclusion from official peace processes.

Demanding a Seat at the Table

From Uganda to Liberia and Somalia, women activists have pressed for a role for women representatives in peace talks, constitution-making processes, and newly constituted political arrangements. These women seeking to influence these processes were generally more educated and urbanised and organised at the national level. In South Sudan in 2013 women from both Sudan and South Sudan lobbied their respective governments and the international community for a role for women in the peace negotiations and in processes directed by the African Union. They demanded a say in shaping the future priorities of the two countries and condemned the exclusive nature of the process and the lack of transparency. They formed a Coalition of Women Leaders from Sudan and South Sudan at the 20th African Union Summit held in Addis Ababa, Ethiopia, in January 2013. They made concrete policy proposals on a wide range of issues and made specific demands regarding women's representation in various bodies involved in implementing the peace agreements. They were especially concerned with how to address women's security, such as through training the military and police forces to be sensitised to women's safety.

Later a South Sudan Women's Coalition for Peace of 50 organisations continued to lobby the South Sudanese government for women to take part in the revitalisation process as negotiators and as part of the technical support team. They called for more women in the Intergovernmental Authority on Development (IGAD) Secretariat and more gender experts in the IGAD Special Envoys Office and the Joint Monitoring and Evaluation Commission. As a result, the 2017 High-Level Revitalisation Process included 11 women as full delegates out of 90, unlike the 2015 process, where women were only observers. By February 2018, the number was increased to 23 and by the time of the Addis Ababa talks in May 2018, there were 39 female delegates out of 120 participants, or one-third. They demanded that the transitional government include 35 per cent women and, in the end, the Revitalised Transitional Government of National Unity formed on 22 February 2020 included 12 women out of 35 in Cabinet posts, three positions short of their demand of 35 per cent. The Coalition doggedly continued to press for a minimum of 35 per cent women in Parliament and all other governmental bodies.

These struggles over representation are consequential because the women's coalition had very specific objectives it wished to see realised. According to South Sudan expert Douglas Johnson (2018), we are 'beginning to see not only in youth groups, but in women's movements and other civil society and civilian organizations a growing demand that there must be some sort of accountability for the atrocities'. Women are insisting that the parties begin to address the issues underlying the conflict, which had to do with corruption, tribalism, and impunity.

In the case of Somalia, women had tried to participate in the Somali peace talks since the 1990s and found themselves systematically excluded. Between 1991 and 1999, women activists were excluded from 13 reconciliation conferences, as were other civil society groups, while warring groups were included. They sought to participate in the March 1993 National Reconciliation Conference in Addis Ababa but were not included. When the male negotiators were unable to reach a consensus, the women activists fasted. In response to the action of the women's groups, the men came up with a peace plan within 24 hours. It outlined provisions for a transitional government, elections, disarmament, and a UN-supervised ceasefire.

The Arta Conference in 2000 in Djibouti marked a watershed. The clan-based selection procedure made it difficult for women to be represented at the conference. In the end about 100 women (out of 2,000–3,000 delegates) were eventually allowed to participate in the conference as a result of the advocacy of women's organisations.[5] At the conference women joined forces as the Sixth Clan made up of women from all clans and lobbied for representation in the Transitional Charter, winning 12 per cent of the seats (25 out of 245) in the transitional assembly.

Informal Peacebuilding Strategies

Because of the kinds of exclusions described above, many women's peacebuilding activities have been relegated to informal and localised strategies. Women activists have mobilised to press for the holding of peace talks in some instances or for a rapid conclusion of peace talks when they were lagging (for example, Liberia in 2003). They have demanded the holding of elections (for example, Sierra Leone in 1996), the holding of free and fair elections without interference from militia (for example, Mozambique in 1994), the delay of elections until soldiers were fully demobilised (for example, Liberia in 2003), and the demobilisation of soldiers with the assistance of civil society and women's organisations (for example, Liberia in 1996 and 2003). In South Sudan, the Women's Platform for Peace, made up of women of all ethnic backgrounds, held press conferences and rallies and petitioned the leaders of warring factions in 2014 in South Sudan, demanding that they reach a peace agreement in 2014 ('South Sudan Women … ' 2014).

Informal and localised strategies involved organising rallies and boycotts, promoting small arms confiscation, conducting reconciliation ceremonies, negotiating with small groups of rebels to disarm, and negotiating with rebels to release abducted children and child soldiers. Many of these activists were grassroots women who lived in rural areas. Others were market women or women engaged in the urban informal sector. Peace activists played a role in preventing the resumption of conflict in various contexts by monitoring and advocating against the sale of small arms, carrying out conflict resolution workshops, participating in campaigns for clean diamonds, and protesting the role of coltan in the conflict in the Democratic Republic of Congo. Coltan is a metallic ore used in the production of mobile phones, laptops, pagers, and other electronic devices. Other strategies during war range from collecting arms to media work, especially through the radio (Tripp et al. 2009).

In the case of Maiduguri in northern Nigeria, local women's organisations negotiated with state security and vigilante groups to get their kidnapped children returned by Boko Haram. They provided information about suspicious movements related to Boko Haram in collaboration with state security and vigilante groups. They made efforts to bring repenting Boko Haram representatives and the government

---

5   Women's Development Organisation (IIDA), Save Somali Women and Children (SSWC), the
    Family Empowerment and Relief Organization (FERO), and an umbrella organisation called
    the Coalition for Grassroots Women's Organizations (COGWO).

together to the negotiating table. They formed groups that advocated for peace and respect in local communities. They organised rallies for peace. They advocated for and provided psychosocial support for women survivors of abuse. They mediated and built community support for pregnant women or children whose husbands and fathers are or were members of Boko Haram. Finally, they organised to provide foster parents for unaccompanied children whose parents were either killed or missing.

Building Bridges Across Difference

One of the most striking features of women's mobilisation in Africa and elsewhere, both in non-conflict and conflict situations, is the capacity of women's organisations to mobilise across ethnic, clan, racial, religious, class, and other differences. In Liberia, women peacemakers at the time of Charles Taylor came together across class, religious, and ethnic divisions in society. In Somalia, it was across clan lines, in Rwanda and Burundi it was across ethnic lines, and in northern Nigeria it was across religious lines. This is not to say there have not been tensions and challenges to such mobilisation, but it has been an enduring feature of the mobilisation we have seen in so many contexts where one would be least likely to see such bridges. Why have women been so central to the bridging of difference strategies?

Part of the explanation has to do with the fact that they are *marginalised and excluded from formal peacemaking and peacebuilding processes* that are recognised by international actors, governments, and rebel militia. Women have generally been marginalised from most forms of power, and therefore they collectively have had less at stake in preserving a status quo that had brought them considerable suffering. Nor are they likely to reap material benefits from continued fighting as they are *not generally beneficiaries of key patronage networks*.

Another part of the explanation for why women so often build bridges across difference has to do with the *way that women are socialised into a division of labour* that often leaves women with the responsibility for caring for the children, the sick, and the elderly. They have responsibility for maintaining the household economy in the last instance, and so the task of maintaining security and of securing water, firewood, and other necessities falls most directly on them. Thus, at the local level, their commonalities may often be quotidian. Relegated to roles as caretakers of the household, they have sought solidarity across differences because of the immediacy of finding solutions to problems of survival that cannot wait for the resolution of peace talks and the development of government policy, such as accessing water, food, and fuelwood.

Unlike men, women similarly share *common gendered experiences during the conflict* that have to do with problems ranging from sexual violence, displacement from land, and difficulty in being represented at peace negotiations, to gaining political representation after conflict. These experiences result in common grievances, making it necessary and more likely that women will build alliances across major societal divisions. Gender cuts across all these differences. Moreover, political power does not map onto gender in the same way that it maps onto class, race, ethnicity, caste, and religion, making gender the only identity that consistently cuts through all of society. However, it is important to recognise that women have also been part of movements based on particularistic identities. Thus, the observation about class and power in relation to gender only points to the *potential* for building crosscutting linkages, not the necessity of this happening.

Moreover, the fact that the category of women intersects with *almost all* other differences often makes it easier to build such alliances because women belong to multiple groups with varied identities. Since women represent these different groups and interests (IDPs, single-headed households, disabled women, etc.) *they bring a wide variety of interests and concerns to bear using their common gender identity* to provide a focus for these multiple concerns. They have the *potential* to recognise these differences and mobilise towards an inclusive strategy.

A few examples from the book highlight this phenomenon. Nigeria's population is evenly divided between Muslims (48 per cent) and Christians (49 per cent). Boko Haram has attacked both Christians and Muslims, convincing women's organisations to combine forces to find ways to create more tolerant communities and build peace (Iyorah 2018). Women's organisations throughout the northern states affected by Boko Haram attacks have built alliances across religious differences. Borno State is the epicentre of the Boko Haram insurgency, which has affected northern Nigeria, Nigeria, Chad, and Cameroon. When in 2014 over 300 girls were abducted by Boko Haram in Chibok, Borno State, a coalition of Borno women's rights groups, both Christian and Muslim, came out in full force to protest the abductions. The head of Nigeria's Market Women's Association ordered the closing of six major Lagos open air markets (Gbowee 2014). A Network of Civil Society Organizations in Borno State, directed by a woman, Fatima Shehu Imam, mobilised along interfaith lines to provide humanitarian aid and assistance to victims of the insurgency. Other groups throughout the country emerged to build linkages along similar lines. The Women of Faith Peacebuilding Network is another interfaith movement of over 10,000 Christian and Muslim women, started in 2011. They organise seminars, meditations, dialogue, vocational training, and skill-building for running businesses. In Jos, over 100,000 Christian and Muslim women marched to protest the Boko Haram massacre of 500 Christians in 2010. They were organised by the Women Without Walls Initiative, led by a Muslim and a Christian: Khadija Hawaja and Pastor Esther Ibanga.

Although one can point to many such examples of mobilisation across different identities, there is no predetermination that women will, in fact, mobilise in this way. In South Sudan, for example, a recent study found that women are victims of violence, but also drivers of intercommunal violence, primarily between the Dinkas, who constitute 35 per cent of the population, and the Nuer, who are the second largest ethnic group. Historically they have fought over cattle and grazing land; however, in 2013, the dismissal of former vice president Riek Machar (a Nuer) by President Salva Kiir (a Dinka) triggered mass violence, resulting in the deaths of thousands of civilians. Communal violence also occurred as a result of tensions related to cattle raiding in order to pay for high dowries, land disputes around laws that prevent women from inheriting land, and tensions related to marriage. Women, according to a survey, were as likely as men to believe that violence is a valid way to solve such conflicts (Iyaa and Smith 2018).

In the midst of this fighting, nevertheless, women activists organised a Bor Reconciliation and Healing Dialogue in 2014, which was the first peace conference since 2013 and was supported by local churches, the UNDP, and the UN Mission in South Sudan. As one participant commented:

> Even though there may be discussions at a much senior political level, it is equally important that at a community level people are coming together, finding methods and means on how to heal what has happened to them, but also find an opportunity to dialogue and discuss and find common ground. ('Dinka and Nuer Women ... ' 2014)

In Bor town, the Jonglei Women's Association organised a 'Women Friendly Space' for women across ethnic lines to organise activities, talk about their concerns regarding peace, conflict and economic opportunities, and find ways to peacefully coexist and build lasting relationships (Iyaa and Smith 2018).

Women who represent different religious, ethnic, and political identities frequently transcend these differences by building strategic alliances. They focus on their common gender-based demands, but they may represent a coming together of many different interests. For example, the South Sudan Women's Coalition for Peace, which is a coalition of more than 50 organisations, includes a wide variety of artisans, environmentalists, women in religiously based organisations, lawyers, media women, disability advocates, South Sudanese living in neighbouring countries, refugee women, and many others. The breadth of the groups is quite remarkable.[6]

---

[6] Anataban Arts Initiative, Association for Media Women in South Sudan, Bahr El Ghazal Women Association (Kampala, Uganda), Centre for Inclusive Governance, Peace and Justice, Community Empowerment and Progress Organization, Consortium of Women's Organizations, Crown the Woman, Ecotech Green Initiative (South Sudan), Ecumenical Women Group (Rhino Camp, Uganda), Equatorial Women's Association (Uganda), Eve Organization for Women Development, Women for Change (Bidi Bidi Refugee Settlement, Uganda), Girls Ambassadors for Peace (Torit), Hope Restoration, Inspire a Sister Initiative (South Sudan), International Fellowship Women Group (Kampala, Uganda), LAWANCI

Women built coalitions across differences in Burundi in the context of peace negotiations and in grassroots mobilisation. In the DRC, women on opposite sides of the conflict held prayer vigils to pressure the militias to honour the 2002 peace accords in Ituri (Kapinga 2003, 25–26). That these coalitions emerged so consistently in so many different contexts along the lines of gender from Burundi to Rwanda, Somalia, South Sudan, Liberia, Sierra Leone, the DRC, and elsewhere highlights the importance of understanding the bases for these coalitions. Certainly, women have also participated in and supported conflict and divisive political movements based on nationalism, ethnicity, religion, and other differences. Women have been fighters, they have encouraged fighters, have assisted them, and have fanned the flames of conflict. Yet women peace activists have also served as some of the most important societal forces fighting to transcend divisive difference. Although sometimes women in these contexts may appeal to ideals of motherhood, women's innate desire for peace, or religious conviction, the fact that women activists were able to mobilise under very difficult circumstances in this way speaks to a broader logic of commonality of interests based on their experiences during the war, experiences of exclusion from peace processes, of not having their concerns addressed, and of sharing experiences of violence, loss, and insecurity.

Women's Rights Activists on the Frontlines against Religious Extremism

The Sahel became one of the most unstable regions in Africa in the 2010s, with over 4,000 deaths reported in 2019 alone and large numbers of IDPs. It is plagued by a deadly combination of the effects of climate change, food insecurity, the increase in extremist and criminal networks, and the shrinking of land available to pastoralists, resulting in communal conflicts between cultivators and pastoralists. Attacks by various jihadists

---

(South Sudan), National Alliance for Women Lawyers (South Sudan), NWERO (Juba, South Sudan), South Sudan Muslim Women's Association, South Sudan Women Campaigners for Peace and Development, South Sudan Christian Women for Change (Nairobi, Kenya), South Sudan Council of Churches (Women's Desk), South Sudan Peace Coalition (Nairobi, Kenya), South Sudan Women's Association in Cairo, South Sudan Women's Association in Uganda, South Sudan Women's Empowerment Network, South Sudan Women General Association, South Sudan Women's Monthly Forum, South Sudan Women With Disability Network, South Sudan Women Refugee Group (Bidi Bidi Refugee Settlement, Uganda) South Sudan Women for Peace (Maga Maga Refugee Settlement, Bweyale, Uganda), Sudan Pentecostal Church Women Group (Juba, South Sudan), SSUDEMOP (Juba, South Sudan), STEWARD Women (South Sudan), Upper Nine Women's Association (Uganda), Voice for Change (Juba, South Sudan), White Shirt Women's Group (Rhino Refugee Settlement, Uganda), Women's Development Group (Wau, South Sudan), Women's International Peace Center (ISIS-Wicce, Kampala, Uganda), Working Women's Association, University of Juba (South Sudan), Young Women Group (Kiryandongo, Uganda), Young Women Ambassadors for Change Bright (Juba, South Sudan), and Young Women's Christian Association (South Sudan).

increased four times in 2018 compared with 2012 in Burkina Faso, Chad, Mali, Mauritania, and Niger (Muggah and Cabrera 2019). The rise, for example, of Boko Haram in Nigeria, Ansar Dine in Mali, Al-Qaeda in the Islamic Maghreb in Algeria and Mali, the Movement for Monotheism and Jihad in West Africa in Mali, Al Mourabitoun, and other extremist groups influenced by Salafism and other conservative ideologies has sometimes placed women on the frontlines of war, not only as victims, but also as prime opponents of some of the more extremist trends in affected societies.

As our cases show, in Algeria and Nigeria women were among the first attacked by extremists, but they were also among the first civilians to respond and create defences. In Algeria, women were a focal point of tensions between Islamists and those who opposed extremism, both symbolically and existentially during the Black Decade (1991–2002). One of the first of the recent wars against Islamist extremism was fought in Algeria. For many women, the struggle against impunity was especially important because of what they experienced during the Black Decade, as they were especially targeted by the Islamist fighters, especially those who worked as teachers, ran businesses, drove, did not veil, and engaged in the public sphere. During this period, Islamists and government forces clashed, leaving 200,000 dead and tens of thousands disappeared and injured. Women had little to lose as they were thrust to the fore of these struggles.

Three forms of women's mobilisation are evident today in Algeria and were seen in the 2019 protests against the regime, which had strong involvement of women's activists and organisations. The first is represented by women's organisations that have fought against impunity of the perpetrators of violence during the Black Decade. The second includes organisations that fought for women's legislative reform, and the third is reflected in the day-to-day struggles women wage against efforts to restrict their presence in the public space and their individual freedom to dress as they please.

Many women's organisations refused to be silenced after the Black Decade and continued to mobilise around calls for justice and an end to impunity for those who had killed, raped, and harmed people during this period. Women victims and the families of those who disappeared during the civil conflict continue to protest and demand answers. They were often beaten by the authorities. They were also arrested because they refused to seek authorisation for their protests on the principle that what they were doing was legitimate and therefore should not require authorisation.

The hard-won reforms that were made after the Black Decade included constitutional reforms regarding labour, political representation, gender equality, and countering discrimination based on gender. They included legislation around sexual harassment (2003, 2004, 2016), quotas at the national level (2011), quotas in regional councils (2012), prohibition of marriage to rapists (2014), prohibition of domestic violence (2017), allowing the nationality of the children to follow that of the wife as well as the husband (2005), allowing a woman to confer citizenship on a non-national spouse (2007), violence against women (2018), and some reforms of the Family Code, although many have felt that these reforms are lacking. These laws represented both the demands of women's groups and part of the agenda of the Front de libération nationale (FLN)-led government that sought to contain and suppress the Islamists, in part, by promoting women's rights as a counterweight to the Islamist agenda after the Black Decade. At the same time, the government's 2005 Charter for Peace and Reconciliation with the Islamists, which granted amnesty to former fighters, represented a finger in the eye of the victims of this period and allowed for impunity in the face of unspeakable atrocities.

The Algerian case shows how, on the one hand, the struggle for women's freedom of movement, what they wear, and how they live their life as well as the struggle for legal rights put them at the forefront of the struggle against Islamist extremism. Women face similar situations in combating violent groups today throughout the Sahel region.

After decades of fighting for legal rights, like the Algerian women, Sudanese women participated in a revolution, which resulted in the ouster of former President Omar al Bashir and the introduction of a transitional government led by Abdalla Hamdok. Already in the first few months, the government overturned the notorious Public Order Act, which limited civil liberties, especially for women. The annulment of this Act was partly in acknowledgement of the key role women played in the protests, in which at times they constituted the majority of the participants. The al Bashir regime had placed numerous restrictions on women's employment, movement, social lives, and how they dressed and veiled. Articles 145–158 dealt with so-called morality, targeting women for consensual sex, dancing at parties, vending on streets, and begging (Amnesty International 2019). The new government also banned female genital cutting, a practice that affects roughly nine in 10 women and children in Sudan. The Hamdok government began to appoint women into key positions, appointing Nemat Abdullah Mohamed Khair as the country's first woman chief justice. There are two women out of six on the Sovereignty Council of Sudan, the country's collective head of state since 21 August 2019: Aisha Musa el-Said and Raja Jicola. These are the first women to hold the position of head of state in Sudan. Musa is a woman's rights activist and Raja is the first Christian (Copt) to hold such a high political office. The Cabinet also includes four women out of 21 members: Asma Mohamed Abdalla as Foreign Minister, Lena el-Sheikh Mahjoub as Minister of Social Development and Labour, Wala'a Essam al-Boushi as Minister for Youth and Sports, and Intisar el-Zein Soughayroun as Minister of Higher Education. These are a far cry from the 50 per cent that women's organisations have been calling for, but they are a start in a country that has had few women leaders in top positions.

Political Representation in Postconflict Contexts

One of the major demands of women in most postconflict contexts has been for a role in governance. This has had gendered implications as women have come to claim on average greater levels of representation in postconflict countries than non-postconflict countries in Africa. Postconflict countries have more gender-related constitutional provisions and legislation than non-postconflict countries in Africa (Tripp 2015). This was not true after earlier conflicts, but by the 1990s international and regional norms and actors had changed political expectations regarding women's rights in a way that influenced constitutional and legislative outcomes.

In general, postconflict countries have double the rates of representation for women in parliament compared with non-postconflict countries. In Rwanda, which experienced major genocide and conflict in 1994, women hold 61 per cent of the legislative seats, the highest rate in the world. Similarly, in Algeria, women's proportion of legislative representation jumped from 2 per cent in 1987 before the conflict between the government and the Islamists (1991–2002), to 32 per cent after the 2012 elections. In Somalia, the number jumped from 4 per cent of women in parliament before the conflict, which started in 1989, to 25 per cent today. Perhaps the sharpest jump was in Rwanda, where the percentage of women in parliament increased after the genocide from 17 per cent in 1988 to 61 per cent in 2020. Except for Tanzania and Senegal, the countries with the highest rates of women's legislative representation in Africa have emerged from major conflict.

It is also no accident that Ellen Johnson Sirleaf was elected after years of conflict in Liberia and became the first elected woman head of state in Africa, while Catherine Samba-Panza was elected Interim President of Central African Republic amid a bloody civil war, and Ethiopia gained a woman president in 2018 after years of instability and conflict. All have been strong advocates of women's rights. The African countries with 50 per cent women's representation in Cabinet are all postconflict countries (Ethiopia, South Africa, and Rwanda).

These developments are tied to societal transformations that took place during war. The decline in conflict after the mid-1990s established new institutions through which women could assert their interests. Peacekeeping negotiations sometimes allowed women to insert their demands; they did so in Africa more than on other continents. Women's organisations influenced constitution-making processes and were able to include more woman-friendly provisions than constitutions revised contemporaneously in countries without civil wars. Women's rights activists saw to it that electoral rules were amended in ways that supported their goals. Similarly, there were far more women's rights reforms passed in postconflict countries than elsewhere, particularly around customary law, land rights, quotas, and violence against women (Tripp 2015).

From Peacebuilding to Stabilisation and Counterterrorism

Accounting for women's peacebuilding strategies matters even more today given the changing military strategies globally that are sidelining peacebuilding altogether. Since the Cold War, liberal peacebuilding has predominated as a strategy to tackle the larger problems underlying conflict having to do with corruption, weak and illegitimate states, feelings of exclusion by sections of the population, and societal divisions (Sisk and Jarstad 2010). It has focused on a wide variety of measures aimed at strengthening national capacity for conflict management (also in some instances local capacities) and reducing the risk of a return to conflict by strengthening both formal and informal political institutions and statebuilding and laying foundations for durable peace and economic development.

In more recent years, however, the UN has been more involved in stabilisation missions and the UNSC has been giving larger mandates to field missions. There has been greater reliance on regional coalitions to fight armed groups supported by international forces. This is evident in the focus on 'stabilisation' in MONUSCO in the DRC (2010), MINUSMA in Mali (2013), and MINUSCA (2014) in Central African Republic. In contrast, in 2001 all the missions in Africa were called 'peacebuilding missions'.[7]

Already in 2005, the US Bush administration had shifted from the global war on terror to a struggle against violent extremism (SAVE). This Preventing and Countering Violent Extremism (PCVE) agenda has gained in popularity. In 2015 UN Secretary-General Ban Ki-moon announced his plan of action to prevent violent extremism in which the terms 'extremism' and 'terrorism' were used interchangeably. Donors are also putting money into these PCVE programmes and UNDP has recategorised some of its established programmes as PCVE programmes. The OECD in 2016 allowed funding to prevent violent extremism to be considered Overseas Development Assistance. In the past, these military and economic types of support were separated, which allowed economic funding to be less politicised. This now means that economic funding can be used for security activities even in countries that have very poor governance and human rights records. US President Barack Obama continued Bush's policy of the global war on terror but changed the strategy to rely more on drone strikes, US special forces, and funding to train local troops in place of building legitimacy, encouraging citizen participation, and promoting values of inclusion. The idea was to limit military engagement and rely more on technological advances as well as more targeted killings outside media attention and political accountability. The number of US special forces in Africa increased from 1 per cent in 2006 to 17 per cent in 2016 (Karlsrud 2019).

---

[7] UN Peace-building Support Mission in Central African Republic (BONUCA); the UN Peace-building Support Office in Guinea-Bissau (UNOGBIS); and the UN Peace-building Support Office in Liberia (UNOL).

President Donald Trump's policy continued in the same vein. However, he had little interest in promoting democracy, human rights, the rights of civilians, or the rule of law abroad (Karlsrud 2019). Trump expanded the types of engagements Obama initiated, conducting 47 airstrikes against Al Shabaab in 2018 (a 200 per cent increase from two years earlier). The White House allowed the CIA to carry out drone strikes against suspected terrorists from an airbase in Niger. Such actions have the potential for backlash among citizens and of galvanising support against the United States. Prior administrations had sought to combine military action with development assistance and support to local militaries. However, Trump had little interest in offering humanitarian and development assistance, which he reserved for close allies. Moreover, he sought to cut support for UN peacekeeping missions he deemed unsuccessful. Some African postconflict governments found this strategy favourable because it helped keep them in power (Gass 2019). President Joe Biden appears to be continuing Obama and Trump's counterterrorism strategies in the Sahel and elsewhere (Coakley 2021).

This focus on counterterrorism has left women's activism and civil society more generally even further out in the cold in spite of strong evidence that the participation of civil society enhances the sustainability of peacebuilding efforts. The earlier liberal peacebuilding strategies were problematic because they focused almost exclusively on statebuilding and involved technocratic solutions, the professionalisation of personnel, standardisation of operating procedures, and honing best practices focused on the state. These types of strategies were carried out to the exclusion of grassroots activities (Mac Ginty and Firchow 2016). Critics of peacebuilding and statebuilding have argued that these strategies, as they have been implemented, have not always delivered results and that they are an extension of Western ideology promoting a free market economy and creating countries dependent on Western aid (Bindi and Tufecki 2018).

Such peacebuilding strategies of all kinds have now been replaced by stabilisation and counterterrorism strategies because the earlier strategies were seen as costly and time consuming. They were premised on the idea that stable democracies are less likely to experience war and will promote peace and security. Promoting democracy, however, is a slow and uncertain process. Such peacebuilding strategies are being abandoned in the current international political climate in favour of seeming quick fixes.

There are gendered consequences to this policy shift to counterterrorism. Not only does it further marginalise the role of women in peacebuilding strategies, but it takes women's interests often quite literally out of the equation. In discussions over the draft UNSCR 2467, which calls for an end to sexual violence in conflict, to hold perpetrators accountable, and to provide support to survivors, the Trump administration removed references to sexual and reproductive health services for survivors because of the administration's anti-abortion position. This also led to the reinstatement of the global gag rule, which former President George W. Bush had introduced to deny US funding to any international organisation that even so much as provided information about abortion options (Reis and Berry 2019). This has serious implications for women's health.

Conclusion, Methodology, and Structure of the Book

Conflict in Africa has changed in nature and has become more intractable as the causes and solutions are more complex. This is happening at a time when donors are withdrawing support for peace initiatives, resulting in the need for more creative and homegrown solutions for conflict resolution and prevention. The changing nature of conflict in Africa, and the fact that conflict today is found primarily in the activities of terrorist groups and in election violence, calls for different types of responses from those that have been tried in the past. The rise, for example, of Boko Haram in Nigeria, Al Shabaab in Somalia, and other extremist groups influenced by Salafism and other conservative ideologies has posed new challenges to these societies. Women often find themselves at the frontlines of war, not only as victims but also as prime opponents of some of the more extremist trends in affected societies. The emphasis on securitisation and counterterrorism by the United States and OECD countries is undermining efforts to focus on peacebuilding, gender, and complexity in dealing with the root causes of conflict.

Our aim in this book is to document some of the key consequences of the gendered nature of peacebuilding: the ways in which the lack of incorporation of women into formal peace processes have hindered peace; how women have been engaged in unrecognised forms of peacebuilding informally in Africa and the contributions and limitations of these forms of peacebuilding; and the ways in which the struggle for women's rights reforms and political representation in postconflict structures is a key battleground internally in African societies struggling to confront conservative Islamist and Salafist influences.

The book tackles these themes through ethnographic research in five case studies. A case study is an in-depth investigation of one unit, which in this case are countries that either have been severely affected by conflict in the recent past, as in the case of Algeria and Sudan, or were facing ongoing unrest, as in the cases of South Sudan, northern Nigeria, and Somalia (Gerring 2004). Most of our cases, with the exception of South Sudan, were Muslim majority countries. We conducted in-depth interviews and participant observation to produce descriptive accounts of how women were excluded from formal institutions. We also show how they sought to engage peacebuilding and governance structures, including informal strategies. We have approached the research of women and peacebuilding from a constructionist perspective, regarding peace processes as contextually defined, contested and redefined in different historical and social settings.

The chapters on Somalia (Chapter 4) and South Sudan (Chapter 2) focus on the ways in which women have been marginalised in formal peace negotiations, leading women to focus on more localised and informal peacebuilding strategies, to fight both for inclusion in formal processes, and to influence formal processes from the sidelines. The chapters on South Sudan (Chapter 2) and northern Nigeria (Chapter 3) discuss the variety of local-level peacebuilding activities women have engaged in. The chapters on Sudan (Chapter 5) and Algeria (Chapter 6) look at the role of women's movements in pressing for legal reform as a means of challenging the Islamist influence, especially the most conservative and jihadist elements in attempting to establish a new status quo. The chapter on Somalia (Chapter 4), and to some extent the chapters on Algeria (Chapter 6) and Sudan (Chapter 5), look at the role of women in shaping postconflict governance through their presence in the legislature and other positions of power. The concluding Chapter 7 looks at the implications of these developments for ongoing and future conflict.

As this introductory chapter has shown, this book takes as its starting point that peacebuilding is gendered just as violence is gendered and that peacebuilding creates gender like violence does. The chapter has argued for the importance of women's engagement with peacebuilding in a variety of contexts: in peace negotiations, in local community contexts, in contexts where Islamist extremism poses a challenge to women's rights, and in postconflict contexts of governance.

In this chapter and those that follow we argue that a number of key features have characterised women's peace mobilisation at all levels in the post-Cold War era and that these issues need to be addressed. First, although women's organisations have often tried to participate in formal peace negotiations and disarmament processes, they have been largely excluded, forcing them to work more at the informal and grassroots level – for example, in community reconciliation and engagement with military with the goal of disarmament. At the local level, women often work to find practical solutions to meet daily needs involving access to water, food, and other resources. At the national level, women activists have sought to be included in peace negotiations, constitution-making processes, and elections, often through the adoption of quotas of various kinds. They have often been relegated to the margins of these processes and have had to seek influence as observers and as advisers rather than as delegates and key negotiators. Demands at the national level emerge out of women's common experiences in conflict relating to sexual violence, access to land, access to a livelihood, inheritance, and political marginalisation.

These common experiences have often led to efforts to bridge racial, ethnic, clan, religious, class, and other differences to create broad coalitions, as is evident in South Sudan. Women's peace efforts have often taken the bridging of difference as a starting point, rather than an end point. In other words, instead of seeing peace as a goal to be reached at the end of talks, they have regarded peace as a process that is achieved by working together across difference around common gender-based and other concerns. The chapter has sought to explain why women are able to create alliances that cut across difference so effectively, even across the most intractable of divisions. It relates this not to any innate capabilities of women or motherhood, but rather the construction of gender identities and roles that open up particular opportunities to women and men and close off others. Their gender identity cuts across all identities in a way that other bases of mobilisation do not, allowing for the *possibility* of creating crosscutting alliances among women.

2

Women Activists' Informal Peacebuilding Strategies in South Sudan

HELEN KEZIE-NWOHA AND JULIET WERE

Introduction

Two years after South Sudan was declared Africa's youngest nation in 2011, the country descended into civil war. Political rivalry and ethnic tensions between Dinka supporters of President Salva Kiir and Nuer supporters of his Vice President Riek Machar, both members of the Sudan People's Liberation Movement (SPLM), culminated in an armed conflict with devastating consequences for the country. The women of South Sudan participated in the formal peace negotiations as representatives of women's groups, civil society, academia, and youth groups, and others as representatives of political parties. In the 2015 peace negotiations, women made up 15 per cent of the delegates, while in 2018 there was a significant increase to 25 per cent representative of women as delegates (CFR 2020b). Women lobbied the negotiators and ultimately were seated at the peace table (Pepper 2018).

Their participation in the formal peace process enabled the inclusion of significant gender provisions in the final peace agreement, such as the 35 per cent provision for women's political representation. Women's informal peacebuilding strategies were equally important. Not only were women able to mobilise for the inclusion of women in formal negotiations and bring attention to the need to include gender-sensitive provisions in the peace treaty, they also mobilised for peace at the community level.

Increasingly, researchers and peace activists have recognised the role of women and women-led organisations in building peace in Africa (Jendia 2020; Westendorf 2018; Hilhorst and van Leeuwen 2005; Porter 2007; Hedstrom and Senarathna 2015; Mazurana et al. 2002). However, there is a dearth of literature on women's participation in peacebuilding in Africa's youngest nation. The scholarship on South Sudan is scant. Notable exceptions include Jackie Kirk (2004) on the role of female teachers in peacebuilding in South Sudan during the North–South civil

29

war. Some scholars have focused on women's exclusion from the formal peace processes during the negotiation of the comprehensive peace agreement between the North and South Sudan in 2005 (Westendorf 2018) and at the start of the peace negotiations in South Sudan in 2013 (Mayen 2013). There is also some scholarship on women's leadership and participation in politics (Arabi 2011; Dahlstrom 2012) and the birth of women's movements in the context of armed conflict (Edward 2019).

Women's informal peacebuilding strategies are, however, rarely documented and recognised in the literature on South Sudan and beyond. This chapter is based on original data collected in South Sudan between 2017 and 2019. It highlights the informal peacebuilding strategies that women activists at the national and community level have used in the period following the 2013 conflict and shows how this has 1) contributed to building peace in local communities with a focus on reconciliation between ethnic groups and ensuring people's livelihoods; and 2) contributed with important inputs and support to women represented at the peace table through, for example, the organisation of marches to bring attention to sexual violence. We argue that women have strategically positioned themselves to build peace by organising across ethnic and religious divides. Especially common experiences of gendered marginalisation and violence have united women in mobilising for peace (Kreft 2018). Women's organisations at the grassroots and national levels provide a potential model for building peace in South Sudan. In the everyday actions of women's groups at the national and grassroots levels, women have been working across divides for peace, by distributing food to those in need regardless of their ethnicity and religion.

Against the frequent assumption within the discourse on Resolution 1325 that any woman can represent all women (see, for example, Pratt and Richter-Devroe 2011), South Sudanese women peacebuilders highlight the importance of diversity, including the grassroots perspective, for ensuring a representative peace process. By representative peace process we refer here both to the numerical representation of women as a group, and to the idea that women's diverse perspectives and backgrounds should be substantively reflected in the collective demands made on behalf of women as a group. The latter has been ensured through dialogue between national and grassroots women's organisations and those represented at the peace table.

Methods

We situate our study within feminist research methodology by putting the voices of South Sudanese women at the centre. By grounding the study in women's lived realities, which is an essential component in feminist methodology (Landman 2006), our action-orientated research aims to generate social and political change. We have collected the data for this study as an NGO working on women and peacebuilding aiming to use the findings generated from the research to develop projects catering to the interest and need of women in South Sudan.

We conducted fieldwork for this study in Juba, Wau, and Bor in South Sudan and Kampala, Uganda, from May 2017 to June 2018 to explore how grassroots women's organisations (GWO) and national women's organisations contribute to peace. We collected data using qualitative approaches through focus group discussions, community meetings, and in-depth interviews. Although our sample is not representative of all South Sudanese women, we have engaged with women from diverse ethnic, religious, class, and political backgrounds. We conducted eight focus group discussions (FGDs) with 111 members of the Women for Faith and Peace Network; the Women's Monthly Forum members; women parliamentarians; women living in Protection of Civilians camps; women from civil society organisations; women living with disabilities; women's groups in Wau State; and various women's groups in Bor State. We conducted FGDs to learn about women's grassroots organisations' activities at the community level and how these activities contributed to peacebuilding. We also conducted 21 in-depth interviews with women activists in Juba, Wau, Bor, and Kampala. The in-depth interviews with women's organisations enabled us to understand more deeply what activities each group carried out and what counted as peacebuilding. We held two community meetings with women refugees in Wau and Kampala to explore women's collective views on grassroots women's peacebuilding efforts. Finally, we held a validation meeting in Juba to share the research findings and receive feedback, which informed our final revision of the findings.

We used content analysis to analyse the data. This allowed us to identify themes and patterns presented in the opinions, experiences, and actions. The chapter is thus presented based on the key themes.

Background: Formal Peace Processes and Women's Inclusion

Women's organising for peacebuilding in South Sudan is rooted in the decades of struggle for the country's liberation since 1955. This context of perpetual armed conflict compounded their marginalisation in economic, social, and political life, but also triggered their mobilisation (Edward 2019). It is within the context of war that South Sudanese women's peace activism took place. Mobilising for a seat at the table in formal negotiations has a long trajectory. In 2005, the SPLM and the Government of Sudan negotiated the Comprehensive Peace Agreement (CPA) without paying attention to the representation of women, which culminated in what Anne Itto (2006) describes as a gender-blind treaty. After South

Sudan's independence in 2011, the country descended into a new civil war and an unprecedented number of peace deals. This time around women were increasingly included at the peace table.

The South Sudan Peace Process

Ethnic tensions and violence were exacerbated by a power struggle between President Salva Kiir and his former deputy, Vice President Riek Machar, in 2013. Leaders of both sides of the political divide engaged in several peace deals, led by the Intergovernmental Authority on Development (IGAD). Between 2014 and 2015, 10 deals were struck, including the August 2015 Agreement on the Resolution of the Conflict in South Sudan (ARCSS), which aimed to end the South Sudanese civil war. The agreements established the Joint Monitoring and Evaluation Commission (JMEC) responsible for monitoring and overseeing its implementation. In July 2016 an eruption of violence led to the deployment of troops from African Union nations. Despite regional and international endorsement, the ARCSS stalled just months after implementation began in 2016. In December 2016, President Kiir initiated a National Dialogue that allowed amnesty for any former rebel returnees (ADBG 2018). However, this action did not bring the desired peace for the people of South Sudan. In June 2017, IGAD leaders endorsed the creation of a High-Level Revitalization Forum (HLRF), which was launched on 18 December 2017, to reinforce the defunct 2015 ARCSS (IGAD, 2017). The mandate of the HLRF was to restore a permanent ceasefire, to fully implement the ARCSS, and to revise the ARCSS in order to hold elections at the conclusion of the agreement's timetable in October 2018 (Verjee 2017).

The first phase of the HLRF ended on 21 December 2017, with the signing of an Agreement on Cessation of Hostilities, Protection of Civilians, and Humanitarian Access. In February 2018, the Sudan People's Liberation Movement in Opposition (SPLM-IO) signed a Declaration of Principles for the peace revitalisation process while the government refused the framework on the basis that it called for sanctioning the parties ('SPLM-IO signs peace declaration ... ' 2018). In May 2018, the second phase of the HLRF ended without a deal on the implementation of the governance and security arrangement ('Phase-2 of South Sudan peace ... ' 2018).

To address this, IGAD developed a bridging proposal that was rejected by SPLM-IO. In June 2018, President Kiir and Dr. Machar met in Addis Ababa with no agreement. Follow-up meetings hosted by President al Bashir of Sudan resulted in the parties signing a deal dubbed the 'Khartoum Declaration of Agreement between Parties of the Conflict of South Sudan' (Modi 2018). The Revitalised Agreement on the Resolution of the Conflict in the Republic of South Sudan (R-ARCSS) was signed by 12 out of 19 armed and political groups, alongside other stakeholders including religious leaders, civil society leaders, women's leaders, youth leaders, and business leaders. Out of 34 signatories to the agreement, six were women, representing 17.64 per cent, which is below the 25 per cent representation of women provided for by the 2011 Transitional Constitution of the Republic of South Sudan as affirmative action in all spheres, as a temporary positive measure to redress past imbalances in women's participation in decision-making (MOGCSW 2012). Yet another peace deal was reached in February 2020 between Kiir and Machar, resulting in the formation of a national unity government. The fragile peace was forged, but only after the death of 400,000 people and the displacement of millions.

Women's Inclusion in Formal Peace Processes

South Sudan women were represented at the peace table through their membership in civil society organisations and women's networks, as members of academia and as youth representatives. During the 2015 peace process, women made up 15 per cent of the negotiators. The government delegation had no women, while the opposition delegation had three women out of 10 representatives.

Women's organisations were represented by the Women's Bloc – a network of women's civil society leaders that served as formal observers and signatories to the Agreement. The Women's Bloc were also members of the Joint Monitoring and Evaluation Commission, a body responsible for monitoring implementation of the Agreement.

In 2018, there was a significant increase in the percentage of women at the peace table: one woman served as a mediator and women made up 25 per cent of official delegates (CFR 2020b). Two women's networks were represented at the peace table, the Women's Bloc and the South Sudan Women's Coalition, which is a network of about 40 women leaders that was established in 2017. Other women participated as members of academia, South Sudan civil society, and youth representatives. Seven women signed the revitalised agreement.[1] The women signed under the category 'stakeholders', made up of 17 representatives in all. The total signatories, excluding guarantors, were 27, so women made up 25.92 per cent of signatories to the agreement. Most of the women represent organisations based in Juba with programmes at the state and community levels.

---

[1]   These were: Mary Akech Bior representing Women's Bloc; Hon. Rebecca Nyadeng Garang, on behalf of Eminent Personalities; Rita M. Lopidia, representing the South Sudan Women's Coalition; Alokiir Malual, representing Civil Society of South Sudan; Professor Pauline Elaine Riek, representing academia; Dr. Emmily Koiti representing youth; and Sarah Nyonath Elijah, representing Gender Empowerment for South Sudan Organisation.

Women's Peace Activism

Building on Wesely and Dublon (2015), we differentiate between grassroots and national women's organisations. The majority of the organisations we interacted with in South Sudan were established after the CPA, while some were established to contribute to peacebuilding following the December 2013 conflict. Although both types of organisations are established by Southern Sudanese women and work at the national and/ or community level, their overall goals and missions differ. All groups work in solidarity for peace, which is seen as being in the interest of women of South Sudan. Working for peace does not necessarily challenge gender inequality but nonetheless it is acting in the interest of women. National women's organisations work for the inclusion of women in the peace talks and for gendering the peace talks and agreements. They thereby work for the strategic gender interest of women, defined by Molyneux as 'those involving claims to transform social relations in order to enhance women's position and to secure a more lasting re-positioning of women within the gender order and within society at large' (1998, 232). Grassroots women's organisations work to create peace at the community level, often catering to practical gender interests that are based on the satisfaction of immediate needs arising from women's placement within the sexual division of labour (*ibid*). This informal peacebuilding is usually less obvious because it is 'intertwined with everyday life' (Mazurana et al. 2002). Women's work at the grassroots level might draw on essentialist notions of womanhood, particularly as nurturers and mothers, which is an important aspect of women's lived experience. Peace activism drawing on essentialised notions of motherhood has, however, been critiqued for reenforcing women's exclusion from politics because it does not fundamentally challenge gender inequality, but rather sustains gender stereotypes, which domesticates women (Coomaraswamy and Fonseka 2004). Although it is not aimed at gender equality in all spheres, we contend that this work is crucial for creating peace at the community level and is an important avenue of women's peace agency (Cockburn 2007).

By grounding the analysis in women's lived experiences of violence and marginalisation, we highlight the diversity of women's agency in peacebuilding. By differentiating between national and grassroots organisations we wish to contribute to the evolving critique of Resolution 1325 in the literature on women, peace, and security that it is assumed that all women in postconflict communities share the same experiences and express the same concerns (Pratt and Richter-Devroe 2011; Adjei 2019). However, we contend that South Sudan may be a model of women's peacebuilding because these organisations and women from diverse backgrounds meet in what Charles Tilly (1978) describes as solidarity for a common goal, namely peace in South Sudan. And peace for South Sudanese women, which we will elaborate on extensively in this chapter, means much more than the absence of war.

Women Activists' Informal Peacebuilding Strategies: Post-2013 South Sudan

The women of South Sudan played an active role in the Revitalised Peace Process. Following the resurgence of conflict in 2013 in South Sudan, even before the warring parties agreed to talk, women activists proactively took action to ensure that the fighting ended. They engaged with the different leaders of warring factions, encouraging them to join the peace table. Through discussions with participants in this study, women activists shared a number of peace strategies. They included the establishment of new women's groups and grassroots women's organisations, lobbying and advocacy for peace and women's inclusion, peace marches and protests, prayer vigils, supporting food security and livelihood enhancement, nurturing relationships across divides, using technology to amplify women's voices, and using external support from African women's peace activists. We discuss each of these strategies in turn. One commonality was bringing women of diverse backgrounds together in social and political action.

Advocacy and Awareness-Raising for Peace and Women's Inclusion

Different South Sudanese women's organisations engaged in various activities to advocate for peace and lobby for women's inclusion in different peace processes. These demands for inclusion were framed within the South Sudan National Action Plan for the implementation of UNSCR 1325, which was adopted in 2015 after a participatory process that included line ministries, civil society organisations, and other stakeholders led by the Ministry of Gender, Child, and Social Welfare with support from UN Women. When the conflict erupted in 2013 and again in 2016 in the capital of Juba, the Women Leaders Peace Network (WLP) developed messages demanding women's inclusion in the peacemaking process and emphasising that South Sudan women want peace. The women leaders further resolved to use the media to denounce the violence, request that the guns be silenced, and call upon all the women of South Sudan to join in nonviolent means to restore peace.

This they did under repressive conditions. The South Sudanese state restricts use of communication platforms. The members of the WLP had to leverage their influence and connections to seek permission from the SPLM to use the media for this purpose. They were thus able to denounce the outbreak of war in the national media. As the Hon. Betty Ogwaro explained in an interview with the authors (9 June 2017):

> We called the women leaders and said, the first thing we must do is go to the media and denounce violence. While at the different media platforms, we urged women to persistently pray for peace in the Republic of South Sudan. On 21 December 2013 we convened and

drafted the media statement; and on 22 December 2013 we were hosted on multiple radio stations. We denounced violence. We petitioned President Kiir and Dr. Riek Machar to stop anything that will lead the country back to war. Our appeal was for them to sit down and negotiate. Various radios gave us free airtime and space to denounce violence, talk about peace and silenc[ing] the guns.

It is evident that organising in contexts of militarism requires creativity. Although among the members of the WLP were legislators and members of SPLM, their move could potentially put them and their positions at risk as they were critiquing an authoritarian state at war.

Women activists carried out advocacy and lobbying under the auspices of a Women's Monthly Forum (WMF). They met monthly and held radio talk shows as a way of providing timely information to women on the status of the conflict and the progress of the mediation process. They urged leaders of the different factions to participate in the peace talks, silence the guns, and stop the fighting. Women in the different states and in refugee settlements engaged in radio call-in shows, amplifying the voice of women to promote peace. After the signing of the 2015 South Sudan Peace Agreement, members of the WMF disseminated copies of the Agreement in eight states of the country. As one female WMF focus group participant explained in an interview with the authors:

> We are a diverse group composed of 82 different groups of civil society organisations. We came together as women of South Sudan to have a common voice and platform. When the agreement was signed in 2015, we decided to move to eight states and educate women and other civilians on the agreement and provide updates on progress of the peace process.

During the radio programmes, speakers, in addition to informing listeners of the progress of the peace process, called for their contribution and participation in the peace process. The radio programmes were used to advocate for the inclusion of women in all peacebuilding activities, invoking the provisions of UNSCR 1325 and the National Action Plan for its implementation in South Sudan. They called on all the women of South Sudan to be active and participate in any process that contributes to peace. The WMF also conducted awareness-raising on the peace process and the gender dimensions of the peace agreement in eight out of the 10 original states of South Sudan through community dialogue that reached women, men, and young people (WMF focus group, Juba, 2017).

In Wau, the Women's Peace Committee conducted awareness-raising on peaceful coexistence and encouraged women, men, and young people to return to their homes because the Protection of Civilian sites were not safe. Community dialogues were held to share information on the peace process, solicit input for the South Sudan women's agenda for peace, and disseminate simplified and translated versions of the Revitalised Peace Agreement. The different levels of advocacy carried out by women's grassroots organisations (WGOs) ultimately helped push leaders at national and local levels to begin peace talks and respect the cessation of hostility agreements.

Peace Marches and Protests

Globally, women have taken to the streets amid seemingly intractable conflict, catalysing public support for peace and creating turning points in movements to end violence. In Liberia in 2003, the Women of Liberia Mass Action for Peace led weekly rallies and sit-ins, uniting women across ethnic and religious divides. Their efforts helped force warring parties to the table to hammer out the deal that ended the brutal Liberian civil war.

Public protests enable women to voice their dissatisfaction with peace processes while soliciting the support of the general population. In Uganda, women under the auspices of the Uganda Women's Coalition for Peace held a Women's Peace Caravan at the peak of the conflict involving the Lord's Resistance Army in northern Uganda and during the follow-up peace negotiations in Juba, South Sudan. The idea of the Peace Caravan was to galvanise support by travelling with a peace torch through the Democratic Republic of Congo, Kenya, Uganda, and then to Juba to deliver the peace torch at the venue of the peace talks ('Uganda Women to Take Peace … ' 2006). Although, the strategy of the peace march by the women of South Sudan is not an indigenous invention, it worked as a powerful tool to generate awareness and solidarity.

The signing of the Agreement on Cessation of Hostilities, Protection of Civilians, and Humanitarian Access (21 December 2017) was an important step towards a resolution of the conflict. However, there were continued clashes among different warring groups, killings, and sexual violence against women and girls. Women activists strategised and agreed to organise public protests on the failure of parties to the peace agreement to respect their commitments. Because the environment was not conducive to freedom of speech, especially on issues related to sexual violence, the women activists organised a silent march in Juba in December 2017 (focus group in Juba 2018; 'South Sudan President …' 2017). They pointed to the fact that there were violations of Article 2.1.10.2 of Chapter Two of the R-ARCSS on permanent ceasefire and transitional security arrangements that called on all parties to refrain from prohibited actions, including acts and forms of sexual- and gender-based violence and sexual exploitation and harassment. Even though the provision was applauded, sexual violence had continued unabated at unimaginably high rates during and after the conflict in South Sudan. Women activists mobilised across religious and ethnic divides, covering their mouths with tape (to signify denial of freedom of speech) and marching in silence, yet their message was loud and clear to demand an end to the war and the suffering of their people. A focus group participant in Juba (2018) described the protest slogans:

We carried posters with different messages, such as: 'Bring back our peace now!', 'Save my future, stop the war', 'Enough of the bloodshed', 'Women continue to be raped and killed; they don't have access to their homes, and there is no humanitarian access for people in need'.

Explaining the idea behind the protest, another participant in the 2018 focus group stated, 'We are tired and fed up of this, and we want our leadership to understand that this is their final chance to bring peace to this country.'

Women from different religious, ethnic, and social backgrounds and from all parts of the country participated in the peace protest, under the banner of 'Give Peace a Chance'. They urged the warring parties to prioritise peace as the negotiations for peace progressed in Addis Ababa. Women peace activists were very conscious and strategic to ensure their message of peace and inclusion was received not just by the public but by the leaders as well. The protests attracted both local and international media attention that enabled the women's message to reach its target audience.

Prayer Vigils

Following cycles of repeated failure to abide by the demands of the peace agreements by parties to the conflict, and thus inability to deliver the type of peace that women agitated for, women resorted to prayer (Gale 2016). Many of the groups interviewed, including the Women's Desk of the Sudan Council of Churches, the Women's Monthly Forum, the Association of South Sudan Media Women, and Eve Organization for Women, among others, said the women of South Sudan found value in prayers as they mobilised across religious and ethnic lines for the common objective of peace.

Women activists of Christian, Muslim, and indigenous religious faiths across ethnic divides organised prayers on a monthly basis to evoke their spiritual strength and the power of God to pray for peace. They organised these prayers in both Juba and other capital cities that host South Sudan refugees, including Kampala, Nairobi, Khartoum, and Cairo. The Women's Desk of the South Sudan Council of Churches also organised monthly prayers in Juba on rotation from one church to another. As Harriet Baka, a participant in the prayer events, explained in a 2017 in-depth interview with the authors:

> Confronted by the conflict, slaughter, and seemingly endless anguish in South Sudan, we wonder how God can allow such things to happen. The Old Testament describes how the people of Israel suffered war, violence, famine, persecution, and exile, and how they tried to find the presence of the loving God of the covenant in all those harsh realities. These prayers are aimed at uniting people to collectively strengthen peace efforts.

The Hon. Betty Ogwaro similarly pointed out in an interview with the authors:

> A lot of efforts have been made by the people of South Sudan for peace to come, but nothing has come. So what we want is to raise our voices to God because no one is here to rescue us. It is only God, that is why we shall continue to pray to God to bring peace to South Sudan.

The prayers provided hope and a platform for women to raise their voices about the urgency for a sustainable peace process. They also provided space to foster empathy, counselling, and solidarity.

The South Sudan women activists were motivated by actions in Liberia, where women organised by the Women in Peacebuilding Network (WIPNET) had strategically held prayers on a daily basis wearing white at a football pitch on the road that the President and other leaders used. The President had eventually agreed to meet the Liberian women and listen to their concerns (Pedersen 2008). Drawing inspiration from the Liberian example, the women of South Sudan from different backgrounds, classes, ethnic, and religious groups kept together in faith and adopted white as their colour for the monthly prayers in all the locations where they convened around their common goal of peace. This gave them hope, built solidarity, and brought all women together. As one WMF woman in a 2017 focus group noted, 'We hold national prayers, we dedicate South Sudan to God, we as humans cannot do much. It is better we ask God to intervene so that we get the real peace from God.' The government of South Sudan was challenged by the actions of the women and the state started organising National Days of Prayer in March 2017. The national prayers were held three days before the official launch of the National Dialogue ('South Sudan President … ' 2017). The women used their prayer events as a platform for building solidarity and continuous advocacy for leaders to respect and implement the signed agreements.

Supporting Food Security and Livelihood Enhancement

Access to food provision becomes challenging in contexts of conflict. Women get cut off in hiding and cannot access their gardens, shops, or markets and yet they carry the responsibility of nurturing and providing food for their family members. Although organised supply of food is handled by the World Food Programme, not all in need are usually reached. In September 2015, UNOCHA reported that 3.9 million people – nearly one in every three people in South Sudan – were severely food insecure and 3.6 million were considered to be 'stressed'. An estimated 30,000 people were facing catastrophic food insecurity (IPC Level 5) in Unity State, leading to starvation, death, and destitution (UNOCHA 2016).

Members of the Women's Desk and Mother's Union of the Anglican Church swung into action on observing large numbers of women and their children displaced in churches and hospital compounds. Through an emergency strategising meeting called by the leaders of the faith-based women's groups, members were requested to mobilise food, clothing, bedding, and other household utensils within their means. They visited the displaced and distributed food and other basic needs to all internally displaced peoples (IDPs) of different religious and ethnic backgrounds. In distributing food, there was no discrimination based on ethnicity.

Apart from providing for the refugees within church premises, they ensured that food consignments to those displaced in the camps reached them at all costs. They trained volunteers in food distribution for effectiveness and risked their lives to reach the most vulnerable people. As one woman of the ecumenical group Women Faith Leaders explained in a 2017 focus group in Juba:

> We planned to deliver food to Nimule where World Food Programme could not reach. There were heavy rains and we had to cross swampy points. I was escorting the trucks with items we received from the churches. The drivers said, there is no way you can reach the camps. Let us distribute the food within Nimule town. I said no, how will the women and their children get to town? We must deliver the food to the most vulnerable in the camp, whether it means death – we have to get there. I was heading this food distribution mission as a woman. We had to cross about seven streams, and it took one to two days to get through each stream. When we finally got there, we found people bedridden. The elderly women could not move. They were not sick but very hungry, having spent seven days without food. Working with the trained volunteers, we distributed food. This is what we did as leaders of the Mother's Union with the support of the Anglican Alliance.

It takes resilience and determination to go against the wishes of one's team and insist that food must get to those most in need. They understood that for the women in the refugee camps, peace also meant their ability to provide for their families adequately, with food being one of the basic human needs.

Beyond the emergency food response and distribution, the Mother's Union organised training in farming for women in Jongole State for Bari Diocese. This enabled women to grow vegetables and maize along the riverbanks for sale and to boost the nutrition of the children, women, and other family members. This gardening brought women together, allowing them to reflect on the conflict as a collective. As one member of the ecumenical group Juba Women Faith Leaders pointed out in a 2017 focus group, 'This tactic worked. Women started saying, we have no tribes, we have no colour, we are mothers, we are their wives, yet they are killing us indiscriminately. This war should end.'

Cognisant of the fact that women and persons with disability are often forgotten in the contexts of conflict and postconflict, the leadership and members of the Association of Women with Disabilities (AWD) did not wait for external support. Working through their village focal persons, they mapped out the impact of conflict on women with disabilities to understand how many women with disabilities were injured, displaced, or abandoned in their homes. They used this information and planned for a support mechanism. An AWD participant in a 2017 focus group stated, 'We reached out to our visually impaired sisters in Bongu village [30 miles from Juba town] with food, clothes, and sugar. This made them happy.' The AWD opened a shop as an income-generating activity. It is from this that they are able to provide support to other members in need of support. Another AWD 2017 focus group participant noted that, 'We do not have donors. We opened up a shop. Noticing that our sisters were in dire need, we needed to take action.'

The focus on livelihood and enhancing the ability of women to provide food for the family draws on the social role ascribed to women as nurturers and providers. Although the engagement of women in emergency food distribution has meant that they have taken on new roles in their local communities, it simultaneously builds on notions of traditional gender roles and women's assigned responsibility within this arena. But women build peace as part of everyday life in the context of armed conflict, and this is an important reminder that they exert considerable agency even if they mobilise within traditional gender roles.

Nurturing Relationships across Ethnic Divisions

The long conflict in South Sudan normalised ethnically based violence, which made it very difficult to broker peace at all levels. The need to bridge the gap became a necessary strategy towards achieving peace. The Voice of Women for Peace and Faith, an ecumenical group, brought together women from different religious denominations for prayers and training on peacebuilding. These activities, which have continued to date, have enabled reconciliation among women from different tribes and religions. Leaders across different denominations mobilised members from their community for joint training and dialogue on peacebuilding. As an ecumenical Women Faith Leaders participant in a 2017 focus group stated:

> We do not discriminate. We include Muslims, Catholics, Protestants, and Adventists because peace is for us all. We look at verses in the Bible and Quran emphasising forgiveness, reconciliation, and peace. We have done this in Rumbek, Yei, Jongole, and Juba.

Women carry the biggest burden of sustaining households during and after conflict. Some of them have lost their husbands and must take care of their children alone. For others, their husbands are engaged in active war at the frontline, while others are in IDP camps. For some who are in public service, their salaries are irregular because the government lacks enough resources to pay civil servants. The Voice of Women and Faith Initiative organises space for women across denominations for dialogue to share the challenges they encounter and support one another. This contributes substantially towards trauma healing for women because such spaces are used to share problems and receive empathy and support in the form of counselling and material resources. A refugee woman leader and activist participating in a 2017 Juba focus group reflected:

> When it comes to the effects of war, I become weak emotionally. My elder sister was raped because of the war. In July 2016, two young Nuer girls aged eight and nine were raped in our presence and we could not do anything; we were helpless. I always say that people have been killed because of their tribe. The trauma is too heavy to bear.

Nurturing relationships was important for women, because it enabled them to reach out to people who they trusted to gather information about the conflict and peace process, and to contribute to an analysis of the conflict that helped in the interventions of various groups. The monthly prayers built sisterhood and became a regular meeting point for most of the women, who gathered to pray and to catch up on latest developments of the peace process. Due to the nature of the conflict that divided people along ethnic lines, building trust was an important aspect that would contribute to rebuilding society.

Using Technology to Amplify Women's Voices

In the digital age, feminist activists employ digital tools to magnify activism and women's liberation efforts. New technologies provide new avenues for participation, influence, engagement, and accountability of peace processes. The field of technology for peacebuilding is growing and contributing to influencing peace process outcomes by strategically targeting policymakers (Puig and Kahl 2013). It enables more engagement of a large population to discuss specific conflict-related issues and make demands of leaders, who are increasingly using technology platforms to collect feedback from citizens.

Women did not allow distance and lack of physical presence at the peace talks to deter their participation. The group interview with the Women Peace Committee at Wau revealed that with the support of the UN Mission in South Sudan (UNMISS), women engaged in advocacy to influence decisions at the peace table. UNMISS organised a Skype dialogue that connected women with stakeholders in the High-Level Revitalization Process (HLRP) in Addis Ababa, allowing the meeting to hear the voices of grassroots women. The objective was for 20 women representing different organisations to express their displeasure at the failure of the HLRP to reach a consensus and to let the international community know they had lost faith in the leadership of the country. The Skype dialogue also enabled them to express their needs and what they considered important for inclusion in the final peace agreement. They raised issues such as the need for justice for survivors of rape, for a cessation of hostilities to address insecurities that made it difficult for women to find food and water, and for a conducive environment to which refugees can return. These recommendations were captured in the final peace agreement (IGAD 2018), including Chapter 2 on permanent ceasefire and transitional security in sub-section 2.1.4, which calls for the protection of civilians and humanitarian access, and sub-section 2.1.10.5, which prohibits acts of hostility, intimidation, violence, or attacks against the civilian population, including IDPs, returnees, and media personnel.

The women activists joined other informal engagements with the broader South Sudanese civil society and established a mechanism to raise the voices of the people and ensure that the delegates at the peace table in Addis Ababa showed a serious commitment to bringing peace to South Sudan. Through a joint peace campaign launched on 15 December 2017, ahead of the talks to push for a final peace agreement, the #SouthSudanIsWatching campaign was intended to show the leadership and the world that the South Sudanese were united as citizens and watching the High-Level Revitalization Forum closely.

The image of glasses was chosen as a symbol of the campaign. Participants put on a pair of glasses, took a photo and shared it on different online platforms using the hashtag #SouthSudanIsWatching. Others used their locations for added emphasis – for example, #WauIsWatching, #JubaIsWatching, and #MalakalIsWatching. The campaign brought many young people and the diaspora on board. The hashtag gathered momentum and reached regional leaders such as the Chair of the African Union Commission, who in tweeting his announcement of the signing of the cessation of hostilities agreement mentioned the hashtag: 'By signing the IGAD-brokered Cessation of Hostilities Agreement, South Sudan leaders recognize the gravity of the situation, and that it is neither morally nor politically acceptable to allow the ongoing tragedy to continue. South Sudan has suffered enough #SouthSudanIsWatching' (Mahamat 2017).

'Hashtag activism' is a term coined by media outlets referring to the use of Twitter's hashtags for online activism. It also refers to the act of showing support for a cause through a like or share on any social media platform, such as Facebook or Twitter (Mbabazi and Mbabazi 2018). Hashtag activism is one way that African women's rights activists collaborate to plan and organise protests and marches, and to rally support to take specific actions geared towards women's liberation that influence policy and effect behavioural change among people.

Another online campaign was led by Crisis Action and many partners in South Sudan and the Great Lakes Region: #SawaSouthSudan. The campaign aimed to connect women activists in South Sudan with women leaders and activists from around the world (SALO 2018). #SawaSouthSudan was a virtual summit convened to celebrate Africa Day on 25 May 2019; it called for lasting peace in South Sudan. The summit enabled online engagement through Facebook, Twitter, YouTube, and the campaign website. The summit, which was both virtual and physical, focused on the impact of war on the population; the role of women in peacebuilding and their inclusion in leadership; justice for survivors of war-related sexual violence; and the role of regional institutions and countries in the region in promoting peace and the protection of women and girls in South Sudan ('World's first virtual summit … ' 2018). Women's organisations in South Sudan joined the campaign, including Eve Organization for Women, Anataban, and the South Sudan Women's Coalition, which had representatives speak during the summit. The event reached more than 115 million people on social media in 25 countries globally. The summit was broadcast throughout South Sudan on Eye Radio and in 11 locations, and the UN Mission hosted viewing events for civil society. The summit received support from leaders, including the US Ambassador to the UN, the Deputy Secretary General of the United Nations, the Executive Director of UN Women, and the UK Special Envoy to the Sudan and South Sudan.

During the summit, participants expressed frustration at the peace talks led by IGAD. The Sawa South Sudan summit produced ideas and optimism for South Sudanese and African leadership to secure progress on key issues, including assenting to African Union sanctions and seeing the worst offenders brought to justice; greater diplomatic leadership from Rwanda's president and chair of the African Union; holding to account regional governments to take all measures to cut off the flow of arms and funds that fuel the conflict; and continuing to build solidarity and activism among and with South Sudanese civil society. To maintain political momentum, the international NGO Crisis Action supported a delegation of three civil society leaders from South Sudan to the UN and Washington.[2]

Increasingly, social media and other forms of technology in peacebuilding are being promoted, because most of the population in postconflict countries are young and most people have at least a mobile phone with access to radio or social media. The use of technology became especially significant in the case of South Sudan because many citizens live in exile or as refugees and this was the only means left for them to engage with the rebuilding process.

Mobilising for Peace

Two additional strategies that supported women's peacebuilding efforts were the establishment of women's organisations and support from African women peace activists outside South Sudan.

Establishment of New Women's Peacebuilding Organisations

In a bid to ensure the inclusion of women in peace processes as well as address the practical and strategic needs of women, many new organisations were formed – some operating at the national level, others

---

[2]   Email communication from Crisis Action, Advocacy and Campaign Manager, 28 May 2018.

at the state levels, and others in IDP and refugee camps. Although some of the groups formed since 2013 remain operational, others that were formed for specific purposes have subsequently ceased to exist, such as the Women Leaders for Peace Network, which was formed to influence women's participation in the peace processes. The major objective of all the groups was to contribute to peacebuilding and most importantly to ensure an end to the conflict. Many of the women interviewed said that the reason they formed the groups was because they believed that women had what it took to stop the war and because of the horrendous human rights violations women experienced during conflict. One of the leaders of one of the groups shared that once the conflict broke out in December 2013, women in Parliament mobilised other women leaders in Juba to form the Women Leaders for Peace Network. As one member of Parliament, the Hon. Betty Ogwaro, explained in a 2017 interview:

> The first thing we did within the Parliament was to quickly mobilise women leaders at all levels, women in Parliament, women directors, women leaders in churches, all women leaders, and told them it is important for us as women to stop the crisis. For men it is easy to take the gun and they don't care what happens; it is us women who bear the brunt.

The women leaders were motivated by the successes they had achieved in previous peacebuilding processes that enabled them to mobilise women to vote during the referendum. Moreover, all women were tired of the war because women suffer most during and after conflicts. The Women Leaders for Peace saw the crisis as another opportunity to engage with political leaders and leaders of the warring parties to take responsibility to stop the war.

The Women Leaders for Peace mobilised women and drafted the women's agenda for peace, which formed the basis for the initial peace negotiations in Addis Ababa in January 2014. They also engaged with the President and encouraged him to increase the number of women at the peace negotiations. Due to lack of funding and fragmentation associated with their organising, this network failed to sustain momentum and has been dormant since the second phase of the talks in 2015. The lack of survival of such initiatives is a clear indication of how such efforts by women are devalued and not recognised.

Another group that was formed following the eruption of the 2013 conflict and subsequent start of peace talks in Addis Ababa is the Women's Monthly Forum, which aimed to close the gap in information-sharing between women leaders advocating for peace in the Addis peace negotiations in 2014 and those working at the country level, including ordinary women of South Sudan. The idea was to ensure monthly updates on the peace process, hence the name. As Veronica Gordon, a founding member, explained:

The Women's Monthly Forum started with five women to provide monthly updates on the peace process; later five more women were invited to join to ensure diversity and inclusion of different women's groups. We then assigned roles and responsibilities to enable effective functioning of the Forum.

Apart from providing monthly updates, the WMF also engaged in consultations during the development of the Women's Agenda, which was supported by UN Women. The issues women raised during the consultations included the need for increased women's representation at all levels of leadership and security for women. All these issues formed part of the South Sudan women's agenda for peace. The WMF also conducted a gender analysis of the 2016 Agreement for the Resolution of Conflict in South Sudan. This study found that several of the chapters in the ARCSS have explicit provisions that safeguard women's rights and specifically create positions for women. For example, a 35 per cent quota was allocated to ensure women's participation in the transitional government. Chapter 6 on the parameters of the permanent constitution contains provisions to ensure gender inclusion. It seeks to guarantee gender equity and affirmative action. This could be a result of the engagement of a gender adviser to the mediator. Although the agreement made efforts to safeguard women's rights in the constitutional process, the transitional government may consider adopting specific gender-related laws or constitutional provisions to guarantee gender equity (WMF focus group, 2016). The WMF also simplified and translated the gender analysis of the agreement and the revitalised peace agreement into three languages: Nuer, Bari, and Arabic. They held radio talk shows and monthly forums and distributed peace-related documents.

Many other groups were also formed at the state levels, and a lot of these groups operated without funding support. They had constitutions to guide their operations, but registration remained a challenge because the cost of US$450 was too high for women in postconflict settings to register their organisations. This meant that they could not conduct public activities, which would have required approval from state security departments and their activities risked being closed down if they did not comply. Moreover, an NGO is expected to have an office and to submit the list of its members, who are usually vetted. It is difficult to vet such a list without including names that the government finds non-partisan. As a result of these regulations, WMF's Veronica Gordon explains, 'Most have remained as community-based organisations. They lack office space and are unable to pay for registration. Many of them get together and partner to raise funds to carry out activities.'

Following the fear and shock generated from the June 2016 conflict, women living in the Protection of Civilians camps in Wau State formed Women Peace Committees with representatives from the 12 counties of Wau and the Protection of Civilians Camps, with a membership of about 160 people as of June 2018. This was out of the desire for peace to prevail and the belief that the conflict in South Sudan would continue to affect women, including widows who had become the mainstay of their households. Their goal was to achieve peace that eliminated ethnic hatred. The Women Peace Committee's (WPC) aim was to build peaceful coexistence among different tribes and promote sustainable development through awareness-raising, using songs and drama to engage with communities. Eventually they gained support from Oxfam and the Community Empowerment for Progress Organization.

Although WPC views itself as a women's organisation, it found the need to engage with men. The idea of bringing men on board came from the realisation that men are involved in conflict directly and should be encouraged to stop fighting, and the desire to encourage different groups to fight for their rights. However, members ensure that women remain leaders of the group, to avoid the possibility of men taking over.

The formation of women's organisations by the women in South Sudan at both national and state levels to build peace and to address the impact of war has significantly contributed to social, political, and economic reconstruction in the country. Many organisations like WPC continue to address issues of economic empowerment, skills in peacebuilding, trauma management, education for women and children, and advocacy for women's participation in decision-making. However, many of the groups did not survive due to lack of funds and means of transportation. The majority of the women who established these organisations did not have the know-how about fundraising or engaging in partnerships with others to conduct their activities. The other challenge was the insecurity in the country that made it difficult for these groups to move around freely and conduct their activities safely. As one 2018 Wau focus group participant explained, 'Sometimes security personnel do not allow us to do our work; sometimes we are arrested and released. This makes us live in fear.'

Women's organisations, which generally remain informal and unregistered, significantly contribute to peacebuilding at the community level. Nevertheless, they face challenges such as lack of funds and restrictions on being formally registered. There is need for more support to these groups to ensure they continue their work in building peace.

Support from African Women Peace Activists

Working in a context of prolonged conflict brings debilitating fatigue, stress, burnout, and loss of hope among women peace activists. In the spirit of sisterhood, African women have innovatively engaged to support South Sudan women peace activists. At the initial stages after the 2013 conflict, women around Africa organised meetings for the women of South Sudan to reflect on conflict and strategise on the next steps. Two such meetings were organised by Isis-Women's International Cross Cultural Exchange (now Women's International Peace Centre) in

Kampala, Uganda, and by UN Women in Nairobi, Kenya. The aim was to show solidarity to the women of South Sudan and provide them with a space to plan the next steps. At both meetings it was agreed that what the women of South Sudan want is peace. Both meetings developed a position paper stating what the women want from any planned peace negotiations. The UN Women meeting also facilitated sharing of experience by women from Liberia, Nigeria, and Kenya to help the South Sudan women plan effectively.

Even in the midst of many failed peace agreements, African women across the continent and the world continued to stand in solidarity with South Sudan women. The #SawaSouthSudan campaign, mentioned in the previous section, brought together influential women leaders from South Sudan, other parts of the African continent, and the wider world in a virtual summit to elevate the voices of South Sudan's women, to galvanise international support, and to foster dialogue around solutions for a lasting and equitable peace. They discussed the human toll of the war, the devastating impunity, and the potential for African solidarity to transform efforts to build peace in South Sudan. 'Sawa' means 'together' and 'ready'.

The Special Envoy of the Chairperson of the African Union Commission on Women, Peace and Security also led a solidarity mission to South Sudan from 6 to 9 December 2016 as part of the campaign to restore the dignity of the women of South Sudan. The delegation met with internally displaced women in the Protection of Civilians camps and representatives from women's groups and civil society organisations. This provided space for women activists to share how the violence impacted women's lives and expressed a strong need for peace and restoration of law and order. It was also an affirmation that their voices on what was happening at the grassroots level were being heard and provoking action and intervention at different levels.

Links Between Women Activists and Women at the Peace Table

From our interviews with women activists, the link with women at formal peace talks had two distinct dimensions. At the initial stages of the peace process in 2014, the women of South Sudan with support from UN Women developed the South Sudan Women's Agenda, which became an advocacy tool for women having a seat at the table. The Agenda was developed from consultations with a wide range of women of South Sudan, as discussed earlier. Members of the South Sudan Women's Coalition ensured there was a direct linkage with women at the peace talks, because they established a feedback mechanism between themselves and those more directly involved. The South Sudan Women's Coalition for Peace is a network of over 50 organisations formed to strengthen the engagement of women with the revitalisation process. In fact, members of the Coalition who were at the negotiations as representatives of civil society, the academia and youth had a 'technical team', drawn from members who supported document analysis that enhanced the arguments and negotiations of women at the table. The technical group also engaged in 'corridor advocacy' with other members of civil society, other women's groups, and the warring parties during the negotiations.

As mentioned earlier, there were videoconferencing sessions that allowed for the voices of grassroots women to be heard in the HLRP in Addis Ababa. Although some women felt positive about being heard during the formal peace negotiations, many of those we interviewed at the local level felt that they were not represented. They stated that most of the women at the national level who were at the peace talks did not know or fully understand their issues. Although they acknowledged that it is good for women to be at the table, they categorically stated that they would prefer to be there and speak for themselves. As a woman who participated in a 2018 focus group in Wau noted:

> The concern is that those women who are there are representing women, but we need women from here to go to the table. Those women don't know our issues so are not representing us. Women at the table are from a national level and do not feel the pains we feel here. We want our own at the table. The women at the national level are maintaining the status quo; we do not want to be represented. Some of those women are the wives of the leaders and their relatives.

This highlights the importance of dialogue with women working at the grassroots level, because only certain women from the political elites will ultimately be included in the formal talks. These women do not necessarily represent the perspective of those at the grassroots. There is a diversity of experiences and a diversity of vision for women of South Sudan at stake. Although there were mechanisms in place to ensure this dialogue, it may not always be reflected in the result of the peace talks. However, there was room for improvement in terms of the feedback mechanism between women at the table and women at the grassroots to provide information and updates and solicit their input. Ultimately these mechanisms and support from the grassroots also strengthened the women at the peace table.

Conclusions

We have differentiated between national and grassroot organisations. National organisations have had the main goal of inserting women around and at the peace table as well as gendering the peace talks. They have largely been successful in mobilising for inclusion by using the framework of Resolution 1325 and the National Action Plan on women, peace, and security, which has as its first goal to 'increase women's effective participation in leadership and peacebuilding and strengthen gender perspectives in the South Sudan's state building and reconstruction' (Republic of South Sudan 2015). The popular concern for security and safety in South Sudan necessitated the building of a powerful coalition of women leaders from South Sudan, which provided the basis on which they were able to leverage their collective voice with IGAD, the defining regional organisation in their area. Equity in numerical representation of women in a patriarchal context where politics is seen as men's business put women's strategic gender interest centre stage. The inclusion of women at the peace table was seen as something benefiting all South Sudanese women because it would bring their experiences to the fore in the text of the agreement, including experiences from the grassroots. Although the dialogue mechanisms between national and grassroots organisations had imperfections, it was a genuine attempt to embrace the diversity of women's perspectives.

Women's organisations have been building peace at the grassroots by bridging ethnic divides, distributing emergency food, and praying, to name some of the strategies employed. This type of peace activism is embedded in the everyday lives and needs of women in the community and thus relates more to women's practical interests. Women showcase agency and take on new roles in their communities at the same time as they adhere to gendered expectations of nurturing. A commonality between the two types of movements is the ability of women to build bridges across ethnic and religious divides. This is essential in a context of a conflict with strong ethnic dimensions, especially between the Nuer and Dinka. Peacebuilding across different ethnic groups is an essential contribution to peacebuilding. This entails emergency food distribution without discrimination as to religion and ethnicity or the mobilisation of marches to put sexual violence on the agenda, something that women of different ethnic affiliations have confronted. We see this coalition-building as a political strategy rather than building on essentialised views of women's peaceful nature. It becomes a necessity to unify women in a patriarchal context where women are sidelined from formal peacebuilding processes. They simply have to strategise differently from men to be heard.

Table 2.1. Women's Organisations Interviewed

No.	Name of Organisation	Year Established	Mandate	Type of Organisation
1.	Peace Building Committee, Wau	2015	Sensitise people living in Protection of Civilians camps on peaceful coexistence	Grassroots
2.	Women Peace Association	2014	Promote peaceful coexistence	Grassroots
3.	Women's Grassroots Network	2014	Build the capacity of members in peacebuilding and reconciliation	Grassroots (network of about 20 small women's associations formed as a result of the conflict)
4.	Monthly Women's Forum	2014	Ensure women's voices are heard and influence peace processes in South Sudan, as well as mainstream multiple engagements by women	National
5.	Women Leaders Peace Network	2013	Galvanise women to advocate for the peaceful resolution of conflict in South Sudan	National
6.	South Sudan Women's Empowerment Network	2005	Promote human rights and seek to achieve social and gender justice and women's participation in decision-making	National
7.	Association of Media Women in South Sudan	2012	Increase the visibility of women's issues in the media	National

Table 2.1. —*continued*

No.	Name of Organisation	Year Established	Mandate	Type of organisation
8.	Eve Organization for Women	2005	Women's leadership and political participation, peacebuilding and conflict resolution, sexual and gender-based violence, and reproductive health	National
9.	Voice of Women for Peace and Faith	2014	Promote peace and women's participation in peacebuilding	National
10.	South Sudanese Network for Democracy and Elections	2009	Promote good governance	National (network of over 150 civil society organisations in South Sudan)
11.	South Sudanese Women with Disabilities Association	2015	Platform for women with disabilities to address their needs and ensure inclusion in nation building	National
12·	South Sudan Women's General Association	2009	Promote the role of women in all aspects of development of South Sudan	National (has state chapters)
13.	South Sudan Women's Coalition for Peace	2017	Promote peace and women's participation in peacebuilding	National (network of over 40 women's organisations)

3

'Ba Sa Jin Mu' (They Don't Listen to Us)
Women and Peacebuilding in North-Eastern Nigeria

AYESHA IMAM, MAINA YAHI, AND HAUWA BIU

Northern Nigeria, where the insurgent radical Islamist group Boko Haram has killed thousands of people, is a context where conflict strongly shapes women's mobility, leadership, and rights. Women in northern Nigeria face the additional challenges of conservative gender ideologies and exclusion from formal peace processes and postconflict governance arrangements. This is despite the efforts of women peace activists in developing the National and State Action Plans, which follow UNSCR 1325 and related resolutions. Nonetheless, women engage in unrecognised or informal forms of peacebuilding. By calling it informal peacebuilding, we acknowledge women's exclusion from political power, which pushes them into and restricts them to informal spheres of activism. In north-eastern Nigeria, women's role in peacebuilding is usually less obvious because it is intertwined with everyday life. This chapter looks at research through the primary lens of activist-researchers with internally displaced women in Borno State of north-east Nigeria. IDP women are seldom if ever considered as actors and more commonly thought of only as victims. The chapter examines how Nigerian women's rights and peace organisations and networks have collaborated across political, ethnic, religious, and other differences and have brought a gendered lens to bear on peacebuilding.

The insurgency of the Jama'atu Ahlis Sunnah Lida'awati Wal Jihad, more commonly known as Boko Haram,[1] is an Islamist group based in northern Nigeria that is also active in Cameroon, Chad, and Niger. Conflict-related deaths in north-east Nigeria are estimated at over 35,000 between 2011 and 2018 alone, over 18,000 of which are due to terrorist attacks. The Global Terrorism Index further reports that Boko Haram is one of the four deadliest terrorist groups in the world over the past 15 years and the deadliest in Africa (Institute for Economics and Peace 2019), even

---

[1] Jamā'atu ahl al-Sunna li'l-Da'wa wa'l-jihād – the Association of Sunnah People for Proselytisation and Struggle. Since 2010 the group has split into several factions but it is collectively referred to in popular usage and in this chapter by the Hausa phrase 'Boko Haram', meaning 'secular education is forbidden'.

with its split into several factions since the upsurge of conflict in 2009 and a decline in terrorist activity since its peak in 2014. Despite military offences in 2015–16 that reclaimed territory, Boko Haram continues its terrorist attacks, including 'suicide' bombings; attacks on villages, convoys, and the military; and kidnappings of civilians. Between January and August 2020, there were at least 13 such attacks, with hundreds killed and many more wounded (the Counter-Extremism Project 2020). The conflict has also displaced more than 2.5 million people (Council on Foreign Relations 2020a), many of whom are still living in IDP camps in north-eastern Nigeria, especially in Maiduguri. Others have been allowed to settle in host communities and with relatives across northern Nigeria.

Even before the current crisis, northern Nigeria was already a field of contestation over women's rights and mobility, due in large part to increasing conservativism over women's dress codes, women's mobility and roles outside the domestic space, polygyny, child marriage, and wives' subordination to husbands, as well as the utility of girls' and women's education[2] (Mahdi 2008; Okoli and Nnaemeka Azom 2019). These conservative gender ideologies are further acted on by the insurgents who not only require *hijab* for women but also prohibit secular education (for both girls and boys) – while at the same time giving women some active roles in the insurgency (*ibid*). This complicates peacebuilding challenges for women themselves, and influences how federal, state, and local government actors, as well as mainstream community groups, frame the inclusion of women as actors in prevention, protection, mediation, and peacebuilding, including reconstruction (Nwangwu and Ezeibe 2019).

Methods

The primary empirical data in this chapter comes mostly from people directly affected by the conflict, specifically internally displaced women and 'returnees'.[3] We ran volunteer-based discussion groups with women in the Bakassi, National Youth Service Corps, and Teachers' Village IDP camps. We also held volunteer discussion groups with internally displaced women living in host communities in the Shuwari, Polo, and 202 Housing Estate neighbourhoods of Maiduguri. The seven discussion groups comprised around 70 women, coming from Bama, Gwoza, Monguno, Damboa, Marte, Konduga, Guzamala, Ganzai, Angwar Doki, Shuwari, Pompomari, Kumshe, Mafoni, Jiddari, Kukawa, Ngala, and Mairi local government areas of Borno State, as well as Michika in Adamawa State. In the IDP camps, we also observed anti-stigmatisation awareness

---

[2]   Mahdi, for instance, points out that 'Up to 1975 hardly any Muslim woman in northern Nigeria wore the hijab, while today one could not miss the growing number of women who wear it.'

[3]   All the women have been given pseudonyms, for their confidentiality and safety, because many of them are still living in the IDP camps.

sessions, community tolerance and mediation training, and psychosocial counselling group sessions.

We also carried out research in Konduga, the capital of Konduga Local Government Area, and spoke with around 20 women there who had returned to their community after fleeing ('returnees') because the army had declared it safe.[4] We held our discussions in the ruined home of one of the returnees. In addition to the discussion groups, we also had informal conversations with internally displaced women.

The fact that two of the three researchers are not only from Borno State, but they are also known activists in Maiduguri for women's rights and community support, facilitated the membership of both the discussion groups and the IDPs in the host communities, as well as strengthening rapport and trust in the conversations.

Almost everyone with whom we spoke had traumatic experiences to tell, whether they shared a personal story or a story about a close relative. We heard painful stories about abduction, rape, and sexual abuse; witnessing husbands, brothers, and sons killed or mutilated and daughters and sisters abducted; and running desperately for days through the bush from remote rural areas with children and without water or food, trying to find safety. They often still did not know the whereabouts of their husbands or children and other loved ones.

Many women have spent years living in crowded IDP camps without enough food, clothing, or medical services, or in host communities and in urban poor neighbourhoods where they live, squat, or could stay in rooms or camp on land owned by relatives or host community members. Typically, as one Polo focus group participant explained, 'we build a shelter in an open plot or uncompleted buildings'. Further, inadequate as supplies to the camps are, IDPs in host communities have little or no state support at all. They depend on domestic work, small-scale trading, sale of craft products, or any source of income they could find, with occasional support from relatives and neighbours.

In addition to interviewing IDP women themselves, we conducted 25 interviews with representatives of women's rights, peace, religious, and community groups; networks, state agencies, traditional leaders, international nongovernmental organisations (INGOs); representatives in security, humanitarian aid, and reconstruction; and policymakers, researchers, and individual activists both in Maiduguri at the local state level and in Abuja, the federal capital territory. Here again, the reputations of the lead researcher and the co-researcher nationally as researchers and activists facilitated the connections with and frankness of discussions.

Following the preliminary analysis of the data from the discussion groups and the interviews, we held a series of five workshops, with the internally displaced women in Maiduguri and select groups of

---

[4] The next day, there was an attack on Konduga by the insurgents. That time, none of our informants or their families were injured or killed.

interviewees in both Maiduguri and Abuja. These workshops fed back into our analyses for critique and revision, and we then worked jointly on developing recommendations based on this feedback. These recommendations are presented later in this chapter.

Background to North-East Nigeria and Boko Haram Insurgency

Most accounts date the founding of Boko Haram to the early 2000s, when it broke away from Izala, the main Salafist movement in Nigeria, and disengaged from the secular Nigerian state and set up an alternative community. At this time, it launched a series of attacks on police stations, prisons, and government buildings, which were quashed by the military. Subsequently, the group was relatively quiet until 2009. This changed amid escalating clashes and retaliatory attacks between Boko Haram members and the police, during which the founding leader Mohammed Yusuf was killed while in police custody. Boko Haram then went underground and re-emerged in 2010 with an explicit strategy of using assassinations, drive-by shootings, improvised explosive devices (IEDs), 'suicide' bombings, direct assault, and kidnapping. It also started targeting not only security forces and government institutions, but also civilians – individuals who criticised them, religious leaders and laity in churches and mosques, teachers and pupils in schools, traditional leaders, health workers in clinics, and politicians and ordinary people in villages, markets, and other public spaces (Kyari 2014).

While building on a history of radical religious protest in northern Nigeria, the Boko Haram insurgency encompasses a much more complicated relationship going beyond the Muslims vs Christians issue that has dominated discussions in the Western media. Before the insurgency, northern Nigeria registered as the most impoverished area on most indicators: average income, access to education, health services, water, sanitation, energy, maternal mortality, infant mortality, and nutritional level. These extreme inequalities have grown worse. Regional inequalities in Nigeria can be traced back to the British colonial administration, when major structural changes in agriculture, transport, and education had profound effects on the socioeconomic development of the then three regions. Since political independence, the activities of post-independence ethnolinguistic elites have perpetuated and widened the regional and individual socioeconomic disparities in the country (Aka 2000; Dapel 2018), as well as widening the gap between the very rich and everyone else, especially the poor, between the urban and the rural, and between men and women (for an overview, see Mayah et al. 2017). Studies also report extremely low trust in government and high levels of perception of government corruption (Pring and Vrushi 2019; Tamir 2019). Nigeria ranks well below the global average on receiving services promptly and without having to pay a bribe, and expectation of being treated courteously by public service officials (Bratton et al. 2019).

Consequently, Boko Haram's condemnation of corruption and immorality, while noting the conspicuous consumption of the (secular 'Western'-educated) Nigerian elite amid oceans of poverty initially made appeals of 'Islamic' justice attractive to many. However, although Boko Haram deliberately and deplorably attacks and targets Christians, it also targets Muslims who do not agree with its views and actions. Boko Haram has killed even more Muslim preachers than Christian clergy and it has killed, abducted, raped, and displaced both Christians and Muslims. Boko Haram does not have the support of the majority of Muslims in Nigeria – 69 per cent of whom are worried about Islamist extremism, and 78 per cent think that suicide bombing and other attacks on civilians can never be justified in the name of Islam (Pew Research Center 2013).

As numerous recent studies point out, the main drivers of extremism leading to insurgency are poverty, regional inequality, environmental stress, migration, youth unemployment, state corruption, and human rights abuses. It is not only religious discourses and differences between Christians and Muslims, or among Muslims (Mustapha 2017; Mustapha and Ehrhardt 2018; Mustapha and Meagher 2020). Although poverty, inequality, and a lack of accountability predate the insurgency, the situation has worsened considerably in large part due to the insurgency. The women we interviewed identified these as the key factors to be addressed in peacebuilding and reconstruction.

One of the main drivers of the increase in poverty in the region is climate change. The people who live in this region experience climate change's severe impacts. The accelerated drying up of Lake Chad has led to increasing aridness in the Savanna Sahel regions (from southern Mauritania to Mali, Niger, Burkina Faso, Chad, and northern Nigeria) and a loss of fishing livelihood, which is exacerbated by insecurity due to Boko Haram attacks and state responses. A combination of drought, an increased average temperature by two degrees in the past 20 years, and the variability in seasonal rainfall patterns (wider swings in rainfall patterns, with too much or too little rain at particular times) makes farming increasingly risky for food security or as an economic endeavour. The interconnected effects of soil degradation and deforestation adversely affect farmers' ability to grow their own food or sell it at the market. The Nigerian government continues to neglect poverty elimination and focus on oil production, a major contributor to federal government revenue (more than 80 per cent), rather than sustainable agriculture and industry, or renewable and decentralised energy production that could address systematic poverty and adaption to climate change.

Security and Economic Effects of the Insurgency

In more than 40 remote villages in the three north-eastern states between 2011 and 2014, Boko Haram was responsible for daily killings, bombings, looting, and destruction of schools, homes, markets, and hospitals. The violence included the abduction of more than 4,000 women and girls. Boko Haram abducted 3,000 women and girls from more than seven local government areas in Borno State. They also kidnapped Nigerians and foreigners for ransom and destroyed telecoms bases, which made communications impossible.

Despite the Nigerian government's halt, reverse, and recovery of Boko Haram's 2014 seizure of territory, the territory outside the zones around the local government headquarters remains largely insecure, because the insurgents resort to hit-and-run guerrilla tactics in a region that is geographically large, without much telecommunications infrastructure, and with underpaid and underequipped armed forces. Despite President Buhari's 2015 declaration that Nigeria has 'technically won the war' against Boko Haram and that it was safe to return to home areas, IDPs are aware of the ongoing insecurity. One Polo focus group participant expressed scepticism:

> Like in Baga town, it was said by one of our relatives, who is a CJTF [Civilian Joint Task Force[5]] that the town is safe. But not the outskirts of the town, because it is still not safe for the people to go to Baga and continue with their normal activities. Because one kilometre from the town is not safe; Boko Haram are there hunting people to either kill or abduct.

Consequently, much of Borno State remains unsafe for residents. Famine looms because most farmers cannot return to their land and farm. Farmers are restricted to growing certain crops and banned from fishing for security reasons. For instance, a Konduga returnee mentioned in a focus group that:

> Due to the presence of Boko Haram around the town, there is no more early-morning fishing as it used to be. Because it is not yet safe for our

---

[5] The Civilian Joint Task Force (CJTF), known colloquially as 'Yan Gora' (those of the sticks because, not having weapons, they used sticks to beat off Boko Haram attacks) was formed in 2013 by young men in Maiduguri to 'protect our community' against Boko Haram and the formation of CJTF units spread throughout the north-east of Nigeria. Members are mostly young men, but women are also members of the CJTF. However, women's participation (and acceptance by their colleagues) varies from group to group – ranging from being active fighters to being restricted to searching women at checkpoints or women's rooms where caches of arms are suspected. The CJTF is credited with successfully preventing Boko Haram from taking over Maiduguri and Biu, and with protecting communities and villages generally. In addition to direct fighting (alone or with the state security forces), the CJTF has provided local intelligence; identified and tracked Boko Haram members; patrolled communities; staffed checkpoints; conducted searches; assisted people with escaping violence; rescued kidnapped girls; transported women in labour to health facilities; and acted as community mediators in disputes, among other things.

men to go fishing in the nearby river, because of the presence of the insurgents at the river. They live across the river where our men used to fish.

Finally, armed insurgents attack lorries containing goods and crops on supply routes.

This lack of security also renders precarious other forms of livelihood and life-sustaining activities, including the small-scale businesses known as *sana'oi* (Hausa, plural), such as gathering firewood in the bush for home use or sale, cooking for sale, dyeing cloth, leatherwork, and harvesting shea nuts for processing or wild fruit and plants for consumption or sale. In rural areas, in particular, it is common to have a *sana'a* in addition to farming, which is practised more intensively in the dry season. The displacement resulting from the insurgency has resulted in the disruption of such means of livelihood, as people flee their villages for safety into local government area capital towns or the state capital Maiduguri, which offer very few amenities to address internally displaced people's needs.

The insurgency has also created trauma for the 13.2 million people of the zone (of whom an estimated 53 per cent of people required humanitarian aid in 2019), as a consequence of repeated attacks resulting in fear, insecurity, rape and sexual harassment, kidnapping, and injuries. The insurgency has contributed to an increase in addictions and substance abuse. The insurgents routinely attack schools and have slaughtered school children – for example, the boys burned in their dormitories at the Federal Government College at Buni Yadi. Consequently, the educational system in the region is in shambles, with schools destroyed or closed, or children withdrawn in fear for their safety and that of the staff.

Gendered Recruitment and Participation in the Insurgency

The insurgency has successfully recruited men and boys to its cause through economic incentives and/or ideology. Increasingly, Boko Haram also uses coercion, forcing men and boys to join as combatants or informants or be killed. Women and girls experience 'participation' in the insurgency differently, primarily through abduction. In 2015, over 2,000 women and girls were estimated to have been abducted in the previous year (Amnesty International 2015). As abductees, women and girls take on both domestic and conflict services. They also face sexual abuse, primarily through forced marriage. Sometimes the 'choice' was between being married or being a slave. For Christian women, the choices were to convert to Islam or be a slave and endure further maltreatment. Leah Sharibu was refused release with 182 other schoolgirls from Dapchi, because she, the only Christian among her fellow students, refused to convert (Leithead 2016; Ogunmade 2019).

Women and girls may also be killed as security force collaborators or as insurgency combatants. Boko Haram has the highest proportion of female 'suicide' bombers of any terrorist group (Institute for Economics & Peace 2019, 16). Sometimes they are forced to become so-called 'suicide' bombers, strapped with IEDs. Many of them are young girls, and to a much lesser extent boys, who are too young to render informed consent, such as Fatimatu in Bakassi IDP Camp, who pointed out that she knew that 'Boko Haram are using the young girls they captured as suicide bombers, because I was a victim as well.'

Once their husbands or fathers become active members of the insurgency, women have few options other than joining Boko Haram. Women's participation in the conflict was often conditioned by the roles played by the men in their lives. It was shaped by societal and cultural expectations that women should depend on men for their livelihoods. For instance, the Muslim injunction that husbands should maintain wives and children has too often been misused to deny girls and women access to education, resources, and means of livelihood. This both renders many women even more vulnerable than men and gives rise to the conditions in which women may find increased autonomy and choices in insurgent groups such as Boko Haram. Some women and girls choose to join or support Boko Haram for economic reasons or to experience greater autonomy in their lives than in pre-insurgency gender relations, or for belief in the cause.

The insurgents recruited women into the organisation into roles such as informants, porters, or those responsible for domestic chores such as cooking and fetching firewood and water. Women also served as recruiters themselves, usually via personal and especially family ties. Women have also become active in armed opposition groups, finding a higher level of autonomy, freedom, and economic returns than in pre-insurgence communities. Wives of Boko Haram leaders frequently had slaves of their own from among the abducted girls and women. In addition, it would appear that attacking villagers and raiding their food and livestock meant a higher standard of food security for many women (and men) in Boko Haram.

Furthermore, young women are more likely than young men to be solicited to join extremist groups (Nagarajan 2017, 37). Gendered stereotypes lead some to believe it may be easier to radicalise or deradicalise women than men by changing their minds, but evidence suggests otherwise. After deradicalisation programmes, many women have returned to extremist groups because they face more stigma than men when it comes to reintegrating into society.

Stigma has several components. First, while both women and men are expected to have *kunya* (contextually translated as modesty, shame, or propriety), strictures on women are stronger than on men. A woman may be accused of being *maras kunya* (lacking in shame, modesty, or propriety) for eating in public or for being deemed to be flirting. For women, in particular, *kunya* is implicated in regulating sexuality, such that women will often not mention their firstborn children (evidence of having had sexual relations), despite being in publicly and socially recognised marriages. For girls and women who have been abducted or who have disappeared returning, especially with a child, raises the question of lacking *kunya* and illicit sexual relations – whether or not that was due to rape, forced marriage, or consent.

Second, returning women (and men) face suspicion over whether they left voluntarily or, even if they were abducted, have been radicalised into Boko Haram and participated in the attacks and atrocities of the insurgents. Implicit is a masculinist assumption that women are easily brainwashed. The use of female 'suicide' bombers by Boko Haram has increased that fear. Women who have voluntarily married or followed husbands who are active insurgents are even more likely to be treated with suspicion and rejection.

Third, there is often a strong deterministic assumption that children whose fathers are active insurgents will inherit the violence of their biological fathers' 'bad blood' (UNICEF and International Alert 2016). Stigma against such children is not only an abuse in itself, but likely to result in self-fulfilling prophecies. For these reasons, girls and women experience forced recruitment and the violence of Boko Haram differently from boys and men and may have a more difficult time reintegrating into society after participating in the insurgency.

Insurgency Impact on Gender Relations in Households and Communities

Due to the insurgency, many men have been injured or killed. Others have lost access to farming land, capital, and resources. This has led women to more frequently become the visible *de facto* heads of households and sometimes the main support for household maintenance. Household gender relations have changed as women's economic contributions to household maintenance have become more clearly needed and more visible – contrary to prevailing social norms, which make women's labour within the household invisible.

Proceeds from women's *work* are most often used to support household members (Imam 1994). They are spent on items such as spices for cooking, clothes for women and their children, medicine, *kayan daki* (bride marriage gifts) for daughters, and assistance with marriage expenses for sons. A study of two villages demonstrated that women's contributions to the household are very much underplayed by both women and men. The undervaluing of women's contributions takes two forms. First, some reproductive labour[6] is almost completely unacknowledged as contributing to household maintenance. Neither women nor men seem to

---

[6] Reproductive labour involves unpaid domestic labour such as cleaning, cooking, and childcare.

count women's labour in household tasks as significant to the household. Just less than half of all women listed cooking as a contribution to household maintenance, and only a third listed any other form of reproductive labour, whether childcare or housework. It is not just that these tasks are reproductive. It is also because they are done by women that they are undervalued. In contrast, 80 per cent of men consider their labour in such tasks as doing repairs and fetching water, fuel, and animal fodder as part of their contribution to household maintenance. In addition to this non-acknowledgement of women's reproductive work, purchasing household necessities is another way women contribute to the household that is downplayed.

One insight that might explain this phenomenon is that husbands' obligation to their wives is defined in terms of economic responsibilities. Thus, for men to admit that they are aided in this by their wives is simultaneously to admit their failure to be good husbands and responsible adults. The change in men's ability to be providers has contributed to an increase in violence against women (especially domestic violence) by men who feel their masculinity is threatened. The increasing tensions in household relations as men have been unable to fulfil their traditional role are also reflected in relations between husbands and wives that question the normative subordination of wives to husbands. A common comment was like that of Sadiya in Bakassi IDP camp that 'our lack of respect for our husbands is due to the fact that they stopped taking care of our livelihood. While they lie under the tree resting, we are the ones moving around the town begging for means of livelihood.' Other changes to household structure include newly created units led by 'separated children', both girls and boys, as well as an increase in youth gangs.

The Boko Haram insurgency has heightened household tensions by increasing vulnerabilities, trauma, and stigma through the violence it has brought. An estimated 15 per cent of people (25 million) in Nigeria live with disabilities. However, across all countries vulnerable groups have greater prevalence of disability (World Health Organisation and World Bank 2011, 27). Many of those vulnerabilities are found in Borno State, including poverty and comorbidities from chronic diseases, and women and older people are especially vulnerable. People living with disabilities experience greater violence in conflict situations because they have less ability to escape. This becomes more pronounced for women and girls living with disabilities, because they are even less likely to have access to support and assistive devices (for example, wheelchairs, hearing aids, spectacles, or children assigned as guides for the visually impaired).

During former Nigerian President Goodluck Jonathan's term in office (2010–15), the military played a role in targeting men and boys from the region as well as women and girls. The military killed and detained men and boys and suspected women and girls of serving as 'suicide' bombers. Men in the armed forces, the police, civilian vigilante groups, and in the community more generally, and politicians have all raped and sexually abused women. The women and girls and their children who survived this sexual violence and abuse experienced more abuse by being stigmatised. The increasing difficulty for already impoverished women and girls to earn a livelihood has also led to 'high-risk coping strategies like transactional sex in exchange for money or food in order to feed their families' (Nagarajan 2017, 48). In the camps of Maiduguri, many turn to survival sex for food or to get permission to leave the camps.

Women in Resistance and Informal Peacebuilding in North-East Nigeria

Women in these communities play multiple protection and peacebuilding roles from resistance to protecting family and community members from attack, helping people escape attack, serving as mediators for conflict among/within the IDP camps, advocating for peace and respect in local communities, and organising peace rallies and marches.

At great personal risk of death, injury, abduction, and sexual abuse, women join 'vigilante' groups at the community level and participate in physical fighting (such as Aisha Bakari Gombiya, who hunts down Boko Haram fighters). Others may join the CJTF to address security issues, like Amina Abdullahi. Nagarajan (2017, 37) finds that although men outnumber women in armed groups, women still participate in vigilante operations. In Biu, for example, women vigilante members make up about 13 per cent of the main office and hold command in some areas due to the hunting skills they inherited from their parents and training in fighting they have received like the men. In addition to accompanying men on joint fighting operations, in Damboa women also prevent spies and IEDs from entering town, patrol the area, and operate checkpoints. Women do face some restrictions because of their gender, though; sometimes they are limited to duties that men cannot execute, such as checking women at checkpoints and markets.

In addition to being associated with armed groups, women have also fought to protect their towns to keep armed groups from entering (Nagarajan 2017, 38). Women negotiate at the local level with Boko Haram, state security, and 'vigilante' groups, with a goal of being left alone and having their children returned. Some women also offer themselves up in exchange for their daughters. They point out members of armed opposition groups to the security forces; negotiate or offer information about suspicious movements or individuals at the local level with state security or with 'vigilante' groups; and try to bring Boko Haram and government officials to the table together, as Aisha Wakil and Hamsatu Al Amin did. They buy time for men and boys to escape when attacks come to their community. They also hide men and boys (including dressing them as women and girls to facilitate their escape) and smuggle them to safety.

Women in Maiduguri organised multiple marches for peace, dignity, and protection and were supported by similar marches and sit-ins across Nigeria. One of the most well-known actions women initiated and sought allies for was the Bring Back Our Girls Campaign (BBOG). Their call, often not fully reported, was for the safe return and protection of all the girls abducted, not only the 276 girls taken from Chibok in 2014. BBOG remains active nationally, with marches, sit-ins, petitions, and public statements, as well as globally with the hashtag #BBOG.

Women and women's organisations have also advocated for and sometimes provided psychosocial support for women survivors of abuse (including mediating and building community support for women pregnant or whose children's fathers are or were in Boko Haram). Women peacebuilders provide economic support for families whose fathers or husbands were killed, injured, or went missing, as well as humanitarian relief for those displaced in general, and organise capacity-building for making a livelihood for women. Sometimes they are able to provide (very) small capital grants so that the trainees can actually use the capacity built. They care for 'separated children' (this includes orphans and those whose parents might still be alive somewhere but are not currently present) and work with 'gang youth'. This work is conducted by myriad small local women's organisations such as Women in New Nigeria, the Borno Women's Development Initiative, the University of Maiduguri Muslim Women's Group, the Borno State Christian Association women's wing, Hope in Legislative for the vulnerable and marginalised, Al Ansar, and Hope for All Foundation. Some projects are also carried out by international NGOs active in the area, like the Norwegian Refugee Council and Search for Common Ground.

However, Nigerian women's organisations, both national and especially state and local community associations, are badly under-resourced. In the current context in Borno State, local women's organisations were doing the work described above with very limited funds, often with donations through personal connections. When INGOs came in with their donor aid, they were given privileged access to IDP camps and set up their own projects and programmes, often ignoring the work that had been done previously by women's groups and hiring women to work on the INGO programmes at much higher salaries.

Women's organisations, sometimes with the support of the humanitarian INGOs, are working against sexual predation of IDP women and corruption in the distribution of limited humanitarian supplies and abuse of power (for example, camp security staff requiring sexual 'favours' before granting exit passes from camps or misappropriating food and supplies intended for camp residents). Hauwa, a resident of the Dalori IDP camp, noted that 'from my experience in the IDP camp in the last three years, I have realised that the security personnel attached to the camp use their position to molest young girls and even older ones whenever there are materials to be distributed.' Similarly, another resident of Teacher's Village IDP camp, Hafsatu stated that 'the problem many of us are facing is the harassment by the security personnel in our camp. If we want to go out of the camp and have to get permission from them, we are asked to go to a room to collect a pass and most times we are sexually assaulted.' Such comments were made about almost every camp, both those staffed by the military and those with CJTF personnel. The internally displaced women work with local women's groups like BAOBAB for Women's Human Rights by speaking out, raising awareness, organising women, and attempting to ensure the accountability of predators.

These women have created a counternarrative against victimhood by serving as actors and courageous survivors, whom authorities should consult, involve, and engage. They do not see themselves as victims requiring charity and pity. Because these women have had to become even better providers out of necessity, they need recognition for their newly expanded roles and support to continue. Yet, instead, women's contributions are being made invisible again. Most commonly, as Laila from the Teacher's Village IDP camp said, 'to be frank with you, the men, especially the camp leaders, never involve the women leaders in the camp when issues of peacebuilding are discussed'.

Women in Formal Peacebuilding and Reconstruction in North-East Nigeria

At the time of this writing, only two women commissioners and four women permanent secretaries serve out of a body of 27. Only one woman serves as the State Emergency Management chairperson and only one woman serves as a member of the House of Representatives, out of 10. The Presidential Committee on North East Initiative, formed by President Buhari in 2016, initially did not include women until there were public protests, which led to the appointment of two civil society representatives who happened to be women. The plan includes some gender-sensitive provisions, including cash transfers, maternal healthcare, psychosocial trauma counselling, and support for women's rehabilitation, but little has been done regarding resourcing, implementation, or monitoring.

The exclusion of women from formal government and political discussions and decisions, including around security or peace reconstruction, is not limited to Borno State. Women across Nigeria are grossly underrepresented in political decision-making. At the federal level in the National Assembly there are eight women out of 109 seats (7.3 per cent) in the Senate, only one of whom comes from northern Nigeria, and 21 women out of 360 seats (5.8 per cent) in the House of Representatives. Women's formal political representation has actually decreased by half over the past two decades from 7 per cent in 2010 to

3.6 per cent in 2020. Currently Nigeria comes 180th out of 193 in the International Parliamentary Union ranking of women's representation in national parliaments.

As a result of such exclusions from the formal sphere, women's political agency has focused on more localised and collective action. Several national women's groups have branches in Borno State. These include both secular groups like the National Council of Women's Societies and BAOBAB for Women's Human Rights, and religious groups like the Federation of Muslim Women of Nigeria and the Christian Association of Nigeria Women's Wing. There are also numerous local Maiduguri or Borno State women's groups, like Women in a New Nigeria, the Borno Women Development Initiative, and the University of Maiduguri Women's Muslim Group. Although most groups run their own individual campaigns and projects, there is a strong tendency at both state and national levels to work together to increase synergy and maximise voice, through networks and coalitions, such as the Legislative Advocacy Coalition on Violence Against Women, which fought for the 2015 Violence Against Persons (Prohibition) Act, the BBOG campaign, and the Women Peace and Security state networks. Members of all the groups, networks, and coalitions mentioned in this paragraph were interviewed in this research project and participated in the policy recommendation workshops. Women's coalition-building efforts between Nigerian Christian and Muslim communities have also been evident in protests against the insurgents' kidnappings and activities, as well as for women's rights generally.

At the local community level, the insurgency itself has disrupted traditional leadership channels for women. Women, more than men, have been physically dispersed from their hometowns where they may have otherwise participated in decision-making through established informal 'traditional' networks. But after relocating to camps and other places for safety, women might not be able to participate in this way any more (Nagarajan 2017, 45–46). Occasionally women leaders are asked to represent women's interests, either through their own initiative or through the intervention of an NGO or INGO, according to a Women in New Nigeria representative. However, this was not the case in any of the camps where we had discussion groups. One informant also noted that none of the IDP camps in Maiduguri had women as camp managers because men dominate the decision-making processes there and choose other men as representatives.

In one of the IDP camps where we held discussion groups, the women leaders in the camp had taken the initiative to form an association to protect women's interests. Through this organisation the women learned skills, like how to identify a land mine. They received humanitarian aid and being in the association allowed them to divide up resources without interference from men. They were also able to monitor the security situation and disseminate information about security throughout the community because, unlike men, they could enter any house. Nonetheless, the women in that camp felt that they were not heard, even when they protested actively. As one said, the camp leaders 'don't listen to us; sometimes we will go out and demonstrate in the camp, yet it does not yield any result' (focus group with internally displaced women from Kukawa LGA). In some cases, internally displaced women have stood in for their husbands who have travelled to farm in a neighbouring state to make decisions for the community (FGD Polo Host community).

Gender relations that discriminate against women perpetuate the risk that women will themselves be actively involved with armed opposition groups, whether by choice or due to their dependence on male connections. For example, women may return to Boko Haram husbands, whether it was initially a nonconsensual marriage or otherwise, by choice for reasons of ideology, autonomy, power, or economic considerations, as well as in reaction to stigmatisation.

In both pre-insurgence and conflict situations, the following conditions remain endemic for women: forced or arranged child marriage, expectation of dependence on men and subordination to husbands, lack of alternatives for livelihood, lack of independent access to land, presence of domestic violence, and lower access to formal, especially higher, education. Peacebuilding that does not involve women and gendered awareness is unlikely to pay attention to the need to reconstruct, not replicate, gender relations. Addressing inequities in gender relations would not only reduce the likelihood that women will support and participate in armed opposition groups as a means of gaining personal autonomy and access to resources. But, even more importantly, addressing inequities is increasingly voiced by women themselves as a legitimate demand and right – including by the mostly poor, rural, and largely illiterate women who were the majority of the discussants in this study.

Women's Recommendations for Peacebuilding and Reconstruction

We asked the focus groups of internally displaced women (both living in camps and living in the community) and women activists working directly with IDPs to discuss what recommendations they would make for peacebuilding and reconstruction. The majority of the women who were IDPs, especially those in the camps, were rural with little formal education. However, some were from rural towns, and some from much smaller villages. A few were, in rural terms, relatively high-status with husbands owning shops or several farms. A very few had some primary schooling and fewer yet secondary schooling and could speak and were literate in English. Most had fled their homes as Boko Haram attacked, and some had been captives of Boko Haram – some escaped on their own, while others were liberated when the armed forces reclaimed territory.

A few had been set up as 'suicide' bombers but had either managed to escape or had given themselves up to the security forces. In contrast, as a group, the women activists had higher economic status and at least secondary school education and were based in urban areas. Nonetheless, this diversity did not make any difference to the recommendations. What follows here are their jointly agreed upon recommendations.

Security and Safety

All the women we spoke to said that it was important to ensure security and safety for IDP women and their families to return home. They also wanted opportunities for internally displaced women and men in camps and for communities to play a role in decision-making about the safety of a particular locality. Security forces should be required to work with local people to ensure the people's safety. As one IDP from Kukawa said, 'The government should engage the youth in the community, to clear the terrorists from their hideouts. They should engage the youth in the clearance exercise permanently; they know all the hideouts where the insurgents hide.' The women were clear that local people know the terrain, the culture, the language, and the people and that security cannot be achieved by the federal army, many of whom are not only strangers to the area, but unable to speak the local languages. The comments by women in the Polo host community focus group reflected the concerns of many groups we interviewed in the region. As one woman said:

> They [Boko Haram] said Ngoshe town was sold to them. They were telling those whom they held hostage that the village is their property, that it was sold to them by some of the villagers, who in one way or the other supported their activities. As we are talking now, Ngoshe village is still under their control. Sometimes the Cameroonian military will engage [Boko Haram], who will run to the mountains and hide. After they withdraw back to Cameroon, [Boko Haram] will come back and continue their hostility against the people.

Another commented:

> The soldiers cannot come to Ngoshe anyhow, because Boko Haram knows the nooks and crannies of the town to the road that leads to the mountains, which the soldiers don't know. So they have an advantage over the incoming army always. Only when the army fires artillery on the mountains – that is the only thing that will destroy them. But yet they are holding some of our family members in their captivity.

Another focus group participant added:

> In every town, there are sympathisers of Boko Haram, so for the military to succeed, they need the same villagers [CJTF] to guide them and fish Boko Haram out of their hideouts.

And yet another:

> The government must take a firm decision to clear Boko Haram out of the caves that they are hiding in. For the clearance to be successful the youth [young adult men who join the CJTF] must be involved.

The women also mentioned the need to ensure safe roads and transport systems, recognising that many of the insurgent attacks were on convoys carrying food and supplies.

The notion of security for women was broadened to include freedom from gender-based violence, not only from armed forces and state security, but also generally in the community and within the household. Given that most violent incidents against women and girls stay at the level of family, community, religious, and traditional leadership, the 'traditional' systems of rights and justice need to be examined.[7]

The women also discussed the need to provide stronger counter-narratives about women's rights to be free of violence, about autonomy, and about anti-stigmatisation campaigns to reduce the marginalisation and rejection of girls or women freed or returning from insurgent hands. The women noted, however, that most of these discussions needed to be aimed at men, since women were more welcoming of women who had left or escaped Boko Haram. Yasmin from Damboa living in the Shuwari community, Maiduguri, for example, reflected a commonly shared sentiment when she said, 'If my daughter is rescued from the hands of Boko Haram insurgents, I will accept her even if she returns with a child.'

For men, however, the situation is more complex, and they make a distinction between wives and daughters. Men seem to be more willing to accept their daughters' return, as exemplified in the comment by Mai Shanu from Bakassi IDP camp:

> I will accept her and the child because she is my daughter, and was forcefully taken away from home by the insurgents. No matter what condition she enters she is still my daughter. I will take her and take care of her like I used to do, when life was normal with us in Bama.

Mai Shanu would also accept living with his wife again because:

> It was not her doing that she was abducted. She is my wife; I will welcome her to my home. We used to stay together before the unfortunate situation separated us. She did not run away by herself. She was abducted forcefully, she was a prisoner in their hands. I will thank God she came back to me and make sure she is okay.

---

[7] There are already programmes across northern Nigeria that engage in raising awareness of women's and human rights with religious and traditional leaders, run by NGOs like the Centre for Women and Adolescents, BAOBAB for Women's Human Rights, or the Development, Research and Projects Centre, several of which have had some success and could be supported to scale up.

However, Mai Shanu did not think he could accept a child of his wife who had resulted from her captivity:

> Hmmm, I will not accept the baby ... Maybe if she comes and the baby is still breastfeeding. [Pause] The truth is that I will not accept the baby. I know the baby is innocent, but I will not have peace of mind if I see him.

A younger unmarried man from the same Bakassi IDP camp responded to a hypothetical question about what he would do if it were his betrothed in that situation. His response was:

> We all know that whenever Boko Haram take away women, they marry them forcefully. And if the husband is killed in a battle, another husband will come and inherit her as his wife. So that is their mode of operation and marriage. Sincerely speaking I will accept her and if she comes with a baby! The baby will be taken care of and, if possible, we shall hand him or her over to the government to take care of the baby.

Neither Mai Shanu nor the other men who made similar comments referred to the notion of the 'bad blood' of the children; on the contrary, Mai Shanu referred to the baby's innocence. Rather it seems more that it would be uncomfortable to live with the daily reminder that their wives had had sexual relations with another man.

Although the women also recommended that there needs to be particular attention to supporting those engaged in 'survival' or 'transactional' sex as well as survivors of sexual violence, there was also some ambivalence about this. Women both recognised the elements of coercion and need involved, and made comments about promiscuity, immorality, and greed.

Livelihood Support

The women were clear on the need for food, seeds, and agricultural input support until the next harvest is reaped and communities are on their feet again. As one Kukawa focus group participant explained:

> We are not happy staying here in the camp for there is no place like home. If we can go back to our villages, we can continue with our little businesses [*sana'oi*] and farming will continue. The government should provide adequate security for us and provide farming support, like seeds, fertilisers, tractors, and pesticides.

A specific point was made about support for women to create and pursue their own economic livelihoods. This support must include skills training and small-scale management plus marketing, equipment, and start-up capital. As a Polo host community focus group participant explained, '[We need] training on skills acquisitions, opening restaurants, trading, selling of provisions, sewing cloth, and selling provisions [opening a provision shop] ... but we don't have the capital to start either.' A displaced returnee from Konduga stated, 'Most of us are traders, but due to the insurgency after they displaced us, we ran for our lives with nothing and now we are back with nothing.' Yasmina from the NYSC IDP camp pointed out, 'We can return to our villages if we are assured of our safety and provided with means of livelihood and capital to start enterprises.' And Yaliya from the Bakassi IDP camp stated, 'We are ready to return to our community if the government can ensure our safety and provide us with capital to continue with our tailoring business.'

Women wanted support for literacy and education, livelihood and functional skills capacity-building, and capital for youth, especially for girls and young women. They recommended including non-gender-stereotyped occupations to improve women's life chances, to lower their likelihood of joining armed opposition groups, and to lower the levels of survival sex (again often referred to as 'immorality').

Infrastructure and Rebuilding Support

Returnees from displacement need assistance in rebuilding their homes and basic provisions to reclaim their lives. The women were quite clear that all areas of recommendations needed to be met, and that mediation talks and community peace discussions were not sufficient without meeting these basic needs. As a Konduga returnee explained, 'Our needs are hospitals, rebuilding of our houses and school, as well as security. If all this is done, we all know that the town can come back to its normal days of peaceful coexistence.' Boko Haram had vandalised or burned almost all the buildings and the roofing had been stolen. As another Konduga returnee explained, 'When we came back, we had to clean out the [rubble and debris in] the house, cut grass, fumigate it, try to repair it … we did it all by ourselves without any help from any INGO/NGO or the government.' Although the first group that returned from Maiduguri to Konduga received roofing sheets, wood, and other building materials, subsequent returnees received no such support. Many returned, only to find their buildings without roofs, walls fallen, or with large holes in them.[8]

Other women called for the provision of free and adequate health care provisions, including 'dignity kits'. These kits generally include bath soap, multiple pairs of underwear, detergent powder, sanitary napkins, a flashlight, toothpaste, a toothbrush, and a comb.

The community and parents call for secure schools with adequate teachers and sufficient supplies. A woman still in Polo, Maiduguri, noted that whether in Maiduguri or at home, 'We need schools that our children can attend and be educated like other children in the city and hospitals with other social amenities' and 'We are not educated to the level of teaching our own children, but we want them to go to school.'

---

[8]   As was the case in Konduga, where we met with women 'returnees'.

Participation, Representation, Discussion, and Decision-making

Women and men must participate in the decision-making processes that affect their lives to guarantee that the results meet their needs – for example, no 'cookie cutter' houses, or provision of pre-defined 'aid' when recipients have self-defined needs and wants. As a Konduga returnee pointed out, 'We the women are sidelined in all the processes of either peacebuilding or planning of anything that will bring development in the town. We the women need to shout out until someone hears our cry.'

To do this, several follow-up points were made, including demands to appoint women leaders who can speak for IDP women in the camps and in the communities. Women also wanted support for women to establish their own groups, organisations, and associations in the form of facilitators or resource persons, capacity-building, and initial funding. They also called for mechanisms to promote discussion and collaboration between women in communities, IDP women, women politicians, and women in government, as well as developing a network of men who will support women's inclusion in peacebuilding and reconstruction efforts. The women were also clear on the need to incorporate women meaningfully in decision-making, planning, and implementation, including in 'traditional systems', local government areas, as humanitarian actors, in government, INGOs, NGOs, the UN system, and other sites of power and influence.

As one local woman leader explained in an interview:

> As the chairperson, I used to talk to people face to face; that is why I know most of the problems they are facing. But the consultation of women should be more because now women are speaking out unlike before ... We have to sensitise the women and tell them of their rights of speech and freedom to life. By doing this the women can be involved in decision-making because they know that they can talk in their community for the sake of peace.

It was also thought to be important to include women in religious affairs. Among both the Christian and Muslim women's rights communities over the past decades, in particular, there has been a good deal of feminist research and advocacy about women's rights in religions (for example, Imam et al. 2005; Medar-Gould et al. 2014), some of which have been taken up by more mainstream groups (for example, Sada et al. 2005).

Community Dialogue

The focus groups addressed the need for dialogue and cross-community building. As the representative from the Women's Wing of the Christian Association of Nigeria said:

> Boko Haram started with a cover of religion. The Christians developed fear because of the killing of Christians, and it affected the relationship

between Christians and Muslims. But it has been conceptualised that the problems affected many people, which is almost everybody. Now the relationship is coming back to life – the Christians and Muslims have to come together and pray and fight the menace of the insurgency. Now we made them [community members] accept even their women who were impregnated by Boko Haram, because it was not their deeds, but terrorist deeds ... Dialogue is one of the ways for Christians and Muslims to come together and plan how to bring out the truth to each other, and achieve a deal on peace and sustain it, without allowing any lies to disrupt the peace process that is being built.

It was clear that the women felt that in building tolerance and respect for rehabilitation and community relations, reconstruction also needed to include accountability for abuses, as well as some clarification of different frameworks of justice (restorative, transitional, and compensatory).

End to Impunity and Calls for Accountability

Many called for an end to impunity for all those involved in the conflict who abused and/or terrorised civilians: insurgents, those from the security forces (military, police, camp security, and CJTF), and aid workers who have abused their positions of authority and trust. A Gava villager from behind the Gwoza mountains said, 'We will not leave it to go without retaliation, since our wives have been married by the insurgents against their wishes. And we know some insurgents who perpetrated acts against our family members.' Feelings against those who committed atrocities against them are, not surprisingly, strong. It is important to discuss how accountability, justice, and resolution can be achieved in their own contexts.

This has been a difficult area in which to progress, as has been evident in South Africa, Rwanda, Liberia, the former Yugoslavia, and elsewhere. There is wide literature on different forms of justice and how to ensure accountability, including those in (post)conflict situations, which is beyond the scope of this chapter to address. However, the point here is that it is important to create spaces to work collectively with the women who, through their courage, strength, tenacity, and strategy, have survived the insurgency. They have not only their lived experiences, but also a deep knowledge of their cultures, diversity, and languages. This issue certainly requires more sustained collective discussion in Nigeria than has so far been the case to respond to the sorts of questions that survivors of atrocities are asking, like Mai Shanu from the Bakassi IDP, who explained in a focus group:

> I cannot accept them [ex-Boko Haram fighters] into our society, because their hands are soaked in blood. They are killers. Having a

peace process with them is not an easy task. They find pleasure in killing their fellow humans. So how sure am I that the Boko Haram member has repented and changed his ways from evil to good and can be involved in a peace process? Let me tell you, Boko Haram members are mostly cult members. They are initiated by their Amir [commander or leader]. If you [a Boko Haram militant] kill more people, you will be qualified to become an Amir in your community or village. One can never underestimate what they can do. For them war is peace, and they go to war to get power in their area, when they become an Amir.

Yet, in the same group session, another man, Said, said he could accept Boko Haram members back into his community. He explained that he was held captive for seven months and was not killed because he had a skill that was important to them (operating grain-grinding machines). He was freed when the military liberated Bama town.

It was, however, notable that in this mixed women and men session, women said very little. Further, although Said's motives for acceptance of militants were not questioned, there were several negative comments questioning the motivation of some women who might be willing to accept 'rehabilitation' of Boko Haram militants. Men, for example, stated that divorcées in Bama deliberately sought out Boko Haram when they took over the town, in order to marry militant commanders and become 'queens', allowing them to have power over abducted women. They also noted a formerly captive woman whose husband divorced her in the camp and 'sent her packing out of the house immediately' because she 'went to the extent of confronting' him when he criticised Boko Haram, saying that Boko Haram are good people. Some men thought that women who had been with Boko Haram had been initiated into Boko Haram and brainwashed into sneaking back even if they have been rescued. Again, this speaks to the need to reconfigure tropes about masculinity and femininity.

Additional Recommendations

We also invited policymakers (state and traditional), representatives of the security forces (military, police, and customs), large humanitarian and development aid INGOs, and national women's organisations and networks to discuss our findings and the recommendations of the women listed above. They agreed with those recommendations and added some of their own.

This group highlighted the importance of researching and addressing the changing gender relations as a result of the conflict, to support communities to prevent and minimise backlash against women's and girls' increased visibility, economic activity, and decision-making. There was already an increase in violence against women. This understanding and awareness clearly needs to be constructed not only with community members, but also among government officials, aid workers, and others.

On livelihood support, this group suggested providing support for the environmental context, including sustainable farming, and supporting the use of the commons, like economic trees and replanting. Further, they felt there needs to be an acknowledgement of the variety of displacement needs and ways to fulfil them. For example, in ensuring livelihood support, rather than the usual individual training in embroidery and cap-making, INGOs could provide adequate support for forming cooperatives, particularly in areas where it is not part of the cultural practice, and they could explore other means and structures for women to gain access to resources for livelihood.

They identified the need to improve education facilities for schools in IDP camps. The group also pointed to the need to support and develop host communities as well as settlements that IDPs would return to. Host communities and individuals in them have frequently allowed the use of land not only for shelters but also for farming, for instance. The host communities where IDPs have been allowed to settle are frequently almost or as poor and underserved with infrastructure, schools, and health services as the areas from which the IDPs fled, and their conditions are further strained by the influx of IDPs. Ensuring the support for host communities' needs is not only just, but also avoids breeding resentment against the IDPs.

Regarding amplifying women's voices, this group suggested using social media to spread information and awareness ('65 per cent of social media users are female' stated one of the Abuja workshop participants); increasing the number of women representatives at all levels of discussion, decision-making, and implementation (for example, at the time of the workshop there were no women in the Borno State Assembly); supporting women's self-esteem and leadership capacity-building; and supporting intergenerational dialogue between women and girls, between men and boys, and with women/girls and men/boys together.

The group suggested increasing access to psychosocial support to address the widespread high level of trauma, including counselling in schools. The paucity of psychosocial counselling is clear. In the IDP camps we visited, psychosocial counselling sessions have been limited to a single group session because there is a lack of trained counsellors. This is possibly helpful, but woefully inadequate. Regarding security, the group noted the importance of ensuring that the CJTF has a clear role that is developed in discussion with them in future peacebuilding and reconstruction.[9]

[9] Despite the CJTF's acknowledged role in protecting communities, there are concerns about how it might further develop. The CJTF has also involved children as fighters (see https://www.hrw.org/news/2013/11/29/nigeria-boko-haram-abducts-women-recruits-children), although subsequently in 2017 it pledged to end this (see https://www.unicef.org/press-releases/civilian-joint-task-force-northeast-nigeria-signs-action-plan-end-recruitment). Other human rights abuses include pursuing personal malice and exacting sexual acts from women (especially IDPs), giving rise to fears that it may devolve to become more of a protection racket, than a community protection group. The government provides occasional support, such as weapons, vehicles, and training to CJTF members. In addition

Epilogue and Conclusions

Although the inclusion of women into peace agreements and reconstruction negotiations globally has been weak despite UNSCR 1325 and related resolutions, it has still been stronger in Africa than in other parts of the world. African women activists, including Nigerian women, were active participants in the campaigns and negotiations that brought about the Beijing Plan of Action,[10] UNSCR 1325, and similar international resolutions and conventions.[11] Women's rights activists fought hard to have their states adopt, accede to, and ratify these instruments. These global mechanisms are regarded as part of a toolbox, along with national constitutional guarantees, to add their weight to national and local struggles for women's rights and protections. From Uganda to Liberia, women activists have pressed for and succeeded in carving out a role for women leaders in peace talks, constitution-making processes, and newly constituted political arrangements, where civil war affected the entire country (Tripp 2015). Unfortunately, in Nigeria, the regional conflicts previously in the Niger Delta or currently in north-east Nigeria have excluded women from peace and reconstruction discussions. Often discussions of peacebuilding and reconstruction have not even included internally displaced men. Neither women nor nonelite men have been party to formal discussion or decision-making.

Yet civil society and women can play and have played critical roles in peacebuilding. When the parties negotiating peace agreements include civil society actors, women's organisations, and those directly affected by conflict, the risk of peace failing is reduced by 64 per cent, regardless of the regime type (Nilsson 2012). Because extremists attack women and women's rights advocates first, women become the most ardent opponents of violent extremism. Women activists broaden their advocacy beyond women's rights to include democratic, legal, and social reforms. Yet the negotiating table only includes combatant and government forces, the entities deemed relevant as those most powerful. Ultimately, peacebuilding is not only gendered but can only be sustainable if it includes women. One of the consequences of ignoring women and the specific experiences and voices of women is an outcome in which peacebuilding and reconstruction frameworks are skewed.

---

to the estimated over 26,000 members of the CJTF, 1,800 receive stipends from the Borno State government through its youth employment scheme, so the lines between state agent and civilian are also being blurred. See also Center for Civilians in Conflict (2019), 'Nigerian Community Militias: Towards a Solution'.

[10] For instance, the provision in the Beijing Plan of Action relating to the girl child originated in the contributions of women's groups at the 1994 Africa regional preparatory conference in Dakar for the Beijing World Women's Conference.

[11] It is often forgotten that those states whose demand for a Women's Rights Convention, similar to the UN Declaration on Human Rights, which eventually resulted in CEDAW, included both Muslim majority and African countries.

Since the workshops, the activist-researchers and IDP representatives have been bringing the research reports and these recommendations to policymakers in the six states of north-east Nigeria where the insurgents have been most active (Borno, Adamawa, Bauchi, Gombe, Yobe, and Taraba) as well as in the Federal Capital, Abuja. So far, among others, the Speakers of all State Houses of Assembly in the north-east geopolitical zone where the insurgents have hit hardest (Borno, Bauchi, Taraba, Adamawa, Zamfara, and Gombe states) have promised to take action. Several of the internally displaced women who participated in the discussion groups and workshops have started or joined women's rights and IDP organisations and become activists in their own right.

However, the process of change is dispiritingly slow. Only Taraba state has enacted the Child Rights Act, passed at federal level in 2003. None of the six states have enacted the Violence Against Persons Prohibition Act, passed at federal level in 2015, after 14 years of campaigning nationally by women's rights and gender activists, although in July 2020 there was a public hearing on gender-based violence following a first hearing of a bill in the state assembly in Borno. The Borno Women's Peace and Security Network, working with the Ministry for Women and Social Development, developed the nation's first National Action Plan in 2014. So far minute amounts of the necessary budget for implementation have been allocated or released, but the mechanisms required to implement it have not been instituted, so it seems to have little influence in policy, practice, or institutional culture, as the data from the women presented above indicates.

Meanwhile, the insurgent attacks continue. The cost is paid in further death, injury, rape and sexual assault, loss of livelihood, and loss of hope and trust. The region continues to be insecure, with millions of people still displaced and unable to return home. The indicators for good health, nutrition, education, and sustainability continue to decline. As many of the women said, '*ba sa jin mu* – they don't listen to us'. But the women still work for change.

4

No Going Back
Somali Women's Fight for Political Inclusion

LADAN AFFI

Introduction

When the Governor of Bay, a region in southern Somalia, visited a school for internally displaced and poor female students in Baidoa, he asked a 15-year-old girl what she was going to do when she finished her education. She replied, 'I am going to replace you' (Ali 2020). For a young Somali girl to have political ambitions is not surprising and represents women's desire to participate in the politics and governance of their country.

In the past 80 years, in which women have pursued a quest for full political participation and representation, Somali women have continued to be treated as a minority, despite making up over half of the population and making critical economic and social contributions to society. This chapter seeks to document women's struggle to participate in the governing of Somalia in the longue durée by examining three distinct periods – the anti-colonial resistance period (1940s–60), the socialist period (1969–91) and the civil war to the present (1991–present). Women were systematically prevented from having any political impact until recently. At each stage, women were welcomed when their activities were needed by society, yet they were repeatedly sidelined once their participation was no longer seen as necessary by those in power. In fact, excluding 'women from sharing in the fruits of these struggles' is a consistent theme throughout the modern history of Somalia (Jama 1994, 200).

Methods

This study is based on fieldwork carried out primarily between 2016 and 2019 in Somalia (Bur'o, Garowe, Hargeisa, and Mogadishu), in Nairobi, Kenya, and Minneapolis, United States. Those interviewed included women activists and women's NGO leaders and staff; male and female members of the 2016 Electoral College; male and female members of Parliament in Somaliland, Puntland, and the federal government; former officials under the Barre government and the transitional federal government; local councillors in the Benadir Regional Government; Cabinet ministers in Somaliland, Puntland, and the Federal Government; clan elders; staff of international organisations and diplomats in Nairobi, Kenya; and diaspora activists for women's rights in Somalia and the United States. Most of the interviews were carried out in person, a few were carried out in groups, and some over the phone. This chapter also draws on textual analysis, particularly of *buraanbur* (women's poetry) as a way of capturing women's political activities, and their hopes and desires for equal political participation.

Background: Clannism, Patriarchy, and Women's Exclusion

The contributions of women to their society have been largely left out of the country's history. Women's historic exclusion from politics is partially due to internal patriarchal institutions such as clannism, clan elders, Somali traditional law that predates Islamic law and civil law (*Xeer* law), as well as externally created structures. The activities of the international community, including neighbouring and regional countries as well as the United States, the European Union, and the United Kingdom, significant actors in Somalia for the past 30 years, have been less about ending the conflict, peacebuilding, and reconstructing the Somali state, and more about pursuing their national interests. Their activities have sometimes led to unforeseen consequences. One of these is the clan-based 4.5 power-sharing agreement, which was introduced at the Sodere Reconciliation Conference hosted by Ethiopia in 1996, dividing up political power between Somalia's four major clans and smaller groupings. It was implemented in the Arta Reconciliation Conference sponsored by Djibouti and institutionalised at the Mbagathi Reconciliation Conference in Kenya. The 4.5 formula is a political power-sharing method that has been the basis for division of political seats at the national and regional levels in Somalia since 2000 (Abdullahi 2018, 33, 229). Similar to Somalia's adoption of a decentralised system, which was first proposed in a document commissioned by the European Commission Somalia office in Nairobi, Kenya (see London School of Economics and Political Science 1995) the 4.5 system was created in Ethiopia. Power-sharing is based on clan membership, with the four largest clans – the Darod, Digil and Mirifle, Dir, and Hawiye – getting an equal share and all the other minorities getting half as many seats as one major clan. This agreement, which privileges membership of the clan, has become a significant barrier to women's political participation (Affi 2020).

Unlike men, whose membership and loyalty to the clan of their fathers is not questioned, women are marginalised and treated like outsiders. They are not considered full members of their clans for two reasons. First, because women are not dia-paying members, they do not formally share in the cost of paying for damage, injury, or death caused by a member of the clan. Although both men and women marry outside their clans, women tend to maintain relations with the clans of their mother, husband, and children, and so their loyalty is questioned, and they are not allowed to represent the clan.[1] However, these multiple connections can facilitate women's role as effective peacemakers, allowing them to largely bypass clannism's violent and destructive elements (Adam and Ford 1998, 22). The benefits of these connections to the society became clear during the civil war.

After the implosion of the Somali state, clan elders were able once again to play a leading role in their communities, applying traditional law, which is specifically discriminatory to women. The clan elders' formal inclusion in the political process is an ongoing challenge that women have been unable to break down. Another obstacle for women is the Islamist parties, previously suppressed by the Barre government, who were able to operate freely during and after the civil war (Elmi 2010).[2]

The revitalised clan structures, the application of *Xeer* traditional law, the open presence of the Islamist parties after the ouster of Siad Barre from office in 1991, and the subsequent destruction of the Somali state created hurdles for women's political participation. What is clear is that in their quest for political participation and representation, women devised different strategies and responses to overcome the barriers of patriarchal culture and institutions, making incremental and steady progress in their inclusion in the political system.

It is important to note that Somali women are not all the same. They come from different regions, are members of different clans (both majority and minority clans), and have different educational and socioeconomic standing. Some live in urban areas and others in pastoral or agro-pastoral communities; some are in refugee camps in neighbouring countries or are internally displaced, while others live in the diaspora. Regardless of these differences, women are 'a significant force of neutrality in what otherwise is a highly politicized social environment' (Adam and Ford 1998, 22).

They come from a society with polarising attitudes towards women. On the one hand, society is open, even encouraging of women's increased presence in the social and economic spheres and the attendant financial responsibility for the family. There is wide acknowledgement that

---

[1] In Somali society, marriage outside one's clan is encouraged for both men and women, yet men's loyalty is not questioned when they marry outside their clan, but women's is.

[2] When a member of the clan injures or kills someone, blood-wealth compensation has to be paid and women are expected to contribute but this is not recognised.

women saved their families and their communities during and after the civil war and that women, whether in the cities, internally displaced camps, or rural areas, exceeded their responsibilities over the past 30 years, while men failed to meet their cultural and religious obligations. On the other hand, most clan elders, religious actors, Islamist parties, and many male politicians reject women's demands for political representation for religious and cultural reasons. Although some women activists may disagree on whether the gender quota is the best way to ensure women's political participation, there is broad and strong support among women from different parts of society that women should be part of the governance of their country, viewing men's leadership in the past 30 years as disastrous (Affi 2020).

In the first nine years of Somalia's independence and again after the collapse of the state in 1991, women sought to overcome patriarchal culture, particularly the incorporation of the clan into the political system. From 1960 to 1969, political parties in Somalia were aligned along clan lines and within Somali culture. Only men could represent the clan, and therefore women were not selected to run for political positions. During the rule of Barre from 1969 to 1991, women – particularly urban women – initially supported his socialist state because of Barre's appointment of women to positions that were previously not available to them, such as vice-ministers and members of the Central Committee of the Somali Revolutionary Socialist Party. They served in the police, the military, and the civil service. In reality, however, for most Somali women, not much changed. When the state became increasingly dictatorial, some women were at the forefront of opposing Barre and joined rebel groups like the Somali Salvation Democratic Front and the Somali National Movement. They joined opposition radio stations like Radio Kulmis, reciting poems meant to encourage an uprising against the government.

When the Somali state collapsed in 1991, women 'emerged as important peacemakers in communities, serving to bridge clan-based divisions' (Jan 2001, 57). They formed organisations focused on the delivery of humanitarian services, although a few unsuccessfully tried to enter the political space, which was closed to all but the warlords throughout the 1990s. This changed in 1999, as efforts began to construct the Somali state. Alongside the 4.5 power-sharing system, a parliamentary gender quota was introduced. Thanks to this quota, in the past 20 years women have slowly pushed into the political sphere, making up 24 per cent of federal parliamentarians in 2016 (Mahmood 2018).

Women's Claims to Political Participation

Many Somali women activists and politicians base their demand for political participation and representation on their claims to citizenship. They regard it as a human rights and social justice issue. These women also believe that the governance of the country cannot be left to men because women's 'participation is critical in rebuilding transformative and inclusive political institutions' (Dini 2014). Many of the women interviewed for this research claim equal participation in the governance of their country because they comprise at least half the population. Paxton and Hughes (2017) label this as the justice argument for women's representation. Building on Pitkin's view of representation (1967), the justice argument draws on three conceptions of representation: formal, descriptive, and substantive representation.

Formal or authorised representation is when women have the same legal right as men to take part in politics, with the right to vote and to be elected for office. Women in Somalia have been advocating for this equality since they joined the fight for independence, which had grassroots support among both rural and urban women. To achieve this, women would need at a minimum the 30 per cent gender quota enshrined in the country's constitution. Formal representation is only the beginning in ensuring women's equal participation in politics, since it does not necessarily lead to equality in numerical representation or in political influence.

The second conception of representation is descriptive or numerical representation, which requires that political representatives should mirror their constituents. The descriptive quota recognises that allowing women to run for office does not mean that they will run or be elected due to significant social and economic disparities facing women, which prevent them from taking advantage of opportunities. Women aspiring to enter politics are often viewed as unqualified in the political arena, facing hurdles in political participation and representation. It is imperative that women are represented in politics in numbers proportional to their numbers in the population. To achieve this, institutional changes to the electoral laws are needed and the inclusion of gender quotas within the legal framework. Descriptive representation does not mean that all women are the same and that they can represent all women but, rather, that women share certain experiences, including being members of a marginalised group. Because of their shared experiences in their economic activities and responsibilities in the household they may develop common interests (Paxton and Hughes 2017). Somali women obtained 24.4 per cent of parliamentary seats at the federal level in 2016 but continue to face difficulties in ensuring their participation across the country.

The third concept is substantive representation, which suggests that women's interests should be advocated for in the political arena. It is not enough for women to have the right to vote, run for office, and be elected. Some believe that the number of women in national legislatures, for example, must reach a critical mass otherwise women may behave like men to avoid being denigrated or marginalised for promoting women's issues (Paxton and Hughes 2017). It was thought that without a critical mass, women would not have the ability to determine their agenda or build a new kind of leadership (Grey 2002). Later, others argued that what matters is not so much a critical mass but, rather, critical acts by women in exerting policy influence and that the quality of women leaders as critical actors is as important as their numeric presence (Bratton 2005; Childs and Krook 2009). Other research carried out by Nazneen and Hickey (2019) demonstrates that critical mass matters when female legislatures are involved in coalition-building. These coalitions can be between female members of Parliament of different political parties or building alliances within broader institutional spaces. Nazneen and Hickey (2019) also find that critical mass is more effective when women legislatures have links with women's movements.

Nevertheless, for a long time, the United Nations suggested that if women comprised 30 per cent of parliamentary and other leadership seats, they could make a difference in advancing women's rights (Paxton and Hughes 2017, 17). This increased to 50 per cent in more recent years as UN Women embarked on a Step it Up campaign. After the 2000 adoption of quotas, Somali women pushed for critical mass, believing that it was the most important factor in pushing for a women's agenda. More recently, as outlined in the Somali Women's Charter, women have demanded 50 per cent of all political and governmental positions.

Improvements in Somali women's political participation have been due to the societal disruptions that have occurred throughout Somalia's history. For example, colonialism disrupted Somali society in significant ways, by bringing urban women under the authority of men and limiting their economic activities (Affi 2004). The adoption of Scientific Socialism by Siad Barre in the 1970s pushed women to enter public spaces and to participate in politics (Davidson 1975).[3] Women's political participation did not last, either during the independence movement or Barre's rule, because the root causes of women's exclusion – the clan and patriarchy – from decision-making structures were never addressed (El-Bushra 2003, 257). It was only after the civil war began to wind down in the late 1990s and state reconstruction began that women were able to enter and take part in politics in a sustained manner.

In her research on African women and political participation and representation, Aili Mari Tripp (2015) pinpoints the factors that determine women's political participation, highlighting the elevated levels of female representation found in parliaments in the aftermath of major civil conflict. Relevant for the Somali case, Tripp finds that it is important that women's roles change within society and that these changes must be accompanied by transformation of gender relations, which Tripp calls gender regime change (2015, 31). Tripp finds that conflict and women's political representation and rights are linked, which emerged in Africa in the post-1990 period. Second, women had a better chance of entering politics after intense conflicts and during conflicts of long duration. The

---

[3]   In Scientific Socialism, Barre sought to use certain aspects of Somali traditions (for example, egalitarianism and self-help) and Islam along with the nation-state to promote the modernisation and development of Somalia.

lessening intensity of the civil war, accompanied by peace talks and constitutional reforms, presented women with an opportunity to assert demands for their rights (Tripp 2015, 41).[4] In addition, women's 'perceived non-involvement in creating conflict afforded them greater legitimacy as leaders during and after conflict' (Tripp 2015, 42). In Somalia, we can see that women's political representation emerged during the 1999 Arta Reconciliation Conference, when women participated in numbers not previously seen. Many of the women in attendance were highly educated and by then had years of experience working in peace, humanitarian, and development work in Somalia. It was also at this conference that women pushed for and achieved the gender quota. Currently, women are demanding that the gender quota across all political and institutional levels be enshrined in the final constitution at 50 per cent (The Federal Republic of Somalia 2012).

The difference in women's political participation before and after the war can be attributed to the civil war. Data from the Inter-Parliamentary Union shows a marked difference in the rates of female representation in Somalia before and after the civil war – it was at 4 per cent before 1991, 8 per cent in 2004, and 24.4 per cent in 2016 (see Table 4.1). According to Tripp (2015), the disruptions that occur during conflict and that lead to gender regime change explain how women became more successful in entering the political space. Part of this regime change was that women's financial responsibility, often as the sole breadwinner, increased their influence within the family and society (El-Bushra 2003, 257).

Each time Somali society experienced disruption, women were able to enter public spaces that were previously closed to them. For example, during both the fight for independence and the Barre government, despite women's entrance into the male domain they were unsuccessful in fully reaching their goal. However, during the civil war as well as in postconflict stages women did succeed in pushing for more political rights. In fact, Somali women only achieved full political rights with men in 2012, with the transition towards a federal system, but these rights have yet to be legally institutionalised and implemented (Abdullahi 2018, 222).

Since Somalia's independence, the clans have been present within the political system to varying degrees. Clan elders are men, whereas women are born into a clan and often marry into another – they are considered transient members of the clan. At all levels of society, men hold decision-making power, with the husband being the head of the family. Any male adult can be chosen as an elder. They might be asked to form a council to resolve conflicts between clans or decide on issues related to marriage, migration, and divorce (Sheikh-Abdi 1993, 18).

---

[4] There is no agreement among Somalis of when the civil war began or when or even whether it has ended. For some, it began in 1978, after the failed attempted coup d'état against Barre and the government began to target the Majerteen clan. For others, it began with the targeting of the Isaaq in northern Somalia in the 1980s. For many, it started when the state collapsed in January 1991 after the ouster of Barre.

Table 4.1. Women's Political Representation from 1960 to 2020.

Date	Members of Parliament	# of Female MPs	Percentage of Women
1960	124	0	0%
1964	124	0	0%
1969	124	0	0%
1979	177	18 (6 appointed by head of state)	10.2%
1984	177	7 (6 appointed by head of state)	4.0%
2004	275	22	8.0%
2008	550	17	3.0%
2012	275	38	14.0%
2016	275	67	24.4%

Source: Inter-Parliamentary Union

Before the arrival of European colonial powers, the clans had their own system of governance, using a combination of Somali traditional law and Islamic *shar'ia* law. Although no formal institutions existed, in times of conflict, a *Shir,* or a meeting of the elders, would be called. This informal government had no formal constitution except that of membership in the lineage concerned, no regular place of meeting, and no official position. Thus, political authority was highly decentralised, reflecting the extreme individualism and independence of Somalis. The clan elders were close to the people and often dealt with people face to face. Decisions affecting society were built on consensus and they were in principle egalitarian, although deep inequalities existed between men and women, between clans, and between generations (Bradbury 2008, 17).

Exclusion of Somali Women in Politics: The Clans and Islamist Parties

Somali women have achieved formal representation and have made significant gains in moving towards substantive representation. However, the 30 percent quota for women at all levels of government has not been institutionalised and remains an informal agreement. For women activists, the gender quota is at the mercy of male politicians and elders because of the absence of legally binding provisions implementing it. This represents a major hurdle preventing women's full inclusion in politics (interview, Nairobi July 2018). Therefore, women activists have focused on including the gender quota in the draft federal constitution once it is adopted. Women's political participation has been hindered by the clan as an institution, clan elders, and Islamist parties, who, although not ideologically aligned, often work together to keep women out of politics.

During the first nine years of Somalia's independence, politics became 'a delicate game of balancing clan interests', and political parties were often organised around the clan (Jan 2001, 57). Banished from the public space during the early Barre years in the late 1960s, clans made a return in the late 1970s. The opposition groups to Barre's government were also organised around clan membership. Since the civil war led to no decisive winners, the 4.5 power-sharing agreement was implemented and was intended to settle the competition for power-sharing that had dogged Somalia by providing the four big Somali clans equal representation in Parliament, while the alliance of other smaller clans received fewer seats (Abdullahi 2018, 155). But the 4.5 system, which was instituted at the same time as the gender quota in Arta, created a dilemma for women as they sought political representation.

This system forced women to appeal to and seek appointments from clan elders, who believed that women were 'unreliable representatives in the political arena, because of their tribal affiliation to their father's and husband's clan' (Parke et al. 2017, 3). In a meeting organised by the United Nations, women activists, political candidates, and politicians identified the 4.5 power-sharing agreement as the biggest setback for women's inclusion in politics. Women saw it as deeply unequal and discriminatory, fostering divisions among women along clan lines (interview, Mogadishu August 2018). In interviews with women across the country, women consistently identified the 4.5 as their biggest hurdle in obtaining political positions, followed by the clan elders. In addition to preventing women from representing the clan, the 4.5 system created a challenge for women to organise as women because their clan membership interfered with their alliances and advocacy for women's rights and political participation. Women elected to the parliament paid more attention to what their clans needed, rather than women's issues, if they wished to retain their position. Women politicians felt this forced them to serve their clans rather than advocating for women's issues (Garowe, August 2017).

There are many Islamist parties in Somalia, and most tend to align with the ideologies espoused by the Muslim Brotherhood or by the Salafis. These parties, such as Al-Ittihad (later renamed I'tisam), Al Islah, Hizbul-Islam, and Al Shabaab, among others, can be seen on a continuum in their views on Islam and its implementation in Somalia (Elmi 2010). The influence of these groups, which had been suppressed during the Barre era, returned in full force after the collapse of the state in 1991. Many

Somalis welcomed the increased presence of Islamic/Islamist discourse, believing that it had 'the potential to wipe the slate clean and defeat clan thinking by articulating the Somali nation as a Somali Ummah inclusive of all Muslim Somalis' (Kapteijns 2010, 28). Whatever their ideological orientations, these Islamist parties often draw on versions of Islam that are foreign to most practising and moderate Somalis. The Salafis, in particular, view women as only wives and mothers. Although groups like Al Islah proclaim that Islam allows women and men equality in social and political affairs, the reality is that women play a secondary role in their organisation (Abdullahi 2018, 208). Demonstrating the dominance of clan identity within Somali society, even the Islamists organise around clan lineages (Elmi 2010, 70).

Fighting for Independence

The arrival of the Europeans and the subsequent anti-colonial resistance provided the first disruption in Somali society, allowing women an opportunity to fight for participation in political life. European colonisers viewed Somali women as nothing more than property; in reality, nomadic women were economically active, often owning small livestock that generated income for them and their families (Choi 1995). When the men were away, women performed their tasks. Neither nomadic nor urban women have ever been submissive to societal oppression (Hasan et al. 1995).

In the war for independence against British and Italian forces, women like Barni Warsame, Halima Godane, Halimo Shiil, Fadumo Hersi Abbane, and Timiro Ukash joined the Somali Youth League (SYL) and later Greater Somalia League (GSL) (Jama 1991). Women supported the independence movement through mobilisation of the population, recruitment of new members, and fundraising for the organisation, as well as providing logistical support (Koshin 2016, 10). Many of these activities led to those women being shunned by society for entering the traditionally male arena, and colonisers did not spare them from imprisonment; some were held for months while they were pregnant, like Timiro Ukash, others received jail terms ranging from three to 24 years. Women were also tortured and killed, like Hawo Osman Tako (Jama 1991, 49). Women who insisted on taking part in the independence movement were often rejected by their families. Some were divorced by their husbands for engaging in masculine activities. Hawo Jibril, who actively participated in the independence movement and fought for women's right to participate fully in the governance of their country, memorialised such women in her poem *Sisters*. Hawo laments that women were excluded from enjoying the benefits of the state because 'even the lowest positions were not offered and our degrees have been cast away like rubbish' (Jibril 2008, 155).

As independence approached, Somali women were optimistic that they would be rewarded for their political and economic roles during the struggle for independence, during which they called for equality with men (Haji Mukhtar 2003, 264). Before the 1958 local elections in Italian Somalia, Raha Ayaanle had been elected to the central committee of the first Somali political party, the SYL. But after independence, rather than being met with the gratitude of the nation, women were to be disappointed and marginalised (Tripp 2015, 23). Despite their attempts to be included in the soon-to-be-independent government, women were excluded. In the 1958 municipal elections, Halima Godane was the only woman to run as a candidate representing the GSL and she was not elected (interview 21 December 2020).

The new Somali state, led by Aden Abdulle, its first president, preserved the colonial and patriarchal institutions that did not recognise women's sacrifices (Haji Mukhtar 2003, 264). Somali men used the same colonial argument to sideline women from political participation. The women, cognisant of their multilayered oppression by the colonisers, the clan, and Somali men, were not silent. Halima Ali Kurtin, a pro-independence fighter, described women's disappointment and anger at their treatment once independence was attained as similar to the state giving 'so much milk; women were still left in hunger' (Jama 1994, 188).

Somali women were caught between a postcolonial state that was, according to Abdullahi, 'nationalistic, hierarchical, centralized and quasi-secular, while the society was clannish, egalitarian, decentralized and Islamic' (2011, 141). But once independence was achieved, Somali women were driven out of the public sphere and their contributions denied.

Even women's desire for equal access to education, employment, and political participation was rejected (Hasan et al. 1995). During this time, in 1959, the Somali Women's Association was created, its leadership consisting mostly of the wives of the leaders of the political parties and whose focus was on social welfare (Hasan et al. 1995).

In 1960, the founding of the Somali Republic provided opportunities for Somali women to be educated abroad, but on their return they were often given lower positions than men with the same skills. According to Fadumo Alin, who studied in both Egypt and Italy, the law dictated that anyone with a university education should be appointed at the director general level or above. Men with a university education were appointed as director generals, directors, and ambassadors (phone interview December 2020). But many women with university degrees were appointed as section heads and restricted to the ministries of health and education. Out of growing frustration over the discrimination they faced, these women established the Somali Women's Movement (SWM) in May 1967. Alin, Raaqiya Haji Du'ale, Hawa Aden, and others created a platform to advocate for women's rights within the family, workplace, and politics (Alin 2012). During this time, advocating for the rights of women remained an elite endeavour, limited to urban areas.

A few women did not wait to be invited to take part in politics. In the last democratic parliamentary election in 1969, Hawa Awale Abtidoon, nicknamed Hawa Yarey, stood for a parliamentary seat in Elbur in southern Somalia. Her candidacy resulted in conflict, the death of the rival candidate, and her loss of the election. While she was disputing the results, the government was overthrown (phone interview, 14 May 2020; Abdullahi 2018, 198).[5]

Socialist Somalia

Siad Barre's 1969 coup d'état and his promise of equality and justice for all provided an opportunity for women to come back into the public space. Although all political organisations were banned, including the Somali Women's Movement, the Women's Section was established within the Political Office in the Presidency of the Supreme Revolutionary Council. Many of the women who were active in the SWM were involved in the Women's Section. Barre adopted socialist policies and sought to remake Somali society into a modern one, and some of the policies implemented by his government were so pro-women that the revolution was nicknamed 'the women's revolution' (Affi 2004). Somali women, especially urban women, used socialism as a tool to achieve equal rights (Hasan et al. 1995).

Barre's government did make tremendous improvements in society, which enhanced women's lives – for example, expanding educational opportunities and making education free and mandatory in 1974 (Castagno 1975). In line with the socialist ideology, all women were expected to take part in the development of the nation alongside men. Some women joined the police and military forces. Young educated women, similar to men, were equally involved in national campaigns, such as the literacy campaign after the 1972 introduction of written Somali using the Latin alphabet and the anti-drought campaign, which saw them sent all over the country to take part in the development of Somalia. Like men, women high school graduates who wanted to work for the government or pursue higher education, including wives and mothers, were expected to take part in national service.

The introduction of the Family Law of 1975, however, was to have a lasting and damaging impact on Somali women. Drawing on both socialist ideology and the United Nations' declaration of the Decade for Women (1975–85), the Family Law recognised the importance of equality between men and women. Barre introduced the law on 11 January 1975, which was designated as Somali Women's Day, with a large celebration organised to showcase the advancement and contribution of Somali

[5]   Hawa Yarey was passionately involved in politics and was known for speaking her mind. During the rule of Siad Barre, she was jailed multiple times (interview, 14 May 2020).

women at all levels (Elmi 2014). In his speech, Barre evoked Hawo Osman Tako and her ultimate sacrifice for the Somali struggle so that 'future Somali generations [could] live in liberty and the pursuit of happiness' (1975). Barre described Hawo Tako as the first Somali woman to die in the struggle for independence in 1948. Her patriotism and death had taught Somali women that they could play a meaningful role in the struggle of their country for independence. For the Somali state, Hawo Tako had come to symbolise the commitment and sacrifice of Somali women for their country and she was the only woman to be honoured with a statue in Mogadishu during Barre's rule (Barre 1975).

Barre heralded the Family Law as one of the stated goals of the socialist revolution, which included the equality of all humans. He saw it also as Somalia's response to the UN's call for women's advancement (Barre 1975). He foresaw opposition to this law from various groups, including clerics. For Barre, this law was an extension and completion of Islam's drive for equality for women. He regarded Islam, like his socialist movement, as 'a correct revolutionary movement' (Barre 1975). The Family Law was intended to address this shortcoming by making women and men equal in all areas, including marriage, divorce, and inheritance (Alin 1977). To ensure that the law was properly implemented, marriages and divorces were to be registered with the government. Customary law, as well as laws issued during the British and Italian colonial period, were abolished (Na'im 2002).

The Family Law elicited an immediate backlash, as Barre had expected, with the clerics organising against the law and mobilising Somalis to hold anti-Family Law gatherings in mosques. The government responded harshly by executing 10 clerics and imprisoning others (Davidson 1975). The Barre government and its ideology continue to be used today as an example of why women should not participate in politics: because their entry into politics means men will lose their lives (Jama 1994, 190, quoting Ibrahim and Adan 1991; Elmi 2014).[6]

In 1976, the Somali Revolutionary Socialist Party was created, and 60 per cent of its 20,000 founding members were women. The following year, the Somali Women's Democratic Organization (SWDO) was established, and a majority of its members were from the SWM. It was headed by Muraayo Garaad and had offices around the country (Rayale et al. 2015). The SWDO called for gender equality and the inclusion of women in all aspects of society. It also advocated for family planning and healthcare and spearheaded campaigns against female circumcision (Haji Mukhtar 2003). However, there was no question that the government was mobilising women to advance its own ideology. Women were seen as a

---

[6] In many discussions on women's participation, clerics will often recall those who were killed due to their opposition to the Family Law, equating gender quotas with men being killed. Also see 'Dood kulul – Sheikh Nur Baaruud iyo Batuulo, Gudoomiyaha Ururke Haweenka Soomaaliya', 13 October 2016, available at: https://www.youtube.com/watch?v=xQ6Ni1nl8OE&t=265s (accessed 19 March 2021).

vehicle to spread the socialist ideology and mobilise the community in support of the government. Still, women's presence at all levels of society increased. A number of women, including Fadumo Alin and Raqiya Haji Du'ale, were appointed as Deputy Ministers. Fadumo Hashi became the first woman to join the Central Committee. Others, like Fadumo Bihi, were appointed as Ambassadors, while Deeqa Oljoog, Dahabo Farah, and Mariam Farah became heads of the Academy of Arts and Sciences (Alin 2012). The benefits of the revolution and of socialist ideology largely went to urban women, who were able to access government services such as schools and hospitals and government jobs. Although women were mobilised through the SWDO, patriarchal institutions such as the clan remained intact. Due to growing opposition and an attempted coup d'état in 1976, the government became more dictatorial, arresting opposition leaders and targeting clans suspected of working against the government. Women were once again at the forefront of the opposition.

Opposing Barre

Women from the Majerteen, whose clan was first targeted by the state, were vital members of the first armed opposition group to Barre, the Somali Salvation Democratic Front (SSDF), which was formed in 1978. They took up arms, cared for the injured, and collected funds and other resources. Marian Haji-Hassan, who was also a founding member of the SSDF, recited poetry in broadcasts on the opposition Radio Kulmis, based in Ethiopia, to mobilise support for the armed opposition to rise up against the government and increase the political awareness of those inside Somalia (Jama 1994, 190). Similarly, when the government targeted the Isaaq, women were critical to the success of the Somali National Movement (SNM), as one former supporter explained in Hargeisa in December 2016:

> Women from the Isaaq clan were a huge part in the struggle and the movement to overthrow Siad Barre. Men tend to downplay our role, but we were integral to the struggle. The struggle would have been thwarted immediately when it began had it not been for women's contributions. Not only did we arrange venues for their secret meetings, but we also mobilised support. We raised funds, we helped to raise awareness about the plight of the people in order to make sure we all had a common front and, most importantly, we were able to keep everything under wraps, which is critical.

When war between the Barre regime and the SNM broke out in 1988 in Hargeisa, resulting in a mass exodus, according to a woman informant who took care of wounded SNM fighters in the field, 'Everyone realised just how important women were to the struggle. We carried and nursed those wounded in combat, cared for those with war-inflicted mental issues, replenished supplies' (interview, Hargeisa, January 2017). Women formed groups like the Alla-Amiin group, voluntarily working with those who had fled the war in northern Somalia, providing food, housing, and schooling, and nursing those who were injured. They also performed songs and poetry mobilising support for the struggle against Barre (Jama 1994). Within the SNM, women took up arms and were killed and injured, as well (interview, Hargeisa, December 2016). All this conflict led to changes within traditional structures, with women increasingly becoming heads of households and with the men abandoning their families because they were unable to support them, or they were fighting for the guerrilla groups or working abroad.

Inside Somalia, women risked their lives confronting the Barre government. In 1988, women in Kismayo, unable to tolerate the excesses of the government, demonstrated in public, baring their breasts to shame men to stand up to the government (Farah 1996, 18). Revealing just how little the government valued women's agency, the government arrested male relatives of the women, believing that the women acted on their behalf (Affi 2004).

Collapse of the Somali State

When the state collapsed in 1991, Somali women took on men's responsibilities in addition to their own. They became indispensable to the survival of their families but also of their communities. According to one interviewee in Hargeisa (January 2017), 'It was left to women to figure out how to keep their families safe, how to feed them, how to care for those injured, shouldering numerous roles and responsibilities, including those that were carried out primarily by their men in the pre-civil war roles in the family, and society led to changes in gender relations.' Women not only cared for their children, but many took on children who were not theirs, caring for orphans and the children of relatives, according to a woman activist who was in Bosaaso during the civil war (Garowe, August 2017). However, their new status and greater responsibility did not translate into an increase in their representation in formal decision-making processes.

During his rule, Barre had ostensibly banned both the clan and Islamist groups, although this pretence was abandoned in the 1980s. After the collapse of the state, both the clan and Islamist politics came back in force, mobilising 'Islamic and clan sentiments' (Abdullahi 2011, 34). Although Islamist groups vary in their views on women's political participation, groups like Ittihad are vehemently opposed to women's involvement in politics, whereas other groups, such as Al Islah, appear theoretically open to women's political participation.

During the civil war, women's numerous clan affiliations led to their rape and death (Jama 2010, 62). But it was also this multiple clan affiliation that could give a woman a 'structural role as peacebuilder, enabling her to act as a conduit for dialogue between warring parties and to exert pressure on them to keep talking' (Jama 2010, 62). Women laid the foundation for peace, but men refused to build on it. One Somali proverb says that women can build peace, but only men can make it; therefore, even if women create the platform for peace, they cannot actually enforce it because women are not included in decision-making forums (Jama 2010, 62).

In Mogadishu, for example, women who were engaged in peacemaking were able to move between neighbourhoods controlled by different militia groups, exerting pressure on the militias to reduce the conflict. In Baidoa, women took it upon themselves to bury those killed in the conflict regardless of their clan affiliation; the men buried only their clan members (Adam and Ford 1998, 22). On returning to Hargeisa in north-western Somalia, which declared independence from Somalia in May 1991, the people found a city destroyed. Across Somalia, the ensuing political vacuum and dire need for the provision of social services created an opportunity for the emergence of active civil society organisations (Abdullahi 2011, 100). While the 'men were preoccupied and entirely distracted by their coveting of international recognition', the women reconvened the Alla-Amiin group prioritising meeting the needs of returnees, according to a former member (Hargeisa, January 2017). Women also sought to bring about peace and security to the city, demonstrating against the *deydey* (armed roaming bandits) and trying to disarm them. When conflict broke out within the clans in Somaliland in 1994, one woman who was present in Hargeisa during this time commented:

> Even the Guurti weren't able to intervene. There was a time when they had gone to the airport to speak with a group of bandits that seized control over the airport; they returned having gotten slapped around by the armed militia. We organised a group of women from all corners of the city to meet with the same group of *deydey*. We knew many of them who didn't see us as part of the government, so they listened to us and we were able to broker agreements on several occasions.

Sado Abdi Amare, a former SNM fighter, was bewildered by the fighting and wrote a poem reflecting the pointlessness of fighting, which she shared in an interview in August 2016 in Hargeisa:

> If foreigners fight, they move apart
> The clothes on me are on
> Oh Deka, what is this fight about?
> What is the conflict between this side and that side?

This did not mean that all women advocated for peace. During the internal conflict in Somaliland and elsewhere in Somalia, there were women who stood with their clans, encouraging the men to fight and collecting supplies for them (Life and Peace Institute 2018). For women like Sado, this made no sense. According to a woman peacemaker, a group of them spoke with the women, asking them why they were supporting conflict (Hargeisa, August 2016). Similarly, in Mogadishu, at the beginning of the civil war, there were women who actively encouraged militias to loot, rape, and kill members of other clans.

The war in Mogadishu, which then spread to the rest of the country, forced Somalis to flee in all directions. In addition to the problems associated with a country in the midst of a civil war, it was women who were left caring for children, the elderly, the sick, and the wounded. Many girls and women were raped in retaliation against their clans, or those of their husbands or children; others gave birth while fleeing. Many Somalis escaped to north-eastern Somalia (present-day Puntland), which was peaceful, in part, because women had taken an active role in bringing peace and security to the region. For example, in the 1993 war between two rival clans that live in Galkayo, leaving over 1,000 people dead in one night, the women took to the streets demanding an end to the hostilities. This led to the Galkayo Peace Accord between the two fighting warlords, Abdullahi Yusuf and Mohamed Farah Aideed, as described by one interviewee in Garowe (August 2017).

Similarly, in Bosaaso, internal conflict within the revived SSDF militia led to a surge in robbery and other crimes. Women, the poor, and unarmed civilians who had fled the war in Mogadishu were subjected to harassment, rape, and looting. The women, led by Lady Hufan Artan, organised a group of young women, who called themselves the Hufan Rangers, and recruited young men to help them patrol the city. They disarmed men and collected funds to enlarge the police presence in Bosaaso, and they pushed to have anyone who committed a crime arrested and imprisoned by the police. Their activities were initially met with resistance, 'but later on people understood what we were doing', as the number of crimes declined, said a former member of the Hufan Rangers (interview, Garowe, August 2017).

The Hufan Rangers, which had 19 members, were also able to solve a bloody conflict over the Bosaaso port that left many people dead and promised to ignite a communal conflict. According to the same Hufan Ranger, the conflict began because there was a disagreement about the order in which boats would dock in the ports and unload their merchandise. Hufan Rangers went to the port every day to try to enforce a fair schedule. They were shot at, and one of their members was killed, but they kept showing up until the boat owners agreed to abide by the schedule set by the women, according to an interviewee in Garowe (August 2017).

In southern Somalia, Hawa Abdi hosted thousands of internally displaced Somalis on her land, meeting their health, security, educational, and food needs, as a famine engulfed the region (Abdi and Robbins 2013). For her humanitarian work, she was targeted by clans, warlords, and Al Shabaab. Many other women garnered local and international attention and appreciation for their peacebuilding, humanitarian, developmental,

environmental, and human rights work after the fall of the government.[7]
Women's participation in the 1995 Beijing Platform for Action led to new ideas and strategies for promoting peace, human rights, and gender equality. In Mogadishu in 1996, women created the Coalition for Grassroots Women Organizations, a network with 30 member organisations, serving to increase the engagement of civil society organisations in southern Somalia (Jama 2010, 63). A year later in Somaliland, Nagaad Network, which today has 46 member organisations, was created to advocate for women's rights. In Puntland, women's groups united under the We Are Women Activists (WAWA) group in 2000. WAWA currently has 46 member organisations and focuses on promoting peace and human rights and increasing women's participation at all levels of society. Because they face similar challenges, these organisations are not limited to their own regions and communicate and exchange strategies with each other.

State Formation and the Gender Quota

Somali women have actively engaged in peacebuilding, humanitarian work, and national development, but the gendered nature of clan-based politics has excluded women from full participation in peace talks (Jama 2010). In response, they have sought, as Tripp (2015) described, 'to disrupt the gendered nature of this process by demanding seats at the peace table and by insisting that their demands be incorporated into the peace agreements' and into state formation (145). Women's political gains across Somalia are mixed and whatever advancements women have made have often been accompanied by efforts to push back on their gains.

Somaliland broke off from Somalia in 1991 and created its own independent and fairly stable state. It does not, however, have international recognition. In the formation of Somaliland, women activists sought greater representation and participation, and according to one woman who was present at the Somaliland National Conference in 1997, women's initial request for participation was rejected (interview, Hargeisa, January 2017). Women demonstrated outside the meeting but were ignored by both politicians and clan elders. In the end, one interviewee explained:

> Women were allocated six non-active seats. We then went to the First Lady and complained to her, imploring her to speak with the President. She did and, as a result, we were given five more seats, making the total 11. There were 550 delegates and only 11 women in attendance, without any influence. If that's not injustice, I don't know what is. (Interview, Hargeisa, January 2017)

---

[7] The women included Hawa Aden, Suad Abdi Ibrahim, Fartun Abdisalan, Ilwad Elman, Rakiya Omaar, Asha Gelle, Asha Hagi Elmi, Lul Bani, Sadia Muse, Amina-Milgo Warsame, Ruqiya Abdullahi Hagi, Habiba H. Jimale, Faiza Jama, Fadumo Jibril, and Maryan Hussein.

Despite their small numbers, women in Somaliland advocated for a gender quota by striving to influence the drafting of the constitution. Their advocacy for gender quotas was met with great opposition. The women observers spoke with all 550 delegates, as one member explained (Hargeisa, January 2017) and the women present 'often interrupted the plenary sessions or spoke out of turn. We got removed several times from the floor or the venue for causing too much trouble.' When they sought to include a gender quota on the agenda of the conference, they were refused and were told this was because the country was 'going through a critical transition and that only a clan-based power-sharing system would get us out of this situation' (interview, Hargeisa, January 2017). They were told that the representation of women was something that could wait until everything else had been settled. Somali women continue to hear over and over again from men in politics that they need to wait until all the other problems facing the country have been resolved. Despite this, one accomplishment for women's activism was the inclusion of article 33 in the Somaliland Constitution, which gives women equal political, economic, social, and cultural rights with men. The same article gives women the rights to be elected and to vote, and to own and sell properties, and forbids violence against women.

When Somaliland held its first democratic election for the Parliament in 2005, the Parliament included only two women out of 164 members. One of the women was elected and another was appointed because an election could not be held in her region, according to one interviewee in Hargeisa (January 2017). Currently, there is only one woman in the House of Representatives and none in the House of Elders. Because elections are one person, one vote, Somaliland women who want to participate in politics face difficulties that they cannot overcome without the implementation of a gender quota. The important roles of clan, culture, and religion mean that most Somalilanders, including women, prefer to vote for men, whose representation and loyalty to the clan is unquestioned. According to an interview with a women's rights activist in Hargeisa, women in Somaliland lost an opportunity to push for gender quotas because they focused more on obtaining recognition for Somaliland (August 2016). After 13 years of lobbying for the gender quota, on June 2018, Somaliland President Muse Bihi and his Cabinet approved a 20 per cent quota for women in the upcoming local and parliamentary elections. This would have given women 18 out of 81 seats in the lower house (Duale 2018). But the bill was rejected by the Guurti, the upper house of the Somaliland Parliament, whose members are exclusively clan elders (Egge 2019).

In neighbouring Puntland, which is a federal state within Somalia, once the regional state formation conference began in 1997 the women were allocated 30 seats as delegates. Like women in Somaliland, women in Puntland contributed in many other ways, as well, including in providing the logistics for hosting the conference delegates. Some women vacated their homes for delegates, while others provided food free of charge. Additionally, 'the women on a daily basis resolved conflicts between the men, between clans, and between groups,' said an observer in Garowe (August 2017). Yet women were excluded from the newly formed state, until Anab Hassan, frustrated at women's exclusion and the denial of their contributions to the statemaking project, recited a poem at a public gathering, telling the clan elders to keep the land and that women would migrate. Anab reminded the elders that women were ready to contribute to the rebuilding of the state, 'but you men ignore our advice and inspirations, you suffocate our intellect, so it never sees daylight' (Jama 2010, 63).

The elders were moved by this poem and Puntland women were allocated five out of 66 parliamentary seats. However, 'each time a woman leaves, the clan replaces with her with a man,' said a former Puntland woman politician (Garowe, August 2017). In the last election in December 2018, women's representation in Parliament fell by 50 per cent. Puntland now has two women in its Parliament, although more than a dozen women campaigned and lobbied; some of the elders who appeared open to appointing women seemed to change their mind in the end and refused to appoint women, arguing that the 30 per cent quota only applied at the federal level. This is part of the broad, serious, and sustained backlash that women experience as they seek to reach the 30 per cent gender quota.

At the national level, Somali women have been pushing for a gender quota since the 2000 Arta Reconciliation Conference, which led to the formation of the Somali Transitional Federal Government. Although women only comprised 9 per cent of the delegates, during the conference they not only advanced their agenda of political inclusion, but also ensured the success of the conference due to their peacemaking role. According to Abdullahi (2018), out of the 810 delegates, 160 were women. According to Maryam Arif Qasim, who was a delegate to the Arta Conference:

> The women's group intervened on a number of occasions when it looked as if there were going to be problems; we were a pressure group. At one point we persuaded a clan who had walked out to return to the conference. On another occasion we persuaded clans to withdraw people they had sent out, to take them back into the fold. (Qasim 2000)

At the conclusion of the conference, women were allocated 12 per cent of the parliamentary seats. At the same time, the 4.5 clan-sharing system was introduced, in which political power is shared along clan lines (Elmi 2014). Aside from the cultural and religious arguments used to oppose women's political participation, the 4.5 system remains the most critical barrier to women's inclusion in politics, as we have seen. It was a clear and adverse response to women's insistence on having a share of the governance of the country, and it remains an obstacle that women have yet to overcome. Women engaged in different strategies, including calling for the formation of their own sixth clan and advocating for the same number of seats as the other clans (Timmons 2004). During the Arta Conference, about 70 per cent of the women present voted on issues, collectively as women, while 30 per cent of the women voted with their clans (Qasim 2000). In reality, out of 245 seats for the parliament, women were allocated 25, which were selected on the 4.5 formula (Jama 2010, 64). This undermined women's efforts to escape from under the clan structure and for women to be included as women, rather than as marginalised members of clans.

At the next reconciliation conference, held in Kenya, the 4.5 system was maintained and even though the gender quota for women was increased to 25 per cent, in reality women were only appointed to 14 per cent of the seats. This increase in gender quota was a response to increased pressure from Somali women as well as the international community. But the male political leaders were not serious about it.

In 2012, the transitional phase ended and the political system was transformed into a federal system. In the agreement, the gender quota was increased to 30 per cent of all political positions at all levels of women. Somalia had not had an election in decades, and it was impossible to implement a one person, one vote system. The new system devised would still have the 4.5 system as the basis of power-sharing and, in a move that made it difficult for women to claim the 30 per cent quota, 135 clan elders were given sole responsibility for selecting who would enter Parliament.

Thus, the selection process became an 'arena where men nominate and select men hailing from their clans to represent the national and all Somalis', according to Dini (2014). This was a major setback for Somali women, because many elders were hostile to appointing women to represent the clan. Women's many connections with different clans, which made them strong and effective advocates for peace, also made their participation in politics challenging. As one civil society activist from Garowe, Puntland, observed:

> Today, we also have the 4.5 formula through which political appointments and decisions are made. Now, traditional men are asked for permission to allow women to participate in politics. A traditional elder will never choose a woman over a man even if she has a PhD. He would rather choose a man who cannot read or write. (Garowe, August 2018; Mohamud 2015, 3)

For many women, the only way to overcome this opposition is to demolish the clan-based system of elders within the political process, which is anti-women. Many of the women who advocate for women's political participation believe that transitioning to one person, one vote will help women in getting elected. Some of these women's activists believe that raising women's awareness will allow women to be elected without the need for gender quota, but there is no evidence that will happen (Jibril, *n.d.).* In fact, the example of Somaliland clearly demonstrates that in patriarchal and clan-based societies like Somalia, women will not get elected without the enforcement of a gender quota.

In 2013, Somali women began to make plans to get the 30 per cent of seats allocated to them in the 2016 federal election. In Puntland, women formed Talo-wadaag, an informal women's group, where they focused on increasing women's representation both in local councils and at the national level. Talo-wadaag coordinated their work at the national level with the newly created Somali Gender Equity Movement (SGEM) in Mogadishu. Through lobbying, organising, and coordinating with each other, and support from the international community, women were successful in increasing their number in the federal parliament. The presence of the Goodwill Ambassadors – a group of women activists led by Asha Gelle, a former Minister of Women in Puntland, who toured the country, speaking with clan elders, highlighting challenges faced by women as well as irregularities during the election – combined with the presence of international observers helped women increase their numbers to 24 per cent. Whether women can increase or even maintain the current numbers in the 2021 election remains to be seen.

Conclusion

The history of Somali women can be described as one of making tentative and fragile progress, but despite the many obstacles Somali women remain engaged with their communities and continue to push for gender equality and greater political participation. They are also aware that to protect their rights, those rights must be enshrined in the constitution and in the laws of the country. In the current provisional constitution, for example, IIDA (Women's Development Organization), a Somali women's NGO, has identified several areas that need to be amended in the constitution, including the gender quota; inclusion of rights that address gender issues; and clarification of the relationship between Somali customary law, *shar'ia*, and international law. IIDA also calls for the establishment of a gender commission and the implementation of gender equality with the truth and reconciliation processes (Legal Action Worldwide 2014).

The next federal election is slated to be held in 2021 and women have been mobilising to increase the gender quota from the current 24 per cent. They have also been campaigning for a way to get the clan elders' influence reduced as much as possible. The expected transition to one person, one vote will not take place. Instead, the 2016 indirect electoral model will be maintained and expanded, with 101 delegates to elect each candidate. Although the federal government as well as member states have committed to maintaining the 30 per cent quota, exactly how this will be done has not been clarified. Also, the doubled registration fee required of candidates, of US$10,000 for the lower house and US$20,000 for the upper, will be a steep financial challenge for women to meet, even if they are given the 50 per cent discount they received in the 2016 election. Additionally, if what happened in 2016 takes place, most women will be unable to afford the massive bribery expected by most electoral delegates in exchange for votes. The continued presence of the elders, who have successfully reduced the presence of women in regional parliaments since 2016, suggests that women will have difficulty in maintaining the 24 per cent of the seats that they currently hold in Parliament. The Goodwill Ambassadors, who played a critical role in the 2016 election in highlighting irregularities affecting women's candidacy, are also missing from the 2021 election. It is not clear how the quota will be guaranteed.

That Somali women are capable of being effective leaders when given the opportunity can be seen not only in the prominent women leaders in Somalia, but also those in the United States, Sweden, Belgium, and the United Kingdom, where Somali women have run for and have been elected to political offices, even during times of increasing political polarisation, right-wing politics, and intense opposition to immigrants and Muslims.[8]

Despite the clan and Islamist forces aligned against them, women are confident that there is no going back. Women have also made inroads into political institutions. For example, Halima Ismail Ibrahim is the Chair of the National Independent Electoral Commission and Safiya Hassan Sheikh Ali Jimale became the first woman mayor of a large city, Beledweyne in central Somalia. She was replaced with another woman, Nadar Tabah Ma'allin in 2020. Galmudug and Hirshabelle regional parliaments elected Fadumo Abdi Ali and Anab Ahmed Isse respectively as their deputy speakers of the parliament until 2020, when they lost the election to men. At the local level, women have done better. For example, in Diinsoor local district in South West State, 50 percent of the members are women (Affi 2020b).

Somaliland will be having their first parliamentary election since 2005 and many women have declared their intention to run. Having failed to obtain a 20 percent gender quota, women candidates have appealed directly to the clan elders. For example, Suad Abdi, a longtime women's activist, was the first woman to be endorsed by her clan elders for the parliamentary election.

[8] In the 2019 US elections, two 23-year-old Somali women, Safiya Khaled and Nadia Mohamed, were elected in Minnesota and Maine to local offices despite encountering extreme racist and anti-Muslim opposition. They follow in the footsteps of Ilhan Omar, who was elected to the US Congress in 2018 and re-elected in 2020, and Hodan Hassan who was elected to state office in Minnesota. In Sweden, Laila Ali Elmi became a member of the national Swedish Parliament in 2018. In Belgium, Sara Mohamed Khalif was elected at the age of 21 to the Leuven City Council.

Movements such as Talo-wadaag and SGEM remain active, engaged, and committed to women's political participation, and new groups like LeadNOW are mobilising to ensure that women remain engaged in the political sphere. The history of Somalia in the past 70 years clearly demonstrates that women are not deterred but will instead continue to participate as they seek full and equal rights in the governance of their country.

5

Sudanese Women's Demands for Freedom, Peace, and Justice in the 2019 Revolution

SAMIA AL-NAGAR AND LIV TØNNESSEN

The world-admired Sudanese revolution is marked by unprecedented contribution and participation of women throughout the country, including women from all walks of lives. The participation of women is not a by-chance event, as Sudanese women own a strong history of resistance in the face of dictatorships and patriarchy. Women were very active resisting the hegemony of the previous regime and its laws and practices.[1]

–Asha Al-Karib, Sudanese activist

Introduction

The popular uprising against the Islamist-military regime of Omar al Bashir lasted for eight months beginning in December 2018 and women were at the forefront of the peaceful protests. Across many areas, women constituted the majority of the protesters (Al-Nagar and Tønnessen 2019). Women from diverse backgrounds in terms of class, generation, religion, education, and ethnicity occupied the streets of Sudan, facing risk of arrest, torture, sexual assault, tear gas, and live bullets. After the ousting of Omar al Bashir on 11 April 2019, a transitional military council (TMC) consisting of al Bashir's former allies took control of the state. At this moment during the protests, women formed a sit-in outside the military headquarters – especially young women. Even after the 'Khartoum massacre' on 3 June 2019, when the military violently slaughtered participants and reportedly sexually abused protesters, women went back to the streets, refusing to back down (Al-Nagar and Tønnessen 2019). Negotiations between the TMC and the Forces for Freedom and Change (FFC) in August facilitated a new constitutional declaration and the formation of the Sovereign Council (consisting of members of both the

---

[1] Interview with Asha Al-Karib, activist and founder of Sudanese Organization for Research and Development (SORD), Khartoum State, 19 August 2019.

FFC and the TMC) as the collective head of state of Sudan for a three-year period and a transitional government consisting of technocrats under the leadership of Prime Minister Abdallah Hamdok.

This chapter aims to understand why women were so visibly involved in the most recent revolution and how it relates to their struggles for peace, justice, and freedom during the dictatorship of al Bashir. Women's activism against discrimination and inequality that hamper their ability to live free of violence and contribute to society as full citizens has a long trajectory. Drawing on recent scholarship on women and the Arab Spring (Moghadam 2018; see also Singerman 2013; Khalil 2014; Al-Ali 2012; Sadiqi 2016), we argue that women's legal and social status before the Sudanese revolution shaped women protesters' demands. Drawing insights from the wider literature on why women protest, we contend that higher levels of gender discrimination and the presence of women's organisations increase the likelihood of women's protest (Murdie and Peksen 2014). As in other revolutions in the region's recent history, women's participation was not spontaneous or momentary, but linked to women's central role in defying these dictatorships through organised movements and what Asef Bayat (2013) has termed non-movements (see, for example, Wahba 2016). Women's rights have been an important political symbol at the heart of what Sudanese Islamists have codified as *shar'ia*, exemplified in the codification of one of the most conservative Islamic family laws in the region and adherence to strict public morality laws. Women's activism against dictatorship represents a long trajectory in Sudan. Women's opposition to al Bashir's regime is, therefore, central to understanding their strong involvement in the revolution.

Although our findings suggest that, at least at the beginning of the protests, women's issues were deprioritised to focus on the demand to overthrow the al Bashir regime, through our interviews with women protesters it became clear that they regarded regime change as pivotal for any positive changes in women's status and situation. The women we interviewed delineated three different women-specific agendas related to the governmental changes they espouse: 1) accountability for sexual violence, 2) freedom to make life choices, and 3) women's political representation in the new civilian government structures. The agenda of women protesters can be traced back to demands for reform by women's rights activists in the aftermath of the Bill of Rights in the 2005 Interim National Constitution. This shows that the demands of what is often described as an urban-based and elitist women's movement have broader appeal to women of diverse backgrounds who regard it as part of their vision for the country in terms of freedom, peace, and justice.

However, it was not until the formation of the sit-in, and especially after women were largely excluded from the negotiations between TMC and FFC, that women's demands for political representation figured more prominently in the slogans and public discourse. Women expressed in the public discourse and through our interviews that their marginalisation during the peace negotiations was seen as a threat to women as a group and a betrayal of what is widely perceived as a women-led revolution (R. Abbas 2020a). Drawing insight from Charles Tilly (1978), who saw threat as an important factor driving the mobilisation of a group into contentious political action, women protesters perceived their exclusion from the negotiation table as a threat and a manifestation of patriarchal culture. This represented what Lisa Baldez (2002) calls a tipping point for women's protest as the event precipitated the coalescence of diverse women's groups into collective mobilisation for political inclusion of women. From this point on, women's issues were no longer subordinated by the overall aims of the revolution but at the very forefront of the public political discourse, where groups of women voiced women-specific agendas through advocacy, art, poetry, social media, and street demonstrations.

The first part of the chapter elaborates on women's role in the 2019 revolution, tracing it back to their involvement in ousting military dictatorships in 1964 and 1985. The second part looks at the centrality of women's issues in the Islamist political project and how women as a group became disproportionately disadvantaged when the al Bashir regime codified a series of laws that were labelled as *shar'ia* law during the early 1990s. Women's groups independent from al Bashir's regime have actively advocated against these Islamist policies despite widespread suppression of civil society. The third part of the chapter analyses the three agendas of women revolutionaries and links these agendas to women's mobilisation for legal reform during the dictatorship of al Bashir.

Methods

To explore women's role in the protests, their motivation for participating in the revolution, and their interpretation of the main revolutionary slogan 'Freedom, Peace, and Justice', we interviewed 68 women protesters and 10 women's rights activists at two critical moments during the revolution: in April 2019 when former President Omar al Bashir was ousted from office, and in August 2019 during ongoing negotiations between the TMC and the FFC. The FFC is a coalition representing the protesters through unions, civil society including women's organisations, political parties, and neighbourhood committees. The sample is of course not representative of all Sudanese women participating in the revolution, but these interviews give us important insights into women's agendas beyond the elite-based women's movement in the country. We asked all interviewees open-ended questions about their role in the protests, motivation, their interpretation of the slogan 'Freedom, Peace, and Justice', and their vision for the future.

We interviewed women protesters face to face and by telephone, with support from a team of research assistants. The interviewees were between 16 and 60 years of age and from a variety of backgrounds in terms of marital status, generation, educational level, political affiliation, and ethnicity. All the interviews were conducted in Khartoum, but the women had diverse backgrounds including origin from Khartoum, Blue Nile, Atbara, Kordofan, and Elgazira. The protesters interviewed mostly included women who had no prior record of activism and protest, including housewives, government employees, journalists, engineers, medical doctors, scholars, university administrators, university students, private sector managers, and small business owners. Some of the women interviewed were women's rights activists or politicians who had participated in sit-ins or other protests previously and were part of organised (social media) groups.

We conducted the interviews in Arabic and Samia al-Nagar translated them into English for coding and interpretation. We have analysed the interview material using thematic analysis, which is a method for identifying, analysing, and reporting patterns (themes) within data. Our inductive approach emphasises the participants' perceptions and experiences as the paramount object of study.

Sudan's Three Revolutions and Women's Role

Sudan's third revolution in 2019 started with strikes and demonstrations in the south-east and north-east of the country. Protests soon spread throughout the entire country with slogans such as 'Freedom, Peace, and Justice'; 'Just Fall, That is All'; and 'Revolution Is the People's Choice'. Growing dissatisfaction with the regime's political and economic mismanagement and oppression under Omar al Bashir, an alleged supporter of terrorism and war criminal, turned into peaceful demonstrations across the country. The Sudanese Professionals Association (SPA) coordinated many of these protests. Established in 2012, the SPA is an umbrella group of trade unions for professionals. It operated mostly clandestinely during al Bashir's regime to avoid arrest.

Women from diverse backgrounds played a major role in the peaceful protests that ousted the dictator al Bashir and after that were persistently present in the sit-in in front of the military headquarters in Khartoum. Although international media outlets have portrayed women's participation in the revolution as exceptional, it represents a long trajectory in Sudan. Before the 2019 revolution, there had been several Arab Spring-like demonstrations, in which women played an active part, in 2011 and 2013 (African Centre for Justice and Peace Studies 2013). Unlike its Arab neighbours in northern Africa, the Sudanese people have ousted military dictatorships before, in October 1964 and in May 1985. In both uprisings, women played an active part.

Women's Participation in Sudan's First Revolution (October 1964)

Sudanese women participated in the October revolution in 1964, Sudan's first revolution. This revolution brought the downfall of the military regime of General Ibrahim Abboud, who had taken power through a military coup d'état in 1958. Professional women, women students, secondary school girls, and even housewives participated extensively in the protests, mainly in Sudan's capital of Khartoum. Although the majority of casualties were men, the October revolution also had a woman martyr, Bakhita Al Hafian, who was shot demonstrating with her children and grandchildren (Al Amin and Magied 2001, 11–12; Al-Gadal 2016, 39–40). At the University of Khartoum, 'posters in the names of female students' declared that they were prepared to sacrifice their lives. Women ululated to motivate protesters, a role they have also taken in Sudan's most recent and third revolution. According to Berridge, women helped 'deter the military from taking action against demonstrators by standing at the forefront of the crowds and humiliating soldiers with chants like, 'Go back to the barracks, you girls'. Although women acted according to socially conservative understandings of femininity by using ululation to support men protesters and shaming soldiers, they also participated as political actors demanding rights (Berridge 2016, 33–34). The Women's Union, the main women's group at the time with a Marxist ideology and close ties to the Sudanese Communist Party, took the opportunity to intensify its advocacy for women's right to vote and stand for election, which was later granted by the new democratic government (1965–69) in 1965. Fatima Ahmed Ibrahim became the first woman to be elected to Sudan's National Assembly (Al-Nagar and Tønnessen 2017a). However, the scant literature on the topic suggests that women's issues were largely subordinate to the national cause of ousting the Abboud dictatorship,(Ibrahim 2015; Berridge 2016).

Women's Participation in Sudan's Second Revolution (April 1985)

As in the October revolution, the 1985 uprising against the dictatorship of Jaafar Nimeiri, who took power in 1969, was led by a national alliance composed of professionals, trade unions, and political parties. Women participated primarily as members of professional unions in preparation for the general strike that occurred during this revolution. Many of them also took part in demonstrations, and housewives allowed secret political meetings in their homes. However, women's rights were not at the forefront of the strikes and uprisings and were considered secondary to the political overthrow of the regime. The new transitional government excluded women from political decision-making, because they constituted neither a trade union nor a political party, and women quickly became discouraged. A move to reserve seats for women in the national legislative assembly was not approved because it was considered 'undemocratic'. *Shar'ia* laws introduced by Nimeiri in 1983 that were restrictive to women were not abrogated by the 1986 democratic government headed by Prime Minister Sadiq al Mahdi. Instead, the government issued a decree stipulating that women in the civil service would receive only two-thirds of the housing allowance of male officials. In addition, a women's committee was instituted at the department of passports and immigration to enforce restrictions on the travel of women abroad (Al Bakri 1995). Although Sudan signed several international human rights conventions in 1986 under the new civilian government headed by Sadiq al Mahdi, the Convention on the Elimination of All Forms of Discrimination against Women (CEDAW) was overlooked. According to activist Asha Al-Karib, 'Women's presence in the transitional and democratic periods [1964–69 and 1986–89] was invisible. There was no effort for women [as a] collective and our agenda was dissolved in the political agenda.'[2]

Women's Participation in Sudan's Third Revolution (April 2019)

Professional and elite women participated in the 1964 and 1985 revolutions, and they also participated in the 2019 revolution. For example, Alaa Salah was dubbed an icon of the most recent revolution after she was seen wearing the national Sudanese dress known as a *toube,* while motivating other women at a protest (Salih 2019).[3] However, although Alaa Salah, a university student, embodies this history of professional women playing a key role in previous popular uprisings in Sudan, this image does not capture the fact that women's participation in the most recent revolution has been much broader than in the earlier ones, in terms of their region, class, and ethnicity.[4] Previous revolutions involved primarily Khartoum-based professional women, but the 2019 revolution involved a more diverse group of women. For example, the women's Food and Tea Seller's Cooperative in Khartoum, headed by Awadeya Mahmoud Koko, played a major role in distributing food to protesters at the sit-ins (Lavrilleux 2019). But at the forefront were young women, or girls as they are called in Sudan. In a country where 61 per cent of the population is under the age of 25, this was a revolution of youth (S. Abbas 2020).

[2] Interview, August 2019.
[3] There has been a critical discussion about coining Alaa Salah as the icon of the revolution. See a summary of the discussion in Engeler et al. (2020).
[4] The image of Alaa Salah as the icon representing Sudanese women has been critiqued. It iconises a particular *kind* of Sudanese woman: northern, Arab, urban, and educated. Malik (2019) underscores that the white tobe, a garment worn by white-collar professional women, is deeply entangled in ethnic and classed structures of Sudanese society and thus far from representative of 'Sudanese women' but of certain women who have been part of the elites since the country's independence. The irony, according to Sara Nugdallah (2020, 90) 'rests in the fact that the image assuming to represent a revolution of change is continuing with the upholding of the very divisions that drove it'.

Some women played an important role in Sudan's third revolution by using *zagharid* (ululation) to motivate protesters. Videos of female protesters reciting poems and chanting revolutionary slogans went viral. This echoes a long tradition of Sudanese women performing praise and lament poems to honour the dead, boost the morale of warriors, and defy ruthless leaders. In addition, housewives played a role from their homes in supporting the protesters – for example, by distributing sandwiches and milk to protesters who were tear-gassed, continuing the roles played by women during previous uprisings. A 35-year-old married female government employee who participated in the protests explained, 'After the gathering of protesters in a specific place, the protest starts by ululation from a lady, and this is the sign for everyone to move and start protesting, and this is the role of the leader.'[5]

Looking beyond women in important but traditional roles, they also took part in the leadership of the SPA, which took a lead in organising protests throughout the country. Especially during the sit-in period, women took on roles that challenged social and political gender stereotypes. For example, they worked night shifts and shared responsibilities at security checkpoints, theatres, political discussion sessions, and kitchens providing food and drink services. They even slept in the camp, something that breaks with prevailing norms stipulating that it is not appropriate for women to be in public spaces without a male guardian because it puts them at risk of sexual assault and bringing shame to the family.

Social media allowed for new ways of participating. Women's groups in the most recent revolution were also vocal and active in challenging gender stereotypes, especially on social media. At one point, chanting protesters described al Bashir as a 'weak woman'. Feminist activists called it out on social media and the slogan did not catch on. They launched the campaign 'Waqt wa naso', which means 'This is the time, and these are its people' on social media to break such gender stereotypes. This followed the suggestion of SPA's service committee that women should take particular responsibility for cleaning the sit-in area because they 'cared more about cleaning'. Women's anger about the sexist attitudes of male protesters mushroomed into anger about how women are treated in all aspects of Sudanese society. The SPA later apologised for urging women (and not men) to clean the streets. And a cleanup day in Khartoum did take place – with both men and women taking part. The Noon movement, which was established during the revolution, called attention to sexual harassment in the sit-in area. *Maydanik* (a gendered word translating to 'her space') were created within the sit-in area as safe zones for women providing victims of sexual harassment with legal and psychological support (Nugdalla 2020). Other groups were also active in creating awareness around women's issues, including representation in political

---

[5] Interview, April 2019.

decision-making bodies in the transitional government and a reform of discriminatory laws codified by the al Bashir regime.

Gender-Discriminatory Policies and Women's Activism against Islamism

The role of women and their demands in Sudan's third revolution cannot be fully appreciated without understanding the regime they were opposing and how its policies had affected women as a group. Al Bashir described the implementation of Sudan's public order law as conflicting with *shar'ia* just before he was ousted from the presidential palace. Even the long-term head of the security forces, Salah Gosh, stated (before he fled the country) that the demonstrations erupted because the government was too strict with the implementation of *shar'ia* laws in Sudan.

Women's rights had served as a symbolic political signifier of the Islamist political project in Sudan, which the country's leaders had called the 'civilisation project' (*al-Mashru al-Hadari*) (Nageeb 2004; Hale 1997; Tønnessen 2011). Women's rights had been at the crux of the 'Islamisation' of Sudan's laws, and these changes had disproportionately and negatively affected women. The civilisation project interpreted Islamic law in a particularly fundamentalist way, and political leaders introduced new *shar'ia* laws that significantly changed women's citizenship rights.

The Islamist state's gender ideology propagated gender equity (*insaf*) (Tønnessen 2011). Gender equity was proposed as a route to women's empowerment that was an alternative to both traditional Islam and Western feminism. Muslim women from certain urban class positions and certain Arabic ethnic tribes became the face of a modern Islam as they combined piety with their presence in the public sphere, including in politics. Resources were put into state institutions (first and foremost, Sudan's Ministry of Security and Social Development) and state organisations (mainly, the Sudanese Women General Union and the International Muslim Women's Union), advancing the state's view of gender equity. After broad mobilisation for a gender quota, Islamists introduced a policy of reserving 25 per cent of the seats for women in national and subnational legislative assemblies to ensure their representation in politics. Not only is women's political role in alignment with Islam but, according to Islamists, complementarity between the hard rational male and the soft emotional female politician is needed in order to make good and sound policies (Tønnessen 2018). The idea of complementarity – that men and women have different rights and obligations because of their biological differences – is central to this gender ideology. However, according to Sudanese Islamists women should only be active participants in the public sphere – obtaining an education, working, and participating in trade and politics – *if* they behave and look pious, moral, and chaste.

But this vision has an important class dimension; for example, it is only possible to combine work and piousness if you are educated and working in blue-collar professions, not if you are working as a street vendor delivering direct service to men (Tønnessen 2019).

During the early 1990s, the Islamist state imposed new legal restrictions on women, particularly on their movement and dress. These laws are collectively known as the 'Public Order Law' in Sudan and have been intrinsically linked with the gender ideology of the al Bashir regime. In December 1991, the hijab became the official dress code for women by presidential decree. Several stipulations in the Criminal Law of 1991 under the title, 'Honor, Reputation, and Public Morality' (articles 145–160), related to adultery, homosexuality, indecent and immoral acts, and prostitution regulated public order. Among other things, it mandated 'decent' attire and behaviour, and criminalised fornication and adultery. Specialised public order police upheld the 'public order' set by these rules (SIHA 2009). In the various states, public order laws were enacted, with varying stipulations. In Khartoum state, the public order law (among other things) introduced regulations aimed at reducing gender mixing in public spaces in order to avoid *fitna,* which is in the Sudanese concept translated into 'sexual chaos', whereby immoral and religiously forbidden behaviour became rampant (SIHA 2009; Tønnessen 2011). For example, dancing might create sexual temptation and therefore should be avoided. Another example was the potential temptation that could be caused by unrelated women and men sitting next to each other on public transport or standing in public queues, which therefore should be segregated. The darkening of windows on private vehicles was strictly prohibited to ensure that they were not misused for immoral acts.

All of these laws and decrees making up the 'Public Order Law' in Sudan underline how moral bodies are disciplined by the state in a fashion that normalises and naturalises particular ways of being. This represses those who do not subscribe to state definitions of the norms of the idealised Muslim woman through various methods of control, marginalisation, silencing, and abuse (Nugdalla 2020). Class and ethnicity often compound such state repression. For example, the Labor Act of 1997 restricts women's working hours but differentiates between women of different classes. *Unskilled* women are not allowed to work during evenings and nights, but *skilled* women like doctors are allowed to do so.

The Muslim Family Law (1991) was a central law introduced by the al Bashir regime that significantly changed women's legal rights. It regulated women's rights within marriage, custody, divorce, and inheritance and has emerged as a contested piece of legislation in contemporary Sudan.[6] It

---

[6] According to Carolyn Fluehr-Lobban, throughout most of the 20th century, *shar'ia* law in Sudan developed through judicial circulars. Before the Islamist takeover and codification of the Muslim Family Law in 1991, these circulars had a pattern of 'an enlightened and liberal interpretation'. In fact, Sudan 'has been a leader in legal reform, anticipating innovations which were not introduced into other Muslim regions until years or even decades later'

has been described as a backlash against women's rights activists, because it (among other things) legalised child marriage (with the minimum age for marriage set at 10 years), stipulated a wife's obedience to her husband, gave a husband the right to divorce his wife outside the courts without cause, and denied wives the possibility of working outside the home without their husbands' permission (Abdel Halim 2011b). It built on the principle of male guardianship (*qawama*) within the family, the idea that the man is the protector, provider, and decision-maker of the household, while the woman is the obedient caregiver and nurturer. It is the most conservative Muslim family law in the Middle East and North Africa, despite decades of mobilisation for reform.

Women's groups and activists who were pushing for an expansion of women's rights and basic freedom and dignity faced an oppressive political environment during the al Bashir regime (Nugdalla 2020). The laws that women's rights activists opposed had been used strategically to silence them (SIHA 2009). For example, 'public order laws' had been used to arrest activists as part of a strategy to ruin their reputations by labelling them 'immoral' and 'promiscuous' because of their attire and behaviour in public spaces (*ibid*). Government security forces, especially the National Intelligence and Security Service, raped and sexually abused women activists with impunity, a trend that continued during Sudan's third revolution (SORD 2020). The Bill of Rights in the Interim National Constitution, which followed immediately after the Comprehensive Peace Agreement in 2005, intensified demands for reform and opened up a political space for women's rights activists. Despite surveillance, harassment, and a violent crackdown on women's NGOs, women's rights activists persevered in opposing the regime's discriminatory policies. Although mobilisation had often been fragmented and reactive to the regime's brutality in, for example, arbitrarily arresting and flogging women, women's rights activists continued to work both visibly and behind the scenes in preparation for the fall of the al Bashir regime. As women's rights activist and Ahfad University for Women Professor Balghis Badri put it during an interview with us:

> Although this regime is oppressive, there have never been so many women's NGOs and there has never been so much awareness. There is more engagement. We have had more exposure to the international community; we have started to learn and see; we have started to mature during this repressive regime. We are ready![7]

Although women with no prior political engagement participated in the 2019 revolution, some of the women did have such experience,

---

(1994, 117). This codification was significant because it marked the transition of family law from the religious field to the political field. With the 1991 codification, family politics became an area of political contestation, with the state rather than the clergy becoming the principal religious authority (Tønnessen 2011).

[7]   Interview, October 2012.

including from women's and human rights NGOs that had worked for peace, justice, and freedom since the inception of the al Bashir regime.[8] Key to many of these groups and movements was the dismantling of the legal architecture legitimised within Islam, which is seen as representing the regime's 'moral preoccupations with women's bodies and movement' (Nugdallah 2020, 84).

Female Protesters' Demands Linked to Past Women's Activism against Islamism

Although the motivations behind the 2018 and 2019 protests were complex and covered a broad range of issues, interviews conducted with female protesters suggest that understanding the al Bashir regime's restrictive laws and discriminatory policies towards women was crucial to understanding why women were so strongly involved in the revolution. However, this does not mean that all female protesters interviewed for this study supported a feminist agenda for gender equality, nor does it suggest that the demands were entirely secular. Although the narratives were clearly anti-Islamist or against the *Inghaz* (which directly translates into 'Salvation', the popular name for al Bashir's regime because it declared the coup d'etat in 1989 a national salvation), our interviews show that this critique is often based on how Islamists either took the strictest interpretation of Islam or outright misrepresented Islam to control Sudan's citizens. The most frequently mentioned examples are the restrictions on women's dress, that women need their male guardians' permission to work for a wage or visit family, and how public interactions between genders are controlled, all in the name of Islamic morality. A 30-year-old university graduate and female protester asserted that 'the regime has used Islam as a way to mask its oppressive nature.'[9] This critique should not be misinterpreted as a call for complete separation from religion. Only one political party, or rather the Aziz al-Hilu faction of the Sudan People's Liberation Movement-North, has demanded a secular Sudanese state ('Sudan's peace talks ... ' 2020).

The diversity of opinion is also reflected in our interview material as it relates to women's demands for justice. We found support for both gender equality and the Islamist concept of complementarity among our interviewees. For example, one married 40-year-old female protester with three children said, 'There is no equality and that is why I went out and participated in the demonstrations ... I believe in gender equality.'[10] But

---

[8] In 2009, the civil society organisations working on peacebuilding were 241 registered CSOs in all Darfur states, in addition to 232 based in Khartoum, and 57 per cent of these organisations were led by women (Partners in Development Services, 2009. 'Mapping and Capacity Assessment of Civil Society Organizations (CSOs) In Darfur.' UNDP: Sudan.)

[9] Interview, April 2019.

[10] Interview, April 2019.

another protester, 29 years old and married, explained that she did *not* protest for gender equality:

> We're protesting for a better life. Not for equality between genders, because at the end of the day we are Muslims. We are asking for our rights, but not in all aspects. We should put in mind that we are a conservative society and our demands should reflect that. Yes, women were active in the revolution since its beginning, complementing men's role inside and outside of the uprising.[11]

Whether female protesters supported a feminist agenda, three specific women's agendas emerge from our rare interview material: 1) freedom to make life choices, 2) accountability for sexual violence, and 3) increased women's political participation and representation. These demands are not new to the political agenda in Sudan. Women's rights activists continually demanded these outcomes during al Bashir's rule, particularly after the 2005 Comprehensive Peace Agreement and the Bill of Rights in the National Interim Constitution, which was a critical political juncture for voicing legal demands. During this time, there was an explosion in women's groups advocating for legal reform. Women's rights retain strong symbolic significance and are at the heart of the codified *shar'ia* law in Sudan. Thus, the polarisation of Islamist women's groups within the government and women's groups independent of the government became more evident to the extent that the al Bashir regime attempted to silence women's rights advocates through different violent measures (Tønnessen and al-Nagar 2013; Tønnessen 2017).

Justice: Challenging Laws Granting Impunity

Demands that the Sudanese state should be held accountable for injustices committed during al Bashir's 30-year reign are widespread. Although peace was negotiated between north and south in 2005 and in eastern Sudan in 2006, the conflict in Darfur that erupted in 2003 was continuous throughout the period that al Bashir remained dictator of the country. After the secession of South Sudan in 2011, conflict erupted along the border between the two countries.

For the women we interviewed, especially those from war zones, demands for accountability are specifically related to sexual violence, which according to the International Commission of Inquiry on Darfur (2005), has been widespread and systematic in the Darfur conflict. Despite the fact that the International Criminal Court (ICC) indicted al Bashir and several of his comrades in 2009 for systematic and widespread sexual violence in Darfur, victims of sexual abuse have not yet seen justice in the country (ICC 2009). One 35-year-old female protester explained, 'Women

[11] Interview, April 2019.

have demands to hold accountable and punish the perpetrators of sexual abuse in Darfur and other parts of the country.'[12] Female protesters from Darfur who participated in the sit-in in front of the military headquarters in Khartoum made a poster with the text, 'Raped women demand prosecution of criminal *Janjaweed* immediately.' The Janjaweed is a militia that operated in Darfur on behalf of al Bashir's regime. It is renowned for its use of sexual assault. Al Bashir later made this militia into the Rapid Support Forces (RSF), legitimising it as an official branch of Sudan's military forces. The RSF's current leader, Mohamed Hamdan 'Hemeti' Dagalo, is a member of Sudan's Sovereign Council, in spite of the fact that the RSF is widely considered to be responsible, together with the national security forces, for the Khartoum massacre on 3 June 2019, which has been described as a 'campaign of terror' to disperse the peaceful sit-in (S. Abbas 2020).

Reports of sexual abuse of female protesters by the RSF during the Khartoum massacre went viral on social media, something we regard as likely to further fuel such claims to justice. The use of sexual violence against female protesters (and the fear of such use) by different branches of the military was a recurring theme in some of the interviews we conducted before 3 June 2019, especially among young female protesters. One 35-year-old married university graduate explained, 'Although women wear proper clothes, they are exposed to verbal abuse and physical violence, and this [the abusers] do with Islam as their cover.[13]

The regime's notorious record for the use of sexual violence to oppress, silence, and engage in ethnic cleansing was on the agenda of women's rights activists long before the revolution started. However, our analysis suggests that this issue first rose to prominence when the ICC indicted the former president and several of his cronies for the systematic and widespread use of sexual abuse in Darfur (Tønnessen 2014, 2017). The idea that state officials should be held accountable for the use of genocide, rape, and sexual violence was a clear message that arose when we asked female protesters what justice means for women, particularly when we spoke with female protesters from areas of the country most affected by war – specifically Darfur, Blue Nile, and South Kordofan. One female protester from South Kordofan, a region where testimonies of sexual violence are also coming to the surface, declared:

> Justice to me is that all of the parties in the previous regime should pay for what they put our nation through. They should be held accountable and punished for the sexual abuse in Darfur and other parts of the country.[14]

Over the past several years, the reform of the section of Sudan's 1991 Criminal Law that deals with rape and *zina* (unlawful sexual relations)

[12] Interview, April 2019.
[13] Interview, April 2019.
[14] Interview, April 2019.

has become a priority for Sudanese women's rights activists. In January 2010, the Alliance of 149, a network of women's NGOs working against article 149 of this law, announced a campaign to reform Sudan's rape laws as part of the UN initiative, Sixteen Days of Activism against Gender-Based Violence. Salmmah Women's Resource Centre, one of the most radical feminist groups active in Sudan, coordinated this advocacy for law reform.[15]

The main focus of the campaign was article 149 and the legal obstacle it creates for rape victims (Gayoum 2011). Until 2015, what the Islamist regime defined as the *shar'ia*-based Criminal Law of 1991 defined rape as sexual intercourse taking place without consent outside a marriage contract. Sexual intercourse outside a marriage contract is punishable with 100 lashes for those who are unmarried and stoning to death for those who are married. Stoning for adultery has never been enforced in Sudan, but people are regularly whipped for fornication. Confusion between rape, adultery, and fornication has serious consequences for rape victims (Abdel Halim 2011a). Prosecuting rape, according to the 1991 law, requires proof of *zina:* a confession or the testimony of four male witnesses, which is practically impossible to obtain. On the other hand, pregnancy is sufficient evidence to prove fornication. This means that the perpetrator of a rape crime almost always goes free, while the rape victim runs the risk of being punished for adultery or fornication if she confesses she had sexual intercourse and cannot prove that she tried to resist, or if she is later found to be pregnant because of the rape (Al-Nagar and Tønnessen 2015). In cases where perpetrators are convicted, it is for the lesser crime of gross indecency (*ibid*).

Another focus in the campaign was to lift immunities against prosecution for criminal acts that members of the police, security, and military forces commit in the course of their duty (Alliance of 149, 2010). Although rape was clearly differentiated from *zina* in a 2015 amendment to the 1991 Criminal Law, the perpetrators of war rape are still protected by immunities in article 33(b) of the National Security Forces Act of 1999, article 45(2) of the Police Act of 2008, and article 34(1) of the Armed Forces Act of 2007 (OHCHR 2007, para. 9). Women's rights activists pointed out other limitations of the 2015 reform, but their campaign was effectively silenced when al Bashir's regime closed down the women's

The Salmmah Women's Resource Centre was founded in 1997 by a group of leading Sudanese activists as an independent feminist resource centre. Its main focus was mobilising and empowering women and women's groups to influence policy and overcome structural, political, and legal obstacles to the advancement of women's equal rights. Other members of the alliance included Sudanese Women's Empowerment for Peace (SuWEP), SORD, Mutawinat, the Alalag Centre for Media Services, the Sudanese Society for Environment Protection, and the Sudanese Observatory for Human Rights. Before the campaign was launched, other Sudanese NGOs were also involved, but they were also shut down. These other groups included the Khartoum Center for Human Rights and the Amal Centre for Rehabilitation of Victims of Violence.

NGO leading the campaign, Salmmah Women's Resource Centre (Salah 2015; Tønnessen 2018). However, immunity continues to be granted even in Sudan's new constitutional charter that protects members of the state from criminal proceedings, including Hemeti as deputy chairman of the Sovereign Council. Hemeti's role in Sudan's transition, alongside other al Bashir–era military generals, leaves little hope of justice during the transitional period. Since the Legislative Assembly has the ability to lift such immunities through the enactment of new laws and a permanent constitution, there is speculation that the delay in the announcement of Sudan's national parliament is deliberate and that the military elements of the Sovereign Council are intentionally delaying the process. Although an all-male committee was appointed by Prime Minister Hamdok to investigate the Khartoum massacre, the process has not been transparent, and the results have not yet been announced (Amin 2020).

With the 2019 revolution, demands for justice for rape victims have surfaced again, especially in the aftermath of the Khartoum massacre and what Hind Baraka, a women's rights activist, called the 'inhumane treatment of women'.[16] Although the investigating committee has not made much progress thus far, women's rights activists continue to bring the issue to the fore. The Sudan Organization for Development and Research (SORD) published a book documenting cases of sexual abuse during the revolution. The women's rights activist Sawsan Alshawia explained to the authors in an interview, 'After the massacre, the protesters' call for justice has been intensified. Justice entails taking all those responsible, RSF, security, and Islamist militia to court, and no one would escape punishment by impunity.'[17]

Women's rights activists continue to bring the issue of justice to the fore internationally, as well. When Alaa Salah, who became the icon of the revolution in international media, spoke on behalf of women's groups to the Security Council on 29 October 2019, she called for an independent international investigation of human rights violations, including sexual and gender-based violence, and to hold perpetrators accountable.

Freedom: Challenging Discriminatory Laws

Many protesters, especially younger protesters, have also articulated that freedom to make life choices is essential for a positive change in women's status. A young female protester said in an interview, 'I specifically want a change of "patriarchal thinking" that justifies restricting women's freedoms and violating their rights.'[18] In particular, two laws codified by the Islamist-military government stand out in the interview material as

---

[16] Interview, April 2019.
[17] Interview, August 2019.
[18] Interview, May 2019.

restrictive and discriminatory to women – the Muslim Family Law of 1991 and the Public Order Law.

The transitional government has the mandate, according to the Constitutional Declaration, to 'repeal laws and provisions that restrict freedoms or that discriminate between citizens on the basis of gender'. At the time of writing, only Public Order Laws in all states were repealed on 26 November 2019, at the same time as the National Congress Party, which was the Islamist political party backing al Bashir, was dissolved ('Sudan's government endorses … ' 2019). This demonstrates the strong link between the former ruling party and its vision for women's rights, especially as it was displayed in the Public Order Law and the high symbolic value of dismantling both. This was one of the first acts of Prime Minister Hamdok's transitional government, but other discriminatory laws are yet to be appealed or revised at the time of writing.

The Muslim Family Law

A female university student asserted, 'Women were tortured by restrictions within the family. I want to be free to decide what I wear and where to go out and when to come back home.'[19] The female protesters interviewed explicitly mentioned certain restrictions in Sudan's Muslim Family Law of 1991, such as those that regulate the age of marriage, a woman's right to choose her husband, her ability to work outside the marital home, her capacity to have custody of her children, and her obligation to be obedient to her husband. This is showcased in the testimony of one of the protesters we interviewed, who is a business owner, married with three children: 'I demonstrate against the family law that will take my children away from me if I divorce my husband. I want to divorce my husband, but I cannot be separated from my children.'[20] Another protester, 22 years old, unmarried, and a student at Ahfad University for Women, said, 'The legalising and permitting of child marriage. I am very angry about that.'[21]

Women's rights activists' call for reform of the Muslim Family Law can be traced back to its codification in 1991, when women gathered behind closed doors to critique it. Since then, many reviews of the law and calls for reform have taken place, including in public spaces.[22] The call for reform reached a peak in 2009 when SORD initiated a broad and inclusive consultative process on family law reform, which eventually

---

[19] Interview, April 2019.

[20] Interview, April 2019.

[21] Interview, April 2019.

[22] A group of female lawyers established Mutawinat (literally translated from Arabic as 'cooperating women') in 1988 to provide legal aid to women and children. The lawyer Samia al-Hashmi currently heads this group. Mutawinat registered as a non-governmental, non-political, and non-religious benevolent company in 1990. Its aim is to better protect women's and children's legal rights in Sudan. Mutawinat is especially focused on offering free legal services to protect the rights of vulnerable women and children of Sudan.

culminated in the drafting of an alternative law that was launched in 2012 (SORD 2012). The alternative law addresses many of the concerns noted by the female protesters we interviewed, including making 18 years the minimum age for marriage, giving a woman the freedom to decide whom to marry, and revoking a man's unilateral right to divorce. The alternative law also stipulates that a mother has custodial rights to her children until they attain the age of legal responsibility and that they remain in her custody even if she subsequently marries another man (Al-Nagar and Tønnessen 2017b; SORD 2012). The al Bashir regime found the alternative law too radical in its demands and did not initiate any reform or amendment of the 1991 Muslim Family Law.

In 2018, the case of Noura Hussein provoked renewed calls for reform by women's rights activists, especially regarding child marriage, forced marriage, and marital rape. Noura Hussein was betrothed to her much older cousin by her father at age 15 without her consent. She ran away and stayed in hiding for three years, but her family tricked her into returning home and married her off by force. After refusing to consummate the marriage for five days, she was raped by her husband with the assistance of his brother and a relative, who pinned her to the bed. When he tried to rape her again the following night – this time threatening her with a knife – she stabbed him to death. She was initially sentenced to death, but mobilisation of feminist activists successfully reduced the sentence to five years in prison and a restitution payment of 337,000 Sudanese pounds (US$18,700). However, it did not result in any changes to the 1991 law (Al-Nagar and Tønnessen 2017b).

There are high hopes that the transitional government of Hamdok will address the issue, especially considering that 13 political parties have signed a petition to adopt the alternative law if there is a regime change in the country. However, because family law is at the very heart of codified *shar'ia* law in the country, it is inevitable that reform in this area will create controversy and potential counter-mobilisation from conservative religious and political actors. As a strategy to bypass those conservative actors who will compete for office after the three-year transitional period, women's rights activists are calling for the transitional government to ratify CEDAW *without* reservations (Salah 2019). This is important because many Muslim majority countries have reservations against article 16 on equality within the family (all countries in the Middle East and northern Africa except Tunisia and Morocco), because it contradicts the codification of *shar'ia*, which constitutes an obstacle for women's rights activists in these countries. Although there are rumours circulating that a range of laws are being reviewed by the Ministry of Justice, we have not seen any reform or amendment of the 1991 law thus far.[23] Women's

---

[23] News circulating about a legal reform allowing mothers to travel with their children without the need for permission from the guardian is not entirely correct. The transitional government abolished article 12 of the 2015 Passports and Immigration Law, including section 3.E, which stipulated that an exit visa shall not be granted to a child who has not

groups have not been invited into a dialogue with the Ministry of Justice concerning legal reform. The transitional government has not signalled whether it intends to reform the 1991 Muslim Family Law or replace it with a secular or civil law. In fact, women's groups have been completely excluded from these processes within the transitional government. Women's groups are disappointed that the transitional government is excluding them in the same manner as the former regime, but they are starting to organise to ensure that their voices are heard. Currently SORD and other women's groups like the Civil and Political Sudanese Coalition (MNSM) and Alalag Center are discussing organising advocacy for family law reform (including through social media), educational/discussion sessions on the 1991 law, and a review of alternative law. They will invite and include the Ministry of Labor and Social Development and Ministry of Justice.[24]

Public Order Laws

Demands for freedom to move in public places and to dress according to one's desire, free of state regulation, were particularly prominent among the women we interviewed. Regulations on women's dress and behaviour in public spaces are codified in a range of vaguely defined 'morality' or public order laws enforced by the public order police, including the Criminal Law of 1991, the Public Order Acts at the state level, the 1997 Labor Act, and decrees mandating the hijab. Public order police are empowered to make arrests under these laws without charge and to imprison alleged offenders without trial (SIHA 2009). One 29-year-old female, married, government employee, and protester declared, 'I'm against all of the laws of this regime ... especially the Public Order Law, which has tortured the Sudanese woman and limited her thinking, freedom, and movement.'[25] Another female respondent, a 19-year-old married student of rural development, spoke out against the strict Islamic dress code: 'The most annoying thing for me is the forced hijab.'[26] The protesters we interviewed also object to the idea that a woman's religiosity is showcased by how she dresses. The young, married student of rural development put it like this: 'I think religion is about your relationship with God ... my relation[ship] with God might be better than theirs and it is not important to show that through the hijab.'[27] Women protest for

attained the age of 18 without the consent of the guardian. Removing this requirement, however, is not enough to allow mothers to travel abroad with their children without the explicit permission of guardians. This is because articles 119-1 and 120-2 of the 1991 Muslim Family Law stipulate that the custodian and child-guardian are not allowed a passport without the permission of their 'male guardian' ('Civil Society Statement ... ' 2020).
[24] Communication with Asha Al-Karib, 13 June 2020.
[25] Interview, April 2019.
[26] Interview, April 2019.
[27] Interview, April 2019.

the freedom to dress and move in public spaces without being considered 'bad' Muslims and immoral women by the state.

It is noticeable in the interviews that female protesters from different class backgrounds, from university students to tea sellers, expressed the restrictions they feel because of these laws. The Strategic Initiative for Women in the Horn of Africa (SIHA 2009) has previously documented the use of *kasha* (sweep and arrest) campaigns against marginalised and vulnerable groups of women who are unskilled workers in the informal sector. They are typically arrested for working during the night, something that is believed to incite promiscuous and immoral behaviour and is prohibited for unskilled workers under the 1997 Labor Act.

Women's rights activists have long argued for abolishing these laws, calling them unconstitutional and unIslamic. Activists who regard whipping as a cruel, inhumane, and degrading punishment refer to article 33 of the Bill of Rights of the previous 2005 Interim National Constitution, which guarantees that no person should be subject to such treatment. Such punishment is viewed by women's rights activists as a tool of oppression and contrary to women's dignity and the fundamental freedom to live their lives as they wish. Several cases of the arrest and flogging of women have prompted activism and received heightened attention by international media. The 'No to Women's Oppression' initiative was established in 2009, in the aftermath of an incident of public order police forces arresting Sudanese female journalist Lubna Hussein for wearing trousers and accusing her of violating article 152 of the Criminal Law, which prohibits indecent and immoral dress and behaviour and provides a punishment of up to 40 lashes.[28] Lubna Hussein called these laws unIslamic: 'Show me what paragraph of the Qur'an, or quote me Prophet Muhammad saying it is the responsibility of the government to punish people in this way' (quoted in Copnall 2009). She stated further:

> Islam does not say whether a woman can wear trousers or not. The clothes I was wearing when the police caught me – I pray in them. I pray to my God in them. And neither does Islam flog women because of what they wear. If any Muslim in the world says Islamic law or sharia law flogs women for their clothes, let them show me what the Qur'an or Prophet Muhammad said on that issue. There is nothing. It is not about religion, it is about men treating women badly.

Since then, other cases, including those of the 'YouTube girl' (flogged in public by public order police in 2010) and Amira Osman (arrested

---

[28] Article 152 states, '(1) Whoever commits, in a public place, an act, or conducts himself in an indecent manner, or a manner contrary to public morality, or *wears an indecent, or immoral dress*, which causes annoyance to public feelings, shall be punished, with whipping, not exceeding forty lashes, or with fine, or with both; (2) The act shall be deemed contrary to public morality, if it is so considered in the religion of the doer, or the custom of the country where the act occurs.'

in 2013 for refusing to cover her hair) have prompted renewed calls for abolishing these laws. For example, the Salmmah Women's Resource Centre had a special focus on law reform efforts dealing with violence against women before it was shut down in 2014. The No to Women's Oppression initiative has had a focus of 1) monitoring women's human rights violations in the country (particularly incidents stemming from the public order law), 2) engaging in advocacy campaigns to support victims, and 3) providing lawyers to represent victims in court and support their cases through fundraising.[29] In conjunction with its membership, SIHA[30] has undertaken research, capacity-building, sub-granting, and advocacy on women's human rights, especially in the area of gender-based violence and the threats faced by female defenders of human rights. In particular, it aims to bring the voices and interests of poor and marginalised women to the mainstream political agenda. Among other things, SIHA submitted a call for urgent reform of Sudan's public order laws to the African Commission on Human and People's Rights (SIHA 2009).

Samia Nihar, a women's rights activist, believes that the oppressive nature of the public order laws has fuelled the revolution, especially among young women. The fact that women bear the brunt of these laws, combined with the campaigns of women's rights activists, has successfully raised awareness of the injustices these laws cause for ordinary women. She explained in an interview:

I do think that the public order law is one of the engines of the revolution because it is the law that directly affected girls and women from the public. Moreover, the public order law is also an example of a law where the women's movement succeeded in showing its awfulness openly, assisted by social media – especially in the cases of Lubna and the 'YouTube girl'. These two cases were the basis for the public feeling of injustice and targeting of women by this specific law. Through these cases, the public order law embarrassed the government very strongly, but the government did not take any action at that time. Other cases followed, addressed by the social media, and public people were concerned by them. In the former President's latest speech, he included a declaration that the public order law was flawed but he was trying to improve the image of the regime too late.[31]

In an attempt to cling to power, al Bashir promised to reform the public order laws. This testifies to how central such discriminatory laws have been to disadvantaging women and, accordingly, why women have been at the forefront of the revolution. However, it is important to note that although the female protesters we interviewed demand freedom to

---

[29] No to Women's Oppression was established in 2009 and is currently led by Ihsan Fagiri.
[30] Established in 1995, SIHA is a regional network that works in Sudan, South Sudan, Eritrea, Ethiopia, Uganda, Kenya, Somalia, Somaliland, and Djibouti.
[31] Email interview, April 2019.

dress and move in public spaces, they make it clear that this does not necessarily entail throwing away their hijab or putting on a miniskirt. Rather, they assert that how they dress and behave should be between them and God, not something the state should control or punish in the name of Islam.

The abolition of public order acts at the state level and with it the notorious public order police was welcomed and widely celebrated as a revolutionary gain for women. In July 2020, the government announced a range of amendments to the Criminal Law, including the articles under the 'Honor, Reputation, and Public Morality' (articles 145–160) part of the Miscellaneous Act. This included the abolition of flogging as a punishment and reforming the formulations regarding dress in article 152 and the definition of prostitution in article 156. Other articles related to the crime of *zina* (fornication and adultery) remain unchanged (Redress 2020). In a civil society statement, several groups (including women's groups) critique the weakness of these reforms and claims that the Criminal Law continues to deny basic freedoms. The statement says the following regarding article 152:

> This amended article, although it removed the phrase (disguised in an indecent dress), still allows policemen to assess the nature of the disobedient act or statement, which allows for the continued interference in personal freedoms by policemen who have the right to assess the matter according to what they deem to be a breach of modesty, without the protections of an objective standard. ('Civil Society Statement … ' 2020)

The process of amending the Criminal Law of 1991, in which the Miscellaneous Act 2020 is the first step, has been driven by the transitional government without report from civil society (*ibid*). Women's groups are disappointed at the lack of engagement and inclusion in the discussion about legal reform.

Inclusion: Expanding the Representation of Women in the Decision-Making Processes

Although Sudanese women had played a key role in ousting military dictatorships before (in 1964 and 1985), their contributions were quickly sidelined in the political negotiations that followed. Women were also largely excluded from the peace negotiations that ended armed conflicts between Sudan and South Sudan in 2005 and in East Sudan in 2006, and they had only marginal representation in the Darfur peace negotiations (Itto 2006). History is repeating itself, as women have largely been excluded from the negotiations between the TMC and the FFC. Only one woman participated in the negotiations. Two women were in the FFC negotiations that culminated in an agreement on 17 August 2019. One represented the National Umma Party (Mariam Sadiq al Mahdi), but she was replaced by a man during the first month of negotiations. The other young woman, Mervat Hamadaneel, representing civil society, struggled alone until the end of the negotiations.

In the transitional government of Abdallah Hamdok, two women, Rajaa Nicola Eisa and Asha Musa Al Saeed (one of whom was nominated by MNSM) out of 11 members have been appointed to the Sovereign Council. In addition, four of the 14 ministers who were initially appointed (including three MNSM nominees) are women holding the posts of Foreign Affairs, Labor and Social Development, Youth and Sports, and Higher Education. This is compared with two women out of 21 in the last Cabinet under the al Bashir era. In addition, a woman was appointed as the chief justice (Mohieedeen 2019). Women's representation in the current governance structure thus falls far below the demand of 50 per cent parity, but in a historical perspective it has more representation of women than any other government. Female protesters and women's rights activists were disenchanted by being relegated to guests at the negotiating table, especially considering that the majority of protesters had been women (Tønnessen and al-Nagar 2020). The appointment of women in the governing structures also falls short of their expectations of gender parity.

Female protesters and women's rights activists perceived their exclusion from the negotiation table as a threat and a manifestation of a patriarchal culture, something that sparked collective mobilisation for political inclusion. At this point, groups of women from diverse backgrounds, many with no track record of political activism, started gendering the revolutionary slogans and discourse for change. As such it represented a tipping point in the revolution as female protesters started demanding rights as women in consolidating a just, peaceful, and free Sudan. For example, young women started to call for 50/50 representation in the decision-making structures of a new transitional government, delivered speeches on women's rights in sit-in forum areas, made art pieces with the slogan 'This is a woman's revolution', stood in front of the building where the negotiations took place carrying posters with slogans, and put up posters in the offices of the SPA, one of the leading organisations of the FFC. In the speeches in the sit-in area, the recognition of international conventions related to women, such as CEDAW, was mentioned (in contrast to Resolution 1325) but did not play a prominent role. This is partly related to historical divisions within the women's movement regarding international human rights and what are considered feminist ideas regarding gender equality (Tønnessen 2013). However, in the post-revolutionary period the demand for CEDAW and the Maputo Protocols has become increasingly pronounced as women's groups have demonstrated for ratification. In a letter handed over to the Minister of Justice, a diverse set of women's groups urged him to take action and state the following:

We strongly believe that the international legal framework will provide a legislative umbrella for the protection of women, in their diverse backgrounds, and will allow them to effectively participate in public life in a way that ensures justice and equity. ('Sudanese women demonstrate … ' 2020)

The slogans used by female protesters and women's rights activists have included the following:

> You thank us in demonstrations and forget about us in negotiations.
>
> If you wait, your rights will not come to you. You have to fight for your rights. 50 per cent is a right for women.
>
> I am a 100 per cent protesting female but am outside the power structures.
>
> I am not only an ululation; I am an existing human being.
>
> If your budget is not balanced, gender will balance it.
>
> We are active partners and not followers.
>
> We are not going to be victims of patriarchy.
>
> Women's political participation is a right and not a donation.
>
> We are 50 per cent and our rights are for 50 per cent.

The exclusion of women from the negotiation table has led to an increased demand from women's organisations to have political representation in the transitional government. The newly established MNSM, initiated by woman's rights activist Sawsan Alshawia, was an attempt to form a platform between diverse women's groups.[32] MNSM and other groups have made women's political inclusion a top priority going forward. Women's rights activist Asha Al-Karib stated in an interview:

> The current women's movement in Sudan is strongly demanding equal participation in the upcoming period. To this end, women are gathering beyond borders of age, ethnicity, and religion to build in solidarity their agenda during this critical juncture of our history. The process for change has already started, but it will be full of challenges, and the road for women will be particularly rocky and tough.[33]

MNSM has made a declaration with the following demands:

> We, the women of Sudan, declare our solid unity in claiming our right to the enjoyment of our human right to political participation including

---

[32] MNSM consists of eight political women's groups, 26 civil society organisations (including young women's organisations), 16 women's sectors of political parties, and 17 civil groups including unions and forums and independent activists. It signed the FFC's Declaration of Freedom and Change and is a recognised body within the alliance.

[33] Interview, August 2019.

through the temporary special measures, which for us can neither be negotiated nor compromised. We, thereof, demand the following:

The representation of women in all governmental institutions, executive bodies, legislative, and the judiciary including at decision making with a percentage of not less than 50 per cent as a temporary measure while giving due consideration to female youth.

The representation of women must be subject to merit and required standards of competency (with due consideration to ethnicity, culture regional geographical representation including conflict affected states, and disability) and in a manner that significantly contributes to the formation of a strong, integral, and inclusive Sudanese Nation. (Quoted in Karama 2019)

Female activists have also initiated a Facebook campaign, 50#qualified women#.[34] The campaign identifies highly qualified Sudanese women residing within the country or from the diaspora as nominees for political offices within the transitional government, including within masculine areas of political decision-making, such as transportation. The initiative is rooted in the experience women had in the aftermath of the stipulation of 25 per cent reserved seats for women in national and subnational legislative assemblies, put in place in 2008. Women's rights activists had high hopes that an increase in the numerical number of women in legislative assemblies would lead to the advancement of women's rights and the gendering of political processes, such as budgeting. However, in the 2010 elections, which were boycotted by the majority of political parties in opposition to the regime, the women elected came almost exclusively from the ruling Islamist political party and did not support gender equality. Women's rights activists realised the hard way the importance of putting women who support the advancement of women's rights into political decision-making bodies.

The initiative is also rooted in the understanding of Sudanese political culture as patriarchal. A common argument in the debate on women and politics in Sudan is that there are no qualified women, especially within political areas that are considered 'masculine' domains. Women are typically marginalised into what Sara Abbas has coined the *hoesh al-nisa*, or 'women's yard'. This refers 'to the traditional division of space in the Sudanese home where women have their own area in the house that they are meant to stick to' (S. Abbas 2010, 6). For example, in the political arena, women typically receive responsibility for areas related to women's issues and children – that is, not finance and defence. During the Islamist era, this was justified with the principle of complementarity, the argument being that, since women and men are biologically different, they should have different roles and women's emotional and caring nature makes them better at caring for vulnerable groups in society (Tønnessen

[34]   See https://m.facebook.com/story.php?story_fbid=2538471939509138&id=100000390711 761&sfnsn=mo (accessed 1 November 2019).

2018). This perspective became apparent in the form that the quota took – reserved seats, where women were nominated on separate lists rather than competing with men. The victory was therefore bittersweet for women's rights activists, according to Abbas (2010, 8), because they had advocated for a 30 per cent quota for women in party lists that also included mechanisms to ensure women's inclusion in the upper half of the list.

In the transitional period, the leadership of the alliance negotiating on behalf of the protesters, the FFC, has come under increased criticism for espousing a patriarchal mentality. A young, female university student activist and founder of the Noon movement, which is one of several newly established civil society groups in post-revolutionary Sudan, stated in an interview, 'The FFC are sexist. The few women who are publicly participating in the current scene are just there as a camouflage or appeasement to silence the international community.'[35] This patriarchal mentality or sexist approach is reflected also in the FFC Central Council, which is responsible for policies and nomination; it only includes three women and 23 men. Although Prime Minister Abdallah Hamdok is widely recognised as a supporter of women's rights, he relies on the FFC coalition for nominations to governing structures in post-revolution Sudan. Recently, the FFC Central Council sent a list to the Prime Minister nominating only men as governors for Sudan's 18 states. Arguments used to support this position were that 'Sudanese society will not accept a female governor' and 'government posts are given to those who are qualified; insinuating that women simply do not have the qualifications to occupy decision-making positions' (R. Abbas 2020b). The Prime Minister sent back the list asking the FFC Central Council to consider nominating women, but the Central Council sent back the same list without adding women. In response, the Sudanese Women Union, MNSM, and No for Oppression of Women prepared a joint list with potential women candidates for governors' posts and sent it to the Prime Minister. Prime Minister Hamdok completely disregarded these nominations, but did appoint two female governors in the River Nile and Northern States.

According to the constitutional declaration, women are supposed to make up 40 per cent of Sudan's National Assembly. Considering that the FFC Central Council has continuously been reluctant to nominate women for decision-making positions thus far, they doubt whether their constitutional right of 40 per cent representation in the legislative assembly will be fulfilled without a fight.

Conclusion: Reasons for Optimism?

How the new interim government deals with women's rights will be central to Sudan's future. Because discriminatory policies have been codified as the 'law of God', legal reforms are likely to meet resistance,

---

[35] Interview, August 2019.

not only from the old political and religious supporters of the al Bashir regime or what is popularly referred to as the deep or parallel state in Sudan (Assal 2019), but also from conservative attitudes within Sudanese society. Legal reform is key to meeting the demands of women, whether they are directed towards lifting immunities for government officials who have perpetrated sexual assault or advancing women's rights and political representation in decision-making in all governing structures.

As it stands now, the Constitutional Declaration does not deal directly with the elephant in the room, namely, the role of religion and Islamic law in the transitional structure, a topic that is politically contested. Although women have been largely excluded from the negotiation table, reform of discriminatory laws codified by the Islamist-military regime is a top priority in the Constitutional Declaration. The exclusion of women from the negotiations, despite their major role in the uprising, testifies to what women's rights activists describe as a patriarchal mentality. [36] If women's rights activists and groups had been given a seat at the table, the declaration surely would have included stronger wording and clearer direction, including a mandate that the country ratify CEDAW. Instead of merely aiming to repeal discriminatory laws, women's rights activists would have demanded stronger protection against gender-based violence, which is currently sorely lacking in Sudan's legal frameworks despite women's demands for accountability and justice for sexual violence and attacks against women before, during, and after the revolution.

Although a repeal of discriminatory laws is on the political agenda in the transitional period, there might be conflicting visions for women's rights in a conservative political and social context, as well as further differences between political actors on what laws and stipulations are indeed considered discriminatory against women. Our interviews show that not all female protesters support gender equality in all spheres, so a radical advancement of women's rights (especially within the private sphere) may evoke resistance even among women themselves. Nonetheless, the transitional period of three years with a technocratic government is an immensely important window of opportunity for women to mobilise for the advancement of women's right, before conservative religious and political actors again compete for office. The fact that Hamdok's government has abolished the notorious Public Order Laws (November 2019) and more recently criminalised female genital mutilation and introduced other criminal law reforms as part of the Miscellaneous Act (July 2020) gives cause for optimism. But women are largely underwhelmed at the slow pace and disappointed at how the FFC continuously sidelines women and brushes away their concerns.

---

[36] Interview, August 2019.

6

The Fight for Democracy and Women's Rights in Algeria

A Long Legacy of Struggle

AILI MARI TRIPP

The uprising that began in Algeria on 22 February 2019, demanding a change in leadership, democracy, and an end to corruption, was a watershed moment in the country's 57-year history since independence. It reflected, in part, the culmination of decades of struggle by two secular movements that have pushed against both the extremist Islamist tendencies in the country and a regime that tried both to contain and to use the Islamists to its own advantage. The near absence of an Islamist presence in the protests and the secular nature of the demands was notable, suggesting that the country has now entered what some call a post-Islamist era (Charef 2017). In Algeria, this has particular significance given the recent history of the country and its experiences during the Black Decade (1991–2002), when large numbers of civilians died at the hands of Islamist militia and even government soldiers. This happened after the country opened up to multipartyism, leading to the electoral successes of Islamic Salvation Front (FIS), which the government could not accept, resulting in the shutting down of FIS and a second round of elections, thus leading to a civil war.

This post-Islamist turn has particular significance for women, who were especially targeted by the jihadists during the Black Decade and were subsequently one of the key forces in pushing back against the Islamist extremist influence. Their role and importance in the post-Islamist trend has rarely been explored, yet in countries like Algeria women's rights activists were key opponents of religious extremism, which they regarded as diametrically opposed to their agenda. Islamism in Algeria, as elsewhere in the region, had become the primary opposition ideology after the 1980s. It replaced nationalism and leftist ideologies (Bayat 2017; Knudsen 2017). The civil and non-religious character of the 2011 Arab Spring uprisings in the region marked a sharp break with the earlier mid-1980s and 1990s, when moral politics within an Islamist paradigm prevailed. The protests that started in 2019 in Algeria followed a similar pattern. These anti-government movements were spurred on by structural changes within the region (as in Algeria), including globalisation, urbanisation, expansion of electronic media, and a new sense of citizenship. A demographic shift towards increasingly youthful and educated societies, and the emergence of a poor middle class further helped created this post-Islamist shift (Bayat 2017). Post-Islamist sentiments recognise the importance of Islam, but more importantly they reflect a pluralism of thought and a secular orientation (El Haitami 2012).

This chapter provides a historical account of why women's rights have been so integral to the fate of the Islamist extremists. It first documents the rise and demise of Islamist influence, which was at its height in 1991 when the FIS garnered millions of votes. It discusses how these trends impacted the status of women and women's rights activism. Then it shows how the uprisings (*hirak*) of 2019–20 have their roots in two secular movements: the women's movement and the Kabyle (Berber) movement. The *hirak* reveals a fundamental shift in Algerian politics. Neither the women's movement nor the Kabyle movement was ever very strong as a result of the regime's efforts to subdue civil society. This chapter discusses three forms of women's activism that have helped lead to the secularisation of society: 1) the movement for accountability of those who perpetrated the acts of violence during the Black Decade; 2) the movement for legal reform; and 3) the acts of everyday resistance by women around protecting their bodies and their right to free movement and to dress as they please.

Methods

In Algeria, I carried out about 40 interviews in Algiers, Oran in the west, and Tizi Ouzou in the east with the help of Nourredine Bessadi in the fall of 2016 as part of my three-country study that included Tunisia and Morocco as well (Tripp 2019). The discussion of the rise of the Islamists draws on this book. The interviews were with leaders and members of organisations like Association des Femmes Cadres Algériennes (AFCARE), Centre d'Information et de Documentation sur les Droits de l'Enfant et de la Femme (CIDDEF), Femmes Algériennes Revendiquant leurs Droits (FARD), Réseau Wassila, and Tharwa Fadhma N'Soumer. I interviewed representatives of various donors and UN agencies like UN Women, academics, journalists, bloggers, and many others. The interviews investigated questions ranging from different frames being used in advocating for and against women's rights to attitudes towards these rights; sources of legislative and constitutional reforms; the strength and autonomy of the women's movement over time; how different government leaders supported or resisted adopting women's rights; and the role of donors and external actors.

Rise of Islamists

Much of Algeria's post-independence history has been a contestation between the Islamists, the Kabyle (Berber), and women's rights activists, mediated by the state, which has been controlled by the ruling party, the National Liberation Front (FLN). Women first broke key gender barriers during the Algerian war of independence when they joined the fight against France. They fought shoulder to shoulder with men during the war of liberation and fully expected to be rewarded with political positions after the war. Yet, after independence in 1962, women found themselves abruptly pushed out of public life (Ahmed 1982).

After independence, Egyptian teachers, as well as some Syrian, Iraqi, and Palestinian teachers, were seconded to help teach in the Algerian school system in the mid-1960s and to help promote Arabic as part of creating an Algerian national identity. Many of the teachers were Muslim Brotherhood sympathisers and were known to be poorly educated themselves (perhaps Egyptian President Nasser's intent was to offload them as the Brotherhood was banned in Egypt). But as Heather Sharkey observes, these imported Egyptian teachers 'seeded Islamism among Algerian schoolchildren in ways that bore bitter fruit during the Algerian civil war of the 1990s, when discontented and underemployed "Arabized" youth filled the ranks of the agitators while standing on Islamist platforms' (Sharkey 2014, 317). To this day, deep tensions exist between those who have been Arabised and Islamicised and the rest (Benrabah 2013).

The education programme started under President Ben Bella (1963–65) resulted in both Arabisation *and* Islamisation to the point that the two identities were regarded as two sides of the same coin (Oulahbib 2016). President Houri Boumédiène (1965–76) at the time had the goal of Arabisation, but not of Islamisation. The Islamist reach, however, expanded during the Boumédiène period and they were able to influence restrictions on women's freedoms, particularly in the areas of family planning and abortion (Ahmed 1982, 165). The women's movement at this time included organisations like the Algerian Association for the Emancipation of Women, SOS Women in Distress, and the Committee for the Legal Equality of Men and Women. Women's organisations pushed back and in 1980 they overturned a ban that required women to travel with a male relative. They also resisted efforts to allow husbands to vote in place of their wives and defended coeducational schools between 1989 and 1991 (Lalami 2014). Most importantly, they resisted government efforts to impose a conservative Family Code starting in 1981.

President Chadli Benjedid (1979–92) faced even greater pressures from the Islamists than his predecessors and he started caving into them through various policies. At the same time, there was an expansion of the

Kabyle movement as well as the independent women's movement, which were both on a collision course with the Islamists (Willis 1996). Much to the horror of the women activists, the Family Code was enacted in 1984, clarifying irrefutably that the state was beholden to the Islamists (Salhi 2010). The law institutionalised polygamy, made women minors under the law, and defined their roles primarily as wives, children, and sisters rather than as citizens. Women could only marry under the supervision of a guardian. They could not divorce their husbands (although men could divorce women) and they could only obtain a divorce through an informal mechanism of *khul'* through which they could give up their legal rights and claims to alimony. Breastfeeding and caring for children until adulthood was a woman's legal obligation. They had to obey and respect their husbands and could only work with the permission of their husbands. Women were reduced to daughters, mothers, and wives and, as far as activists were concerned, they were not considered citizens in their own right.

The Family Code represented an effort by the government to sacrifice women's rights in order to appease the Islamists. Thus, the FLN played secularists and Islamists along with other conservatives against one another to mediate the different political tendencies within Algerian society (A30.10.16.16). Since independence, the FLN had systematically eliminated any democratic opposition as it solidified its position as a one-party state. It choked civil society. As Messaoudi and Schemla explained in 1995, 'Apart from the Berber cultural movement, it has been the women, and they alone – who have been publicly questioning the FLN since 1980–81' (57).

The Black Decade of Conflict (1992–2002)

Algeria adopted a new constitution in 1989 under President Chadli Benjedid, allowing for the formation of multiple parties beyond the FLN. This political opening also allowed for the formation of all kinds of associations and made it a little easier for civil society and women's organisations to mobilise. Three women's associations formed in this period: the Association for the Emancipation of Women, the Association for Equality before the Law between Women and Men, and the Association for the Defense and Promotion of Women's Rights. These organisations were particularly concerned with the rise of the Islamists as well as the Family Code and violence against women.

However, the opening of political space also allowed the Islamist groups to increase in influence. In 1989, FIS was formed, and it had soon gained a following of tens of thousands of supporters, drawing particularly from the urban poor. It emerged as the leading Islamist party, which had grown rapidly in a relatively short period of time as a result of the networks of mosques they controlled and social services they provided to the poorest individuals, taking advantage of the economic crisis in the 1980s. The government legalised FIS, thinking that this would make it easier to control the party and prevent the further radicalisation of society. FIS quickly took control of 55 per cent of communal councils and 80 per cent of regional councils (Willis 2012, 170). Soon it was poised for similar victories in the national assembly. The authorities started arresting and imprisoning most of the party's leaders. FIS nevertheless claimed the majority of votes in the first round of the 1991 election. It was certain to win in the second round, but the authorities annulled the results of the first round and cancelled the second round altogether. FIS was banned in 1992, President Benjedid was forced out of office, and a state of emergency was declared.

FIS's two central concerns had to do with 1) Islamicising and Arabising the educational system and 2) focusing on the role of women in society with the aim of keeping women in the home to fulfil what they perceived as their central role as mothers and wives. They also sought to dictate women's clothing and social relations. They felt women and men should not work together and should not mix in schools and universities. They opposed birth control. They saw women in the workforce as taking jobs away from young men (Willis 1996, 1999). The Islamists targeted women's rights, in particular, and demanded changes in the Family Code, arguing that educated women were French stooges. Many of the Islamists wanted (and still want) a return to the perceived golden age of Islam at the time of the Prophet Mohammed (A30.10.16.16).

The Islamist movement regarded the women's movement and the Kabyle movement as beholden to the West. This had what was tantamount to treasonous implications given Algeria's bitter war of independence against France. The Islamists portrayed themselves as the true nationalists and Islam as a religion that had helped Algerians fight for their independence. Women were attacked in public spaces for dressing indecently by throwing acid on them or attacking them with knives. When women went to the police, they were told they brought it on themselves. Passage of the regressive 1984 Family Code had not seemed to satisfy the Islamists, even though it contained major concessions to them. Nevertheless, they felt it was not Islamic enough, calling for *shar'ia* law and the creation of an Islamic state.

With the political opening in 1989, women's organisations had begun to mobilise and coordinate activities among themselves. They were among the first to protest the ascent of FIS and called for the cancellation of elections because they felt that many women's votes were stolen by proxy FIS votes (men saying they were voting on behalf of their wives), bringing Algeria to the brink of becoming another Islamic republic like Iran and Afghanistan (A16.10.11.16). They had watched what had happened in these countries and had seen their own society being slowly

'Talibanised', as some explained in interviews. At the time of the rise of FIS, about 3,000 Algerians who had fought in Afghanistan returned to Algeria, adding fuel to the growing civil conflict.

Women's rights activists felt that FIS had planned to use democratic means to undermine democracy. As feminist author Cherifa Bouatta cautioned, 'Winning elections alone is not democracy' (Bennoune 2013). Islamist violence directed particularly at women further convinced women activists that FIS never had any real democratic aspirations. The prospect of a FIS victory brought over a million citizens to protest in the streets of Algiers, and women were at the forefront of these demonstrations. Women feared the Islamists were threatening to do away with the constitution, women's rights, and other freedoms. Many women and others felt physically threatened by the impending victory of FIS.

Meanwhile, as FIS grew in influence, they targeted women. They used mosques to preach their views and were able to convince large numbers of unemployed youth that women should return to their homes to produce fighters for the cause of Islam and leave their jobs to the men. They sought a moral cleansing in society and saw women as the prime focus of this project. The opposition by many women to the 1984 Family Code was seen as evidence of the moral corruption of secular women since they opposed polygamy. Women's rights activists who demonstrated against the Islamists were seen as the epitome of the repudiation of national values, as Abbassi Madani, the FIS leader put it (Salhi 2011).

The first attacks by FIS were cultural. They took down satellite dishes, which people used to watch cable TV from around the world, and installed loudspeakers through which they preached hate and threatened those who did not follow their edicts. Men who wore beards started wearing Afghani garb and women started wearing *hijab, niqab, jilbab, khimar,* and *chadors*, all of which had been alien to Algerian society. In some areas, they segregated boys and girls in schools and forced girls out of physical education. They harassed people on beaches and in swimming pools and prohibited wedding ceremonies and celebrations involving music. They issued death threats against singers and actors and closed down cinemas and theatres. Fear was pervasive in the towns where the Islamists were in control (Salhi 2011).

These forms of cultural control were soon followed by attacks on police and state officials, especially after the state of emergency was declared in 1992 and the government banned FIS after annulling the December 1991 parliamentary elections, fearing that FIS would win (Salhi 2011). After the attacks on state security personnel, others became targets including students, journalists, intellectuals, feminists, and leftists. Lists of women who were to be killed were posted at the entrances of mosques. Women were the key civilian targets, and they were killed in the most brutal ways: They were decapitated in front of their children; tortured and then killed; gang raped; and shot in broad daylight. Teachers were killed in front of their students. Thousands of schools were burned down. Leaders of feminist organisations were targeted. The prime targets included women who worked: women who worked in government, women who owned business and beauty salons in particular, teachers and university lecturers, and women artists and singers. FIS also targeted women who were unveiled. Women were forbidden from going to *hammams* (public bathhouses), where they could congregate and talk among themselves. Then the killings moved to massacres, bombings of buses, attacks on whole villages, kidnappings, and rapes of young girls. Girls were abducted to become sex slaves. Today there remain thousands of parents who do know where or why their children were taken.

As a result of the extremist discourse of imams in mosques and of Islamists more generally, 'Algerian society at large has started to look at females who did not wear headscarves as loose women, disrespectful of Islamic rules and often labelled as prostitutes. This explains the tremendous increase in the number of veiled females in Algeria,' according to Zanaz (2019).

The Black Decade almost destroyed all women's associations. In 1994, there were 14 nationally registered associations. Of these 14 associations, only two or three remained after the decade was over. Activists either were killed, ceased their activities, or fled the country. It was not until the 2000s that the movement reappeared (A3.9.26.16). The Black Decade took an incalculable toll on Algerian society. Fighting between the government and Islamist groups resulted in the deaths of approximately 200,000 people and the disappearance of 7,000 others. Fighting diminished after 1997. Many citizens remain traumatised for life.

The Decline of Political Islamists

A former Foreign Minister, Abdelaziz Bouteflika, won the presidential elections in 1999, 2004, 2009, and 2014 and attempted to stabilise the country. Part of this effort involved trying to neutralise the Islamists. Algeria pursued a policy of reconciliation and reintegration with Islamist fighters after the civil conflict. At the same time, it invested in housing, jobs, health, infrastructure, and youth policies to pacify citizens, who had been traumatised by the war.

In 2005, Algeria signed a Charter for Peace and National Reconciliation with Islamists and granted amnesty to former fighters who agreed to stop fighting. Some jihadists were given financial incentives and jobs to further incentivise them to cease their activities and reintegrate them into society. As a result, 15,000 jihadists abandoned violence (Ben Mansour 2002). Some fled the country. Many leaders who were coopted lost their following.

The Charter was passed on 27 February 2005 while the Parliament was in recess. In a public referendum, 97 per cent of the electorate voted in favour of a reconciliation charter. Those who are deemed to violate the

Charter can be imprisoned for up to five years for any statement or activity concerning 'the national tragedy' that 'harms' state institutions, 'the good reputation of its agents', or 'the image of Algeria internationally'. Not surprisingly, for the victims of this era, the reconciliation was a finger in their eye. It was an exercise in impunity.

While Algerian society overall is very conservative, having been influenced by the Wahhabi or Salafist tendencies after the 1980s, the political influence of the Islamists has diminished considerably. Already this was evident with the rise of Daesh. The number of ISIS fighters who went to fight in Syria and Iraq from Algeria to join the Daesh fighters was negligible compared with that of other countries in the region. Even the Salafists themselves have changed. No longer do they call for jihadism and violence and accuse people of apostasy as they did in the 1990s.

It should be noted that some former Armed Islamic Group (GIA) members resurfaced in 1997 to form an offshoot called the Salafist Group for Preaching and Combat, a group that subsequently merged with local al-Qaeda affiliates in 2007 and rebranded itself as AQIM. The Algerian army estimates that there are still between 500 and 1,000 jihadists belonging to AQIM. They are involved in sporadic, localised attacks, and the government regards them as a nuisance. However, they do not have popular support (Ghanem 2019).

Those Islamists that are active, like the group Dawa Salafiya, are considered 'quietists', who focus on preaching and avoid politics. Some argue that their influence is growing as a result of a new generation that has found an identity with the group. They are attracted to their anti-Western message, their rejection of violent extremism and of the Islamist politicians who have been coopted, and their opposition to the FLN regime that has monopolised power (Ghanem 2019; Olidort 2015).

The decline of the Islamist parties and their political influence in elections was evident in 2012 when the Islamist Green Algeria Alliance claimed only 47 seats, or 6.2 per cent of the seats in the legislative elections. They had a similarly poor showing in the 2017 elections, whether due to their own weakness, the rigging of the elections, or both. The Islamist Green Alliance collapsed and the Movement of Society for Peace (MSP), known as Hamas, which is close to the ideology of the Muslim Brotherhood and is the largest of the three parties, formed an alliance with Front for Change. However, they won only 6 per cent of the seats. The MSP, which today is divided, had participated in the Bouteflika government along with the ruling FLN and National Rally for Democracy (RND) between 2004 and 2012. The 2021 elections resulted in the lowest voter turnout ever of 23 per cent due to intense disillusionment with the FLN. The MSP capitalized off of this disenchantment with the FLN and gained seats in the parliament, having recast itself as a "moderate" party willing to work with the government. Nevertheless, today the Islamist parties are regarded as irrelevant, divided, plagued by defections and splinter groups, and lacking in consensus around clear objectives

(Fabiani 2017). Parties like MSP have been so coopted by the government that they are unable to play a role as serious opposition to the ruling party (Ghanem 2019).

Further indications of the decline were evident in April 2019, with the relatively small turnout for the funeral of Algerian Islamist leader Abbassi Madani, whose FIS dominated the country's first free elections in the 1990s. Attendance by Islamists was low compared with the numbers of people gathered for the farewell of pro-democracy leader Hocine Ait Ahmed in 2015 and artists of the popular Chaabi music, such as Amar Ezzahi in 2016 and even Matoub Lounes in 1998 (Ghanmi 2019).

The presence of the Islamists in the 2019–20 *hirak* protest movement was minimal. Many of them demonstrated on the outskirts of Algiers, Kouba, El Harrach, and Bourouba, transforming the protesters' calls for a 'free and democratic Algeria' to a 'free and Islamic Algeria'. Often they found themselves driven out of the larger protests. On International Women's Day MSP president, Abderrazak Makri, was condemned by the protesters. Another Islamist leader Abdallah Djaballah, president of the Front of Justice and Development, and a party deputy wanted to participate in the 15 March demonstration, but they were met with cries of *'Djaballah dégage!'* ('Djaballah get out!'). Protesters early on dismissed the regime's efforts to scare them by saying that their marches would ultimately lead to a takeover by Islamists.

Recent surveys of protesters confirm this decline in interest in Islamist approaches. A Brookings online survey of 9,000 Algerians targeting protesters (4,200) and military personnel (1,700) between 1 April and 1 July 2019 found that Islamist ideology of any kind did not appeal to those surveyed (Grewal et al. 2019). Moreover, according to the survey, Islamist leaders like Ali Belhadj, Abdallah Djaballah, Abderrazak Makri, and Kamel Guemazi drew negligible support. The survey obviously did not reflect the entire population, and it was administered through Facebook in a country where 50 per cent of the population has Facebook accounts. But it nevertheless captured a politically significant cross-section of the population; thus it would have captured Islamists involved in the protests.

Even the demonstrations themselves reveal several cultural dynamics of resistance that fly in the face of Islamist cultural norms. This was evident in the use of the Kabyle dialect in the banners, displaying of Amazigh flags, and Kabyle clothing, evocative of pre-Islamic culture of the region. This was especially the case in the Kabyle region. In other regions, women sometimes wore the traditional white *haik* garment in the demonstrations to evoke nationalist sentiments and opposition to Gulf religious influences such as the full body covering, the *niqab*, which is not considered Algerian. The *haik* is rarely worn today except by a few older women. Recently the Algerian government banned the wearing of the *niqab* by women in public sector jobs as a security precaution, but it is more likely to have been a measure to further marginalise the Salafists.

The prominent and ubiquitous display of the Algerian flag in all the demonstrations also emphasised the national and patriotic dimension of the protests. In a society that had been so deeply divided, Algerians cloaked themselves in the Algerian flag, partly as insurance and protection from the state, but most of all as an assertion of national unity.

Women's Rights Activism (2019–)

With the protests against the regime, starting in 2019, the women's movement emerged once again as a key secular influence. Le Collectif de la Société Civile pour une Transition Démocratique (the Civil Society Collective for a Democratic Transition) emerged as the most powerful network within the *hirak* protest movement. It included about 30 associations and citizens' organisations, a large number of which are led by women like Mouwatana, Tharwa Fadhma n'Soumer, SOS Disparus, Djazairouna, and Wassila Network.[1] The Algerian uprising showed how women reclaimed public space as citizens. They overcame the enormous weight of fear and came out in the hundreds of thousands week after week throughout the country. Like men, women were undaunted by the riot police, their tear gas, and provocations.

The protests began with demands against then-President Bouteflika's bid for a fifth term in office. After he withdrew his candidacy, the protesters demanded that the oligarchy that had backed Bouteflika step down. One by one, various members of *le pouvoir* (the powers that be) were removed from power or arrested. The protests demanding democracy, dignity, an end to corruption, and transparency continued until COVID-19 forced them to come to a halt. The new president Abdelmadjid Tebboune, who was elected in 2019, was regarded as a continuation of the status quo, as was evident in the low turnout for the election and the extraordinarily low turnout (22 per cent) for the 2020 referendum on the new constitution.

The *hirak* brought together people from all walks of life, all ages, and political persuasions, which is even more remarkable given how divided the country was during the Black Decade. Islamists participated in the demonstrations, but as citizens, not as Islamists. The protests were held every Friday so that the term *vendredir* (to Friday) became a verb. Women were on the frontlines of the *hirak*. The presence of women in the protests had particular significance. In the past they were not as visible in such movements, in part, because the strong Islamist influence discouraged

---

[1] Other organisations in the network include Rassemblement Actions Jeunesse (RAJ), Ligue Algérienne pour la Défense des Droits de l'Homme (LADDH), Comité Soutien Vigilance du Mouvement 22 Février (CSVM-22 FEV), SOS Culture Bab El Oued, Comité National pour la Défense des Droits des Chômeurs (CNDDC) , the Collectif des Jeunes Engages pour l'Algerie, Agir pour le Changement et la Démocratie en Algérie (ACDA), Conseil National Economique et Social (CNES), and Syndicat National Autonome des Personnels de l'Administration Publique (SNAPAP).

such action on the part of women. This changed with the *hirak*. Women were also said to have helped ensure that the protests remained peaceful, as protesters chanted *silmiya* (peaceful). The appearance in the 2019 protests of women leaders like the iconic heroine of the Algerian independence war, Djamila Bouhired, gave protesters added encouragement.

After 8 March, International Women's Day, the demands for democracy were combined with demands for women's rights, as protesters marched with banners stating, 'No free and democratic Algeria without freedom of the women'. One Algerian commentator, Hamid Zanaz, explained that the slogan 'Democracy = women's rights' meant 'No to a religious state. No to applying *shar'ia*. No to Islamists' rule and no to fundamentalist colonization' (Zanaz 2019). Thus, the links between women's activist demands and the post-Islamist tendency were clear.

Three forms of mobilisation were evident in the *hirak* that had their roots in Algeria's recent history. The first is represented by women's organisations that have fought against the impunity of the perpetrators of violence during the Black Decade. The second includes organisations that fought for women's legislative reform. The third is reflected in the day-to-day struggles women wage against efforts to restrict their presence in the public space and their individual freedom to dress as they please. All of these movements reflect the new post-Islamist orientation of women's rights activists.

Women's Fight Against Impunity

The protest against impunity was ever present in the 2019–20 uprising. Women carried banners showing female heroines and martyrs, including women like Nabila Djahnine, who was murdered at the age of 30 on 15 February 1995, in Tizi Ouzou, where she was an architect and President of the association Thighri n'Tmetout (Cry of Woman). She was a feminist who had participated in mobilisations against the 1984 Family Code.

For many women, the struggle against impunity was especially important because of what they experienced during the Black Decade, because they were among the first targeted by the Islamist fighters, especially those who worked as teachers, ran businesses, drove, did not veil, and engaged in the public sphere. During this period, Islamists and government forces clashed, leaving 200,000 dead and tens of thousands disappeared and injured. 'Women mobilised, they protested. They were in the vanguard in confronting the Islamists. Indeed, they played a big role and gained the respect of everyone, including those in power,' explained one activist in an interview I conducted in Algiers (A8.10.30.16). As another activist said to me, 'We had nothing to lose, we had absolutely no other choice [than to protest].' Women in Algeria had seen what happened to women in Iran and Afghanistan, and they were determined that Algeria not follow suit. As one activist said: 'At the time, women were already emerging on the streets to shout, "Neither Iran nor Afghanistan, Algeria is Algerian!"' (A2.10.31.16).

Women formed organisations like Djazairouna in Blida, which was established in 1996 by women whose families had been targets of Islamist terrorism. The overall objective was to provide moral, psychological, and legal assistance to victims of the Black Decade. The association, which included both men and women, attended the funerals of the victims of violent extremism. In the past, only men attended funerals, but women now started going as an act of protest to insist that the victims were not guilty and that the only culprits were the extremists. They also provided comfort to the families of the deceased. When Djazairouna was formed, there were not many people attending funerals because if they attended the burial of someone who had been killed by the Islamists, they would later find themselves on a list to be targeted. The organisation continued to mobilise after the Black Decade to bring attention to the need for justice for the families who had lost loved ones and suffered at the hands of the Islamist militia.

After the Black Decade, the government sought to neutralise the Islamists through repression, by monitoring the activities of religious leaders and curtailing their political engagement, and by signing the 2006 Charter for Peace and National Reconciliation that granted amnesty to former Islamist fighters. In addition, the government promised to forgive and forget all crimes committed during the Black Decade on all sides, including the government security forces. A quid pro quo was foisted on civil society actors, who were told that the government would provide stability in exchange for their silence. The country's leaders used the charter with the Islamists to suppress protest in the country, threatening at the outset of the 2019 protests that there would be a reemergence of jihadi Islamists and a breakdown of the country into a Syria-like civil war.

As a result of the charter, there never was a truth and reconciliation process. The crimes committed during the Black Decade were swept under the rug, and victims and their families suffered in silence without any right to speak out about the atrocities that were committed in this period of Algeria's history. No one was called to account and perpetrators live freely with impunity. Wounds inflicted by the government were similarly left to fester, including the atrocities of the Berber Spring of 1980, the suppression of the October 1988 protests, and the Black Spring of 2001. As Algerian scholar Meryem Belkaïd wrote of the 2019 *hirak*: 'Transitional justice is one of the goals of our uprising. It does not necessarily appear explicitly in our slogans but that's basically what we all want. We have already begun our reconciliation by going out on the streets of the country every Friday, communicating, looking at each other again in the eye' (Belkaïd 2019).

Many women's organisations refused to be silenced after the Black Decade and continued to mobilise around calls for justice and an end to impunity for those who had killed, raped, and harmed people during this period. Women victims and the families of those who disappeared during the civil conflict continued to protest and demand answers. They were often beaten by the authorities. They were also arrested because they refused to seek authorisation for their protests on the principle that what they were doing was legitimate and as such they should not require authorisation. For example, activists from the Tharwa Fadhma N'Soumer and Djazairouna associations were arrested while protesting near the Grande Poste in Algiers on International Women's Day in 2017 to denounce inequality in Algerian society and honour the women who died during the Black Decade.

The protests against impunity were part and parcel of the uprising. They even found their way to the Cannes Film Festival in 2019. Five actresses in the film *Papicha* held up pins on the runway, saying 'yatnahaw gaâ' ('they must go') referring to the Algerian regime. *Papicha* (Algerian slang for a 'pretty, cool girl') is based on the experiences of Algerian filmmaker Mounia Meddour during the Black Decade. It tells the story of Nedjma, an 18-year-old student in 1997 who resists the pressures by the Islamists to wear a *niqab* at a time when unveiled women were being attacked. Nedjma loves fashion and resists by creating a fashion show of traditional Algerian costumes, evoking nationalist themes of resistance as a challenge to the foreign character of the Islamist challenge (Smail 2019). This kind of open engagement with the Black Decade is a brave move in the Algerian context.

Fight for Legislative Reforms

A second area of mobilisation of the women's movement involved pressuring the government to reform the Family Code and to take other measures to improve the status of women. They were able to obtain some key constitutional reforms in 2016 that gave women equality with men, including quota laws. As a result, after the 2012 elections, women held 31.6 per cent of the parliamentary seats and 30 per cent of the Cabinet after 2014, the highest rate among Arab countries at the time. Today, four generals are women, also the highest proportion within Arab states. Women also make up about half of the judges (Kimani 2008), 44 per cent of magistrates, and 66 per cent of justice professionals in lower courts (IDLO 2017). Algeria also made legislative gains in the areas of violence against women, electoral quotas, and nationality laws.

Although women make up almost 57 per cent of university graduates, they constitute only 18 per cent of the total workforce. The gains in representation proved to be precarious as the rate of women parliamentarians dropped to 8 per cent with the 2021 elections as the quota was ignored. In spite of some gains, Algeria still has a long way to go towards gender equality, given women's aspirations. As one *hirak* protester stated, 'I am here today, with my daughters, with all the children of the people, in order to recover this Algeria which is lost' ('Au premier rang ... ' 2019).

In the past, only Tunisia had made significant advances in women's rights after independence in the MENA region. Today the Maghreb countries, Algeria, Tunisia, and Morocco, have converged in the types of women's legal reforms they have adopted around quotas, sexual harassment, the prohibition on the marriage of victims to their rapist, nationality issues, violence against women, and other such legislation. They have also been more successful in moving their women's rights agenda forward than Middle East countries due in large measure to the coordinating and strategising efforts of women's organisations in all three countries. As one Algerian activist who was active in a key coordinating organisation, Collectif 95 Maghreb Egalité, put it:

> Collectif Maghreb Egalité has been particularly effective in [coordinating women activists in the three countries]. The Maghreb countries, apart from Tunisia, which already had an advanced Family Code, worked on a code of the Maghrebian family, which we call the 100 measures and which we went to present in Beijing. Through this Maghrebian Code, we have gone further than those of our respective countries and we have presented a document which we called a White Paper, which included all the international conventions ratified by our countries and where we spoke of 'Maghrebines under reservation.' That is to say, the reservations made by our countries when ratifying these Conventions, in particular CEDAW. So we went to Beijing and organized a parliament that included more than 2,000 women and we presented the 100 measures with the obligation for each of us to return to our countries and work on this Code. The work of the Collectif Maghreb Egalité has served to support the work in each country. (A3.9.26.16)

The 2005 Family Code

Family law has always had a particular place in the legal history of the region. Colonial influence ensured that while other areas of law were transformed, family law remained subject to Islamic jurisprudence (*fiqh*). Even though unified legal systems and personal status codes were introduced after independence, the imprint of Islamic law and the historic centrality of the family in the Mediterranean region weighed heavily on the new legal frameworks.

After being elected to his second term in 2004, Algeria's President Bouteflika committed himself to making women's rights reforms despite fierce opposition from the Islamist parties. The focus of women's mobilisation for a long time had been on violence against women and on reforming the Family Code and Bouteflika was highly cognisant of this. Organisations like Collectif 20 Ans Barakat (20 years is Enough!) had been active in 2003 in trying to overturn the Family Law. In 2005, under pressure from women's organisations, Algeria amended the 1984 Family Code, but it was still far from acceptable to most feminists.

With the 2005 Family Code, women gained more rights in marriage, divorce, and citizenship, bringing it further in line with the international treaty of women's rights, CEDAW. Consent became an important part of the marriage contract. The notion of women's obedience tomen was abolished and replaced by reciprocal rights and duties of men and women in the marriage. The male guardian's role became symbolic – they could no longer force women to marry against their will or oppose their choice in marriage. The legal age for marriage was changed from 21 for men and 18 for women, to 19 for both sexes. The new code no longer prevented women from marrying non-Algerians and Algerian women married to foreigners could transmit their citizenship to their children. Men and women had reciprocal rights and duties, and they were to share their roles as head of household. This replaced an earlier clause that required the wife to obey her husband, who was regarded as head of household.

Many of the reforms in the 2005 Family Code appear to be a compromise between Islamists and women's right advocates, mediated by the state. Algeria abolished repudiation as a form of divorce, but polygamy was still legal, though subject to conditions. The husband would have to secure the permission of the first wife/prior wives in order to marry another wife. He would also need the permission of a magistrate (Marzouki 2010). One of the main concerns has to do with divorce (article 54) by *khul'*, which allows the wife to divorce her husband only if she pays an amount that does not exceed the dowry. As the law stands, even if she has a third witness, the woman can be repudiated, while she herself cannot ask for the divorce other than through *khul'*. Many women's associations found this provision to be degrading, because the woman was obliged to pay for her freedom. Custody of children is given to the wife and the husband is asked to provide rent or housing. However, the Penal Code and the Family Code have yet to be reconciled, and so the husband cannot be prosecuted if he does not provide housing (A7.11.10.16). Thus, some argue that the code left hundreds of women homeless after divorce, resulting in many women living in the street, often with their children. There are many women with dependent children but without a fixed home because they cannot return to the family home with their children as was the case in the past. And even women who could afford to rent encounter difficulties in renting apartments as divorced women. This is also the case for single mothers. There are few homes for women in distress. A woman also still needed a guardian when she married; although technically the new Family Code allowed women to choose their guardian, it was not clear that in practice they would be able to do so given familial pressures (A3.9.26.16).

Because of all these deficiencies in the Family Code, some argued that the president had used women's rights as a bargaining chip in his controversial Charter for Peace and National Reconciliation, which gave amnesty to Islamist militants and security forces who had blood on their hands from the time of the Black Decade. They felt he broke his promises to women's rights organisations in order to appease the Islamists and gain their backing for the amnesty (Rachidi 2007).

Despite these deficiencies in the Family Code, Algeria stands out in other areas of family law reform. Those marrying under the legal age (now 19 for both men and women) without permission can find their marriages voided in Algeria, where only 3 per cent of teenage girls marry under the legal age of 19. Unmarried women can travel outside their home in all MENA countries, but married women are legally restricted in all countries except for Algeria, Morocco, Tunisia, Libya, Lebanon, and Mauritania (World Bank 2015).

In other areas of legislative reform, Algeria adopted a quota law in 2012 for women in the national, regional, and local assemblies. It has a list proportional representation electoral system, and adopted a somewhat unique quota arrangement that includes both legislated candidate quotas and reserved seats. Women must make up 20 per cent of the candidates on party lists for the People's National Assembly when there are four seats; 30 per cent when there are five seats or more; 35 per cent when there are 14 seats or more; and 40 per cent for 32 seats or more. Finally, a 50 per cent rate applies to seats reserved for nationals living abroad. The law does not specify where the women are to be positioned on the list. A similar system is in effect for the Wilaya People's Assemblies (WPA) elections. In elections for the Communal People's Assemblies, women's representation is set at a minimum of 30 per cent in areas with a population greater than 20,000. One women's rights activist explained:

> We launched an advocacy campaign in partnership with political parties and with the voluntary sector to tell the President that we want a quota of women in Parliament and not less than 30 per cent. We first had the constitutional revision in 2008 and then we had the law in 2012, so it's a process. There is the work done by the associations, but a political will is needed to make it work. (A3.9.26.16)

Even Islamist women worked on this issue together with secular feminists, as they had at times on issues of violence against women. It was rare in Algeria to find civil society organisations working together, but the Islamists also stood to gain from this policy.

Women's organisations like CIDDEF had provided training for women candidates before the elections on how to give a speech, approach voters, organise public events, and other such campaign strategies. According to Nadia Ait Zai, founder of CIDDEF, the election results of 2012 were a major victory for women:

> The women's associations acted as pressure groups, and this pressure was effective. The information and documentation center of CIDDEF, for example, has been working systematically on this issue since 2003. We participated in a Maghreb-wide study on the subject of women in politics and pushed for changes at the highest level. The President has received our suggestions favorably. (Sabra 2012)

This was similar to other efforts for policy reform. She continued, 'At CIDDEF, we work on advocacy: advocacy on inheritance, advocacy on the elimination of reservations and advocacy on the marriage of minors. We are doing research which allows us to tell the public authorities "here is my research and here are my proposals."' As a member of the Maghreb Egalité Collective, they had learned and borrowed from the other two Maghreb countries as well as shared their experiences with activists in the region.

While the Maghreb countries stand out in terms of the amount of legislation regarding violence against women (VAW), the most striking difference is in the adoption of comprehensive legislation, which has occurred only in the Maghreb countries. The Maghreb countries converged when it came to these general laws regarding violence against women. Algeria passed a law regarding violence against women in 2015, Tunisia followed suit in 2017, and Morocco in 2018. Algeria and more recently Tunisia have also passed legislation around marital rape, and the provision is being debated in Morocco.

One of the areas where there has been increasing legislation in the region relates to women's citizenship rights. Only Algeria and Tunisia in the MENA region allow women to pass their citizenship to both their husbands and children. Algeria reformed its citizenship laws in 2005 to allow a woman to confer citizenship to her children and 2007 to her spouse.

Only a few Arab countries meet the international standard of a minimum of 14 weeks of maternity leave. The only countries that meet the standard are the Maghreb countries Algeria and Morocco and the greater Maghreb countries of Libya and Mauritania. Tunisia is an outlier here, with only four weeks of paid maternity leave. Within the MENA region, Algeria along with Tunisia, Bahrain, and Morocco have the most lenient abortion laws, but only Tunisia allows abortions without restriction. All these four countries also have the highest levels of contraceptive use among women of childbearing age.

In 2014, Bouteflika presented Parliament with legislation to establish a fund for widows to provide for their children. In 2016, he called for reconsideration of Algeria's reservations to CEDAW to correspond to existing legislation (*APS* 2016).

Everyday Protests

While there have been such changes on the legal front, equally vigorous contestations are taking place on the cultural front, especially on the part of young women. The impact of these quotidian protests was evident in the 2019 uprising, in which notably large numbers of young women participated.

Conservative young internet users launched a web campaign in 2015 in Algeria 'Be a Man' ('Sois un homme') also known as 'Purity', inviting men to make sure that their wives and daughters wear 'decent' clothes. 'Do not let your women go out with a daring outfit', they implored their readers (*APS* 2016). The initiative was launched a few weeks after a law student was denied access to an examination room because her dress was deemed 'too short'. 'The inquisitors are back,' announced the Algerian daily *El*

Watan in March 2015 ('Les inquisiteurs sont … ' 2015). Some promised that they would be 'merciless' with those who would not hide their bodies enough. 'We are going to take a picture and publish the pictures on the web so that it's a lesson for them,' said one of them in a post in support of the campaign. 'We are going to disfigure them by pouring acid on their faces,' another wrote, according to the national newspaper (Verduzier 2015). Such threats are taken seriously in a country where during the Black Decade non-veiled women were beheaded and targeted by extremist Islamists. The Minister of Justice said that investigations were going on into these threats and promised that Justice would face 'those who want to take us back to the '90s' ('Appels a l'agression … ' 2018). Women responded by going to the beaches in droves wearing bikinis, bringing a swift end to the campaign.

Not surprisingly, women swimming in bikinis evoked considerable public response. They were finding it harder to wear bikinis, even though a few years earlier they might have been in the majority, especially in the Kabyle region (Agerholm 2017). In Annaba – also known as Hippo, the ancient home of the early Christian theologian St. Augustine of the fifth century – women organised protests against an online campaign in which men posted photographs of women in bikinis to mock and expose them for contradicting what they believed were Algerian religious values. A closed Facebook group of 3,200 members formed in response to push back against this form of religious conservatism. Women in bikinis swam together alongside others in one-piece swimsuits and burkinis in protest.

'In the past, women's bodies had no place in public spaces,' said Yasmina Chouaki, an activist from Algeria's Amazigh-speaking Tharwa Fadhma N'Soumer feminist group. 'When women were obliged to leave their private spheres, they were forced to entirely cover their bodies.' She continued: 'Today women and their bodies seek to win a place in all public spaces. On the beach, there is a kind of bargaining going on between the woman and society through clothing' (Ghanmi 2017; Verduzier 2015).

For most swimmers, there is no issue. But as Algerian sociologist Yasmina Rahou pointed out: 'Algerian society is finding itself between the hammer of Islamist extremists who want beaches for women under the watch of police squads … and the anvil of turning women's bodies into market products of some unbridled form of modernization by Westerners' wants' (Ghanmi 2019).

Some women took to social media. One launched a Facebook page entitled *'Ma dignité n'est pas dans la longueur de ma jupe'* ('My dignity is not in the length of my skirt'), in which men and women published photos of their legs in support of the law student wearing a short skirt ('Trop courte ma jupe … ' 2015).[2]

One woman blogger I interviewed talked about how bicycling ended up being a daring act for a woman in her rural neighbourhood. Another protest over women's right to occupy public space involved a woman,

---

[2] https://www.facebook.com/groups/728956213879776

Ryma, who was verbally assaulted and beaten for jogging before Iftar (sunset meal) during the Ramadan fast in Algiers. A man said to her, 'Pourquoi tu cours? Ta place est dans la cuisine à cette heure-ci!' ('Why are you running? Your place is in the kitchen at this time.') After the assault, she went to the police to complain, and they asked her why she was jogging and did nothing to pursue her aggressor. Ryma then took to social media (Berkani 2018). The next day, on 9 June 2018, over 300 women and men of all ages as well as some NGOs came to out to walk with her in protest (Rahmouni 2018). They carried slogans like '*Ma place est où je veux, pas dans la cuisine*' ('My place is where I want to be, not in the kitchen') at Sablettes beach in Algiers to defend her right to occupy and run in a public space ('Afin de protester … ' 2018). This incident occurred in a context where over 7,500 cases of violence against women, including 730 abandonment proceedings, were reported to police during the first nine months of 2017 in Algeria. The lack of response from the police in this case does not bode well for the legislation that has been passed around violence against women.

These kinds of protests infuse the daily life of society. They reflect an important part of the women's movement and an unwillingness, as during the Black Decade, to cave into intimidation and be forced out of the public space and into submission. Young women, particularly in urban areas, are social media savvy and, unlike the 1990s, more aware of international trends.

Young women are more educated than in the past. Women in Algerian universities today exceed men by 12 per cent, with a female to male ratio of 1.46. Already in high schools, women are surpassing boys. In 2018, 65 per cent of the girls compared with 35 per cent of the boys graduated with a baccalauréat, the diploma that allows students to go to university. The percentages have been steadily increasing and in 2014 almost 68 per cent of girls succeeded in their bac exams (Benfodil 2018). This has resulted in boys going into the business world in greater numbers, while women pursue university degrees in larger numbers. 'For girls, it is clear that studies have emerged as the royal road to a form of emancipation from the patriarchal shackles, an instrument of social liberation, in short,' as one feminist put it (A16.10.11.16). The number of women graduates in science, technology, engineering, and maths (STEM fields) is almost the same as men – 49 per cent women, 51 per cent men. Women make up 70 per cent of the country's lawyers, 60 per cent of judges (up from 18 per cent in 1988) and the majority of doctors. Women are moving into areas traditionally dominated by men such as driving buses and taxicabs, pumping gas, and waiting tables.

Women are marrying later and starting their families later. About 60 per cent of women use contraceptives – 3 million women out of a total of 5.3 million married women of childbearing age. As a result, they have more time to gain an education. Young women travel, they watch films from abroad, and they congregate in groups in restaurants and coffee houses, which in the past were the domain of men. At the same time, younger women activists are not as concerned about legislative reforms and associational membership as older women activists, and instead they focus more on such daily battles to change the culture.

Conclusion

The extremist Islamist presence in Algeria has diminished considerably since the early 1990s, when its political influence was at its height. The government adopted a strategy to diminish its impact through a charter and through political, military, and legislative strategies. Part of this strategy involved adopting women's rights laws and policies. Women's rights activists themselves also brought pressure to bear on religious extremists. They have become a force in what might be considered a post-Islamist era.

Women activists are challenging extremist Islamist ideologies in the Maghreb region, especially ones that target women, their bodies, and their rights. At least three forms of mobilisation have persisted since the Black Decade, becoming especially visible during the 2019–20 *hirak*. These include mobilisation for an end to impunity for attacks on women and others based on an extremist religious litmus test; demands for legal gender-based reforms; and direct action against social restrictions – on women's bodies, their clothing, and their occupation of public space. The reforms after the 2019–20 Sudanese revolution against restrictions on women's dress and behaviour similarly reflect this pushback in the region, as do gender-related reforms adopted in Tunisia and Morocco after 2011.

The Algerian *hirak* has revealed not only a popular desire for a democratic Algeria, but also one that guarantees gender equality. Women's mobilisation since the 1990s played an important role in leading up to the *hirak*. Their mobilisation reflects a rejection of Islamist extremism and patriarchal efforts to control women's bodies and how they dressed, worked, and studied. They challenged those who did not want them to mix with men and controlled what spaces they could occupy. Women's mobilisation challenged these restrictions directly, reflecting a desire to move into a post-Islamist era that embraced religion in a way that allowed for an end to the impunity of the perpetrators of violence during the civil war. They demanded legislative reform that promoted gender equality in the family and society in defiance of extremist Islamist pressures; and, finally, they engaged in everyday forms of resistance that directly combatted repression against women and their bodies and freedom to occupy public space.

7

Conclusions
Women's Peace Activism in Africa

LADAN AFFI AND LIV TØNNESSEN

Exclusion from Postconflict Governance: Women's Struggle for a Seat at the Table

This book has shown how the failure to recognise women's many contributions becomes a major cost in peacebuilding efforts. The exclusion of women from formal peacebuilding processes, including political decision-making in postconflict governance structures, is a commonality across the cases presented in the book. This is in spite of their participation being recognised as an essential aspect of inclusive social justice in peace processes and UNSCR 1325 mandating their inclusion at all levels of decision-making in peace processes for the maintenance and promotion of peace and security. Women are excluded, their proposals and needs are viewed as incidental rather than essential, and successes are measured without taking into account that some outcomes may not serve to improve women's lives as much as men's. The case studies in this book show how women's marginalisation in peace mediation and larger peacebuilding processes is often symptomatic of their inferior status in their communities and politically institutionalised hegemonic masculine norms. By hegemonic masculinity we refer to 'a set of values, established by men in power that functions to include and exclude, and to organize society in gender unequal ways … ' (Jewkes et. al 2015, 113).

In Somalia, access to political office is mediated through clan membership, but since lineage is traced through the father, women are considered transient members who belong to neither their father's clan nor their husband's. Women's multiple clan connections have made it difficult for them to participate in the clan-based politics of the country (Affi in this book; Affi 2020a; Dini 2010).

In north-east Nigeria, women's compounded marginalisation complicates women's inclusion as full actors in peacebuilding and politics more broadly. The north-east of Nigeria is a heavily patriarchal society where the region's religious and cultural norms have defined women's status through reproduction and largely confined them to domestic roles. Womanhood has become a central theme in male-dominated political struggles, especially when the female body is perceived as a battleground in a global conflict between Islam and 'the West' (Okoli and Nnaemeka Azom 2019).

However, gender inequality does not tell the whole story and needs to be considered alongside other intersecting factors. Cultural, religious, and legal inequalities combined with poverty and a historic disenfranchisement of this region in Nigeria have contributed to compounded marginalisation with higher rates of women's illiteracy and child marriage and lower school attendance in this region compared with the rest of the country. This context of compounded marginalisation and conservative Islamist ideologies of the domestication of women is acted on by the Boko Haram insurgency. Nigerian women have been caught up in the conflict between the state and Boko Haram, where both sides have inflicted violence on women (Imam, Biu, and Yahi in this book; Imam, Biu, and Yahi 2020).

The specific ways in which women are excluded from and included in hegemonic masculine institutions and how this is implicitly and explicitly justified by social norms must be understood in the local context, including the legacy of the conflict itself. In Sudan, a patriarchal mentality institutionalised by conservative Islamism over the past three decades sidelines women as emotional and limits their right to be heard to 'women's issues'. And when women are included, it is usually women with urban, Muslim, and educated backgrounds from specific ethnic groups known in Sudan as riverine. Meanwhile Islamists in Sudan have included certain women fitting this profile in politics through a reserved seat quota in the national and subnational assemblies since 2008, which has been facilitated through an Islamic vision of biological complementarity between men and women and the need to have both 'soft' and 'hard' elements included in decision-making. However, it is only certain 'soft' political matters that require women's nurturing and caring emotions; typically these are an extension of women's domestic role as a wife and mother. When the going gets tough in 'hard' politics, especially in peace negotiations historically and today, 'women's issues' are deemed irrelevant and women's 'emotions' are not welcome. They are juxtaposed to men's 'rational' efforts to divide the spoils of war among themselves (Tønnessen 2018). As Dianne Otto has pointed out, 'If women are admitted on the understanding that their special contribution arises from their womanly instincts, it follows that their political agency will be limited to what is made possible by that representation and restricted to "feminized" tasks involving nurturing and mothering' (2006, 139). Rather, women's full inclusion should be, as the Somali chapter argues, based on principles of justice and human rights.

Exclusion does not only refer to whether women are given a seat at the table, but what issues are considered worthy of discussion. 'Women's issues,' such as gendered violence and attacks on women's bodily integrity and dignity during armed conflict and authoritarian Islamism, have been sidelined as 'soft' issues, even when they are clearly not.

The research showcased in this book contributes to the larger literature on women's exclusion from peacemaking, detailing how these processes are fuelled by essentialist notions of women regarding them primarily as victims of conflict, rather than as active participants who bring other perspectives to the table. Depending on the war narratives in various conflicts, protection of women and children as victims of war takes centre stage in formal peacemaking, rather than including them and their perspectives and acknowledging their agency (see for example Karam 2000; El Jack 2003; Skjelsbaek 2001; Adjei 2019). Exclusion is in reality what Westendorf (2018, 433) describes as a deliberate strategic tactic and 'a highly visible marker of the broader exclusivity of such processes'. As such, formal peace processes reinforce existing power structures and political elite dynamics, which 'limits the space for broad societal engagement in official peacebuilding and has contributed to the entrenchment of conflict and instability' (*ibid,* 435).

However, processes of exclusion also ignite the mobilisation of women and the creation of political alliances across divides. This is a common thread throughout the book, whether mobilising for a seat at the table or engaging in informal peacebuilding at the grassroots. In the context of exclusion–inclusion in formal peacebuilding processes, we see mobilisation across divides as a political strategy of a marginalised interest group. As Mollie Pepper puts it (2018, 61), women are 'key players in peacebuilding because of their civil society activism', something that 'places them around the table, if not at the table'.

When dominant masculine norms are geared towards viewing politics as men's terrain only, our case studies show that women fight for inclusion and by doing so challenge societal gender stereotypes. In many cases they succeed in mobilising for a seat at the table in formal peacebuilding processes. In Somalia, women not only created a sixth 'clan of women' in a patriarchal society, but they moved from absolute exclusion to winning 25 per cent of seats in Parliament via a constituent assembly (Affi in this book; Affi 2020a). Similarly, the popular concern for security and safety in South Sudan that necessitated the building of a powerful coalition of women leaders from Sudan and South Sudan arguably provided the basis on which they were able to leverage their collective voice with IGAD, the defining regional organisation in their area (Kezie-Nwoha and Were in this book).

These findings support the growing literature suggesting that social rupture caused by armed conflict creates opportunities for gender role transformation and institutional openings in peace talks and constitution-making to enhance women's rights and representation (see, for example, Berry 2018; Tripp 2015; Webster et al. 2019). Amani El Jack argues that 'the social upheaval caused by conflict creates the potential to redefine gender relations' (2003, 41). Tripp (2015) argued that, for the most part, the Sub-

Saharan African states with the highest levels of women in politics and the strongest legal protections for women are those that experienced war after 1985. Civil conflict is also associated with higher rates of women's legislative representation in Sub-Saharan Africa (Hughes and Tripp 2015), and globally (Hughes 2009).

However, our case studies also illustrate in important ways how women's inclusion and participation in formal peace processes are curtailed. In some contexts, women face what has been described in the literature as 'male backlash' (Finnoff 2012); 'post-war backlash' (Pankhurst 2008); 'patriarchal backlash' (Berry 2017); or 'retrogression in gender relations' (Cockburn 2013). In Somalia, women faced what Affi (in this book; see also Affi 2020a) describes as a political backlash where religious actors and clan elders in collusion with male politicians do their best to circumvent the gender quota; many simply refused to appoint women. Also, the formation of new regional states entailed a distribution of some clans across different regional states, which was a disadvantage for women. For example, if a sub-clan is in one region, one seat was reserved for women for every three seats. But once the sub-clan ran for election across two different regional states, the seats were divided between the two and the seat allocated to women may be lost (Affi 2020a). As well, in the 2020–21 federal parliamentary election, sub-clans that appointed women in 2016 insist that other related sub-clans should take their turn and give seats to women. Thus, we may see a situation where more clans refuse to appoint women and the gender quota declines. The backlash against women during the decades of demanding their rightful share in political decision-making has a long trajectory in Somalia.

In Sudan, military forces within the state reacted to women's participation in the 2019 revolution with various forms of gender-based violence. Women protesters were in the majority in the streets in many locations throughout the country and in numerous ways challenged traditional gender stereotypes in the process. They were met with harassment and threats that the Rapid Support Forces and Islamist security officers would ruin their reputation. Sometimes they were called prostitutes and had their hijab forcefully removed and their hair shaved. The aim was clearly to frighten women protesters and force them back home. These acts, especially forcefully removing the hijab, are a direct threat to women protesters that other parts of their bodies are at risk of sexual abuse (Tønnessen and Al-Nagar 2019). Sexual abuse later became a reality during the Khartoum massacre on 3 June 2019.

Our field-based contributions on gendered peacebuilding, therefore, acknowledge that power hierarchies and unequal gender dynamics before and during conflict can be reproduced in postconflict governance structures. Deeply patriarchal institutions such as religious, ethnic, and clan structures and legal discrimination continue to challenge women's political gains in the transition following conflict.

Women's Informal Peacebuilding

The chapters of this book demonstrate the ingenuity of women and how they create spaces within patriarchal structures to relieve the immediate effects of conflict in their local communities. Through a variety of strategies and avenues, women are engaged in informal peacebuilding.

In the context of violent terrorism in north-east Nigeria, women courageously buy time for men and boys to escape when Boko Haram attacks their community. They also hide men and boys, including dressing them as women and girls to facilitate their escape and smuggle them to safety. Although women have largely been excluded from peacebuilding discussions, they have negotiated with Boko Haram at the local level to have abductees returned and even offered themselves in exchange for their children.

Women in Borno have organised and participated in numerous marches, rallies, campaigns, and protests to draw attention to abuses and to demand participation and action for peace. One of the most widespread actions they took involved the Bring Back Our Girls campaign. Originally intended to be a one-day march in 2015 to bring back the Chibok schoolgirls, the movement includes a call to bring all girls and women home. Under the hashtag #bringbackourgirls, it became globally known and highlighted the plight of women and girls who had been abducted by Boko Haram and who still remain missing. Local women's organisations also mediate and build community support for returned abductees who are pregnant or have had children and whose fathers are or were in Boko Haram. There is a stigma especially against women who have children born to Boko Haram fathers, even if the pregnancy was against their will. This is a major obstacle to reintegration into community life, which women actively work to change (Imam, Biu, and Yahi in this book; Imam, Biu, and Yahi 2020).

South Sudanese women have been grossly underrepresented in formal peace negotiations. However, they have been active in informal peacebuilding at the local level, where peace means rebuilding society. Such informal peacebuilding is radically different from formal peace negotiations where male warlords and political leaders in new positions of power divide the spoils of war, according to Kezie-Nwoha and Were (2018). While national women's groups have lobbied for a seat at the table and demonstrated for a gender-sensitive peace agreement, often by using social media and public demonstrations, the work of women's groups at the grassroots is intertwined with everyday life in attempts to alleviate suffering and create reconciliation between warring ethnic groups. Church spaces have been one arena for mobilisation. The Voice of Women for Peace and Faith initiative organises space for women across denominations to discuss, share the challenges they encounter, and support one another (see Kezie-Nwoha and Were in this book; Kezie-

Nwoha and Were 2018). This has contributed heavily towards trauma healing for women as such spaces are used to share problems and receive empathy and support in the form of counselling and material resources. Also, members of the Women's Desk and Mothers' Union have mobilised within the contexts of churches and communities for emergency provision of food and basic necessities for the internally displaced of different religious and ethnic backgrounds. Beyond the emergency food response and distribution, the Mothers' Union organised training in farming for women in Jongole State, enabling women to grow vegetables and maize along the riverbanks to boost their families' nutrition as well as for sale. The focus on women's role in securing the family's livelihood entailed taking on new responsibilities, but at the same time ultimately draws on the social role ascribed to women as nurturers and providers.

Fully acknowledging women's contributions to peacebuilding requires a shift of focus away from formal negotiations towards their activism around the peace table and beyond. By referring to informal peacebuilding, we acknowledge women's marginalisation in relation to political power that confines them to informal spheres, which means that their contribution to peacebuilding often goes unrecognised as such. According to Mazurana and McKay (2002) women's role in peacebuilding is usually less obvious because they are 'intertwined with everyday life'. Informal does not suggest that it is less important, and it goes beyond women's effort to push for inclusion in formal negotiations. Informal peacebuilding largely takes place at the grassroots level, more often than not without international funding. Our findings suggest that women cleverly work across divides for peace and as such represent a model for peacebuilding more generally. It recognises the significance of peace actors at communal levels and their agency, rather than viewing them as the objects of top-down peacebuilding processes. In the scholarship on local peacebuilding, Mac Ginty and Richmond (2013, 767) describe local agency as 'small-scale mobilization for peace in practical terms ... ' Local agency is one particular form of agency that relates to 'transformative processes aiming to improve the social conditions of everyday life,' according to Kappler (2015, 875). Our book, and particularly the sections on women's informal peacebuilding, contributes to this literature by adding a gender dimension. Despite the central role that this literature affords to the agency of local actors, it has not been gender-focused (Mueller-Hirth 2018).

The chapters in this book, especially those on north-east Nigeria and South Sudan, show that women take on new roles in their communities – for example, as heads of households – in patriarchal contexts where this signifies a transformation of traditional gender roles. However, these women may not hold liberal goals aimed at gender equality, but mobilise for peace within themes of, for example, motherhood, which oftentimes draws on essentialised conceptions of womanhood or traditional gender frames. Many women constructed their roles as peacebuilders in relation to experiences as mothers; the Bring Back Our Girls campaign and the communal work by women to negotiate the return and reintegration of abducted children illustrate this point well. In these informal peacebuilding activities, women exert considerable agency and at times transform social relations in their communities by using motherhood as a frame of mobilisation. To think of women's peacebuilding agency in terms of a 'gendered responsibility for peace' along the same lines as Mueller-Hirth (2018), we contend that women are empowered but simultaneously constrained. This argument provides empirical nuance to the existing literature, which is critiqued for framing of women as biologically more dispositioned to peace because of their reproductive role and for reenforcing rather than transforming gender inequalities (see, for example, Cockburn 2007; Cohn 2008).

Women Stemming the Tide of Extremism

This book has examined contestations over women's rights, which conservative Islamist extremists actively and sometimes violently participate in across various countries in Africa. A common thread shared by these groups is attacks on the rights of women and girls, whether directly with violence in the form of kidnapping, whipping, or sexual attacks, or through the codification and implementation of regulations presented as Islamic law often juxtaposed to 'the West'. Under flagships such as limiting women's rights to education and more generally women's right to participate in public life and to decision-making over their own bodies, the emergence and popularity of such groups reenforces ideas of women as primarily wives and mothers. Women's civil society groups are important actors in stemming the tide of violent extremism, but are seldom recognised as such in security dialogues and counter-extremism programming. In Nigeria, national strategies to counter violent extremism ignore women's civil society organisations as major stakeholders. Instead, women are seen as predominantly victims of, and promoters of, violent extremism (Nwangwu and Ezeibe 2019). But as the chapters in this book show, especially those on Algeria and Sudan, women's groups have a long history of countering violent extremism.

Since independence, Tripp (in this book; Tripp 2019) demonstrates how the women's movement in Algeria has tried to curtail the influence of Islamist extremists during the years of civil strife (1991–2002) and beyond. Many women stood up to extremists during the Black Decade as they were among the first targeted by the Islamist fighters for working as teachers, running businesses, driving, not veiling, and engaging in the public sphere. Many women's organisations refused to be silenced and continued to mobilise around calls for justice and an end to impunity for those who had killed, raped, and harmed people during the Black Decade. Algerian women were caught between the state and an Islamist agenda that resulted in their rights being severely restricted – for example, in the 1984 Family Code, which sought to remake women into only wives, mothers, and sisters. The involvement of women in the 2019 uprising was the culmination of decades of struggle on the part of women, which have taken at least three different forms: civil society mobilisation for reform, direct challenges to Islamist extremist provocations, and cultural wars in defence of personal liberty. Women's groups were active in efforts to pressure the government for reform of the Family Code in 2005, although demands continue for further reform of the code. They obtained some key constitutional reforms that gave them equality with men and greater political representation. The 2019–20 protests were notable for the strong presence of women and the lack of a strong Islamist presence, which defined the country for so long.

In Sudan, a popular uprising in 2019 ousted the dictator Omar al Bashir, who had ruled the country with an iron fist for three decades and during that time forcefully introduced conservative Islamisation processes that have disproportionately disadvantaged women as a group. Women of different and diverse backgrounds were among the majority of protesters across the country. Although women had diverse visions for gender relations, ranging from gender equality to gender complementarity, they were in various ways protesting the extremists' violent use of conservative or restrictive religious interpretation to limit their rights and personal liberties in private and public spheres. The notorious public order laws controlling women's bodies and movement in the name of Islam have become the heart of what is seen as fundamentally unIslamic government measures to restrict women's lives.

Al-Nagar and Tønnessen (in this book) show how women's activism against discrimination and inequality has a long trajectory. Women's rights have been an important political symbol at the heart of what Islamists have codified as *shar'ia* law, and women's opposition to al Bashir's regime is central to understanding their strong involvement in the revolution and its aftermath. Rejecting efforts to use conservative religious interpretation to limit their rights and everyday life, female revolutionaries and women's rights activists delineated three different women-specific agendas related to the governmental changes they espouse: 1) accountability for sexual- and gender-based violence impunity in the context of the many armed conflicts during the al Bashir era, but also related to the Khartoum massacre, when forces within the military sexually abused women protesters; 2) freedom to make life choices, including the abolition of public morality laws; and 3) women's political representation in the new civilian government structures. Thus far, women have been able to push for some reforms in Sudan's current post-revolution. The constitutional declaration of August 2019 promises a repeal of discriminatory laws codified by the Islamists and 40 per cent representation of women in the national legislative assembly. To date, the public order laws have been repealed, female genital mutilation/cutting criminalised, and in the Miscellaneous Act of 2020 women are granted the right to travel out of the country with their children without the written approval of a male guardian.

Women have been at the forefront of fighting Islamist extremism in

Algeria and authoritarian Islamism in Sudan and they have a vested interest in continuing this struggle through civil society activisms as well as in everyday life. There are reasons to believe that these insights from Africa can be transferred to other contexts, especially given the common narrative and biologically determined conception of gender shared by extremist groups across religions and regions, propagating the idea that women belong in the home and under the control of men. This is important, especially taking into consideration that the concept of extremist violence often goes undefined and in the public imagination is narrowly focused on radical Islamist groups.

As a new focus area within the women, peace, and security agenda, women's engagement in countering violent extremism is increasingly being brought to the forefront (Aroussi 2020). In this discourse women are often looked upon as victims in subordinate and passive subject positions rather than important agents in organised groups that challenge extremist doctrine and engage in cultural wars in defence of personal liberty in their everyday lives. According to Asante and Sheperd (2020, 311), the representations of gender roles and identities in relation to counterterrorism and countering violent extremism largely 'fix women in subordinate and passive subject positions'. Our book demonstrates women's agency by foregrounding their (everyday) activism in countering violent extremism. By centring the experience of women, we are nuancing and mirroring some of the current criticisms against the women, peace, and security agenda in at least three important ways.

First, we contend that the struggle for women's rights is integral to keeping violent extremism in check. However, it is also important to note that fighting violent extremism does not necessarily entail a fight for gender equality in all spheres. Within the group of women revolutionaries in Sudan, Al-Nagar and Tønnessen find that not all protested for liberal goals of gender equality in all spheres. Not all Sudanese women share the same experiences with authoritarian Islamism and express the same concerns with it. Some of the women protesting al Bashir did not protest against Islam, but against what they deem to be an authoritarian regime's misuse of Islam. Some of the women protesting did not protest for gender equality but for a reinterpretation of complementarity in which women should be allowed more space to work and earn a living and for women to move freely in public places. This reminds us of the feminist critique of UNSCR 1325, that it is premised on the assumption that all women in postconflict communities share the same experiences and express the same concerns (Pratt and Richter-Devroe 2011).

Second, the violence and insecurities experienced by women in contexts of violent extremism go beyond 'conflict-related sexual violence' and so does their activism. The meaning of 'security' in the women, peace, and security framework has been critiqued by feminist scholars who find its overemphasis on conflict-related sexual violence problematic (Ní Aoláin, Haynes, and Cahn 2012; Eriksson Baaz and Stern 2013). This 'securitization of gender' has, according to some feminist scholars, depoliticised gender inequality and detached conflict-related sexual violence from the context within which such violence emerged, which transgresses war and peace (Jansson and Eduards 2016; Eriksson Baez and Stern 2013; Houge and Lohne 2017). As Peterson (1992), Tickner (1992), and many others have highlighted, the role of gendered ideologies in producing and reproducing violence and structural insecurities becomes well illustrated in cases elaborated in this book where violent extremist groups have taken control of the state or pockets of the state, as is the case in Nigeria. Women rally against sexual violence, insisting on legal reforms and ending impunity across our case studies. In parts of Somalia, women have successfully pushed for the adoption of a sexual offences bill. Women activists in South Sudan organised a silent march in Juba in December 2017 to highlight sexual violence. They covered their mouths with tape to signify denial of freedom of speech and protested in silence to demand an end to sexual violence, which continues at high rates despite the recent ceasefire agreements. Although sexual violence is high on the agenda, the experience of women and their activism as demonstrated in this book illustrate that they experience violence against them as a continuum (Cockburn 1998, 2004; Enloe 1993, 2010). In Nigeria, women call attention to the abduction of girls by Boko Haram and sexual slavery, but also domestic violence. Imam, Biu, and Yahi (in this book) call attention to the fact that the notion of security for women in north-east Nigeria includes freedom from gender-based violence, not only from Boko Haram and the Nigerian armed forces, but also generally in the community and from domestic violence within the household. The change in men's ability to be the family's economic providers, a role that is traditionally ascribed to men in this area, has contributed to an increase in domestic violence because it threatens their masculinity.

Third, it is not only violent extremists or rebel movements that exert violence against women. In northern Nigeria, women also suffered from gender-based violence committed by the government security services and vigilantes inside and outside refugee camps. In the process of consolidating a transitional government in Sudan, women have been sidelined by non-Islamist political forces. The Forces for Freedom and Change (FFC), the coalition representing the protesters, has marginal representation of women despite the fact that women were the majority of protesters during the revolution. The FFC is a powerful and highly patriarchal institution mandated to provide Abdallah Hamdok with nominations for key positions in the postconflict governance processes. Framing the exclusion of women within a conservative Sudanese culture, women face many of the same patriarchal attitudes as during the dictatorship of al Bashir. The structural violence they experience during the dictatorship has not ended with the negotiation of a peace deal. It presents itself, as Eisenstein (2007) explains, as a parallel form of war on women in times of conflict as well as peace.

BIBLIOGRAPHY

(2006). 'Uganda Women to Take Peace Torch to Juba', *Sudan Tribune*, 9 November, available at: http://www.sudantribune.com/spip.php?article18573, accessed 19 March 2021.

(2007). 'From Peace Torch to Peace Treaty: Ugandan Women Promote an Inclusive, Sustainable Peace,' UNIFEM, 7 May, available at: https://reliefweb.int/report/uganda/peace-torch-peace-treaty-ugandan-women-promote-inclusive-sustainable-peace, accessed 19 March 2021.

(2014). 'Dinka and Nuer Women Meet for Peace in Bor', *Radio Tamazuj*, 2 August.

(2014). 'South Sudan Women Leaders Threaten Protests as Peace Talks Stall', *Radio Tamazuj*, 6 August, available at: https://radiotamazuj.org/en/news/article/south-sudan-women-leaders-threaten-protests-as-peace-talks-stall, accessed 19 March 2021.

(2015). 'Algérie: La campagne "Ne laisse pas tes femmes sortir avec une tenue osée" fait fureur sur le Web', *20 Minutes*, 26 May, available at: https://www.20minutes.fr/monde/1616211-20150526-algerie-campagne-laisse-femmes-sortir-tenue-osee-fait-fureur-web, accessed 19 March 2021.

(2015). 'Les inquisiteurs sont de retour', *El Watan*, 25 May, available at: https://www.elwatan.com/edition/actualite/les-inquisiteurs-sont-de-retour-25-05-2015, accessed 19 March 2021.

(2015). 'South Sudan War: A Long List of Broken Deals', *New Vision*, 13 August, available at: https://www.newvision.co.ug/new_vision/news/1332521/south-sudan-war-list-broken-deal, accessed 19 March 2021.

(2015). '"Trop courte ma jupe?": l'Algérie montre ses jambes', *France24*, 14 May, available at: http://observers.france24.com/fr/20150514-trop-courte-jupe-algerie-montrer-jambes-polemique, accessed: 19 March 2021.

(2016). 'Dood kulul – Sheikh Nur Baaruud iyo Batuulo, Gudoomiyaha Ururke Haweenka Soomaaliya', video, 13 October, available at: https://www.youtube.com/watch?v=xQ6Ni1nl8OE&t=265s, accessed 19 March 2021.

(2016). 'South Sudan Conflict: African Union Approves Regional Force', *BBC News*, 16 July, available at: https://www.bbc.com/news/world-africa-36833875, accessed 19 March 2021.

(2016). 'South Sudan Humanitarian Needs Overview', UNOCHA, 6 January, available at: https://reliefweb.int/report/south-sudan/2016-south-sudan-humanitarian-needs-overview, accessed 19 March 2021.

(2017). 'Communiqué of the 31st Extra-Ordinary Summit of IGAD Assembly of Heads of State and Government on South Sudan,' IGAD, 12 June, available at: https://igad.int/communique/1575 -communique-of-the-31st-extra-ordinary-summit-of-igad-assembly-of-heads-of-state-and -government-on-south-sudan, accessed 19 March 2021.

(2017). 'South Sudan President declares National Day of Prayers for 10 March', *Sudan Tribune*, 2 March, available at: http://www.sudantribune.com/spip.php?article61770, accessed 19 March 2021.

(2017). 'Women Take to Streets to Demand End to South Sudan War', *Al Jazeera*, 9 December, available at: www.aljazeera.com /news/2017/12/women-mouths-taped-shut-demand-sudan-war-171209214901540.html, accessed 19 March 2021.

(2018). 'Afin de protester contre l'agression de Ryma: un "footing citoyen" organisé hier à Alger', *Algérie Monde Infos*, 10 June, available at: http://www.algeriemondeinfos.com/2018/06/10/afin-de-protester-contre-lagression-de-ryma-footing-citoyen-organise-hier-a-alger/, accessed 19 March 2021.

(2018). 'Appels a l'agression des femmes non voilées: Tayeb Louh confirme l'arrestation d'un des auteurs', *Algérie Monde Infos*, 19 June.

(2018). 'Phase-2 of South Sudan Peace Revitalization Talks End Without Deal', *Sudan Tribune*, 24 May, available at: http://www.sudantribune.com/spip.php?article65466, accessed 19 March 2021.

(2018). 'SPLM-IO Signs Peace Declaration of Principles as Juba Declines', *Sudan Tribune*, 10 February, available at: http://www.sudantribune.com/spip.php?article64693, accessed 19 March 2021.

(2018). 'World's first virtual summit building solidarity and solutions for the women of South Sudan', *SawaSouthSudan*, 25 May, available at: https://www.sawasouthsudan.com/media-1, accessed 19 March 2021.

(2019). 'Sudan Appoints Its First Woman Chief Justice', 10 October, *Dabanga*, available at: https://www.dabangasudan.org/en/all-news/article/sudan-appoints-its-first-woman-chief-justice, accessed 19 March 2021.

(2019). 'Sudan's Government Endorses Draft Law Banning Al-Bashir's Party', *Sudan Tribune*, 27 November, available at: https://sudantribune.com/spip.php?article68592, accessed 19 March 2021.

(2019). 'Video: Au premier rang des mobilisations algériennes, les femmes revendiquent leurs droits', *France Info*, 13 March, available at: https://www.francetvinfo.fr/monde/afrique/algerie/election-presidentielle-en-algerie/video-au-premier-rang-des-mobilisations-algeriennes-les-femmes-revendiquent-leurs-droits_3231293.html, accessed 19 March 2021.

(2020). 'Civil Society Statement in Response to the Law of Various Amendments', *Sudan Tribune*, 14 August, available at: https://sudantribune.com/spip.php?article69702, accessed 19 March 2021.

(2020). 'Sudan's Peace Talks Are Stalled by Govt Ambiguity over Secular State: Al-Hilu', *Sudan Tribune*, 3 January, available at: https://www.sudantribune.com/spip.php?article68806, accessed 19 March 2021.

(2020). 'Sudanese Women Demonstrate for Gender Equality, Urge CEDAW Ratification', *Sudan Tribune*, 3 January, available at: https://sudantribune.com/spip.php?article68800, accessed 19 March 2021.

Abbas, Reem (2020a). 'Women Led the Revolution and Continue to Push for Change', *The Elephant*, available at: https://www.theelephant.info/videos/2020/09/23/sudan-women-led-the-revolution-and-continue-to-push-for-change, accessed 19 March 2021.

Abbas, Reem (2020b). 'A Year After Bashir's Fall, the Struggle for Sudanese Women Continues', Wilson Center, Blog of the Middle East Initiative, available at: https://www.wilsoncenter.org/blog-post/year-after-bashirs-fall-struggle-sudanese-women-continues, accessed 19 March 2021.

Abbas, Sara (2010). 'The Sudanese Women's Movement and the Mobilisation for the 2008 Legislative Quota and Its Aftermath', *IDS Bulletin*, 41(5), pp. 100–108.

Abbas, Sara (2020). 'The Weight of Feelings: Khartoum's Revolutionary Moment', *Discover Society*, available at: https://discoversociety.org/2020/04/01/the-weight-of-feelings-khartoums-revolutionary-moment, accessed 19 March 2021.

Abdel Halim, Asma (2011a). 'Gendered Justice: Women and the Application of Penal Laws in the Sudan', in Lutz Oette (ed.) *Criminal Law Reform and*

Transitional Justice: Human Rights Perspectives for Sudan. Farnham, Surrey: Ashgate, pp. 227–42.

Abdel Halim, Asma (2011b). 'A Home for Obedience: Masculinity in Personal Status for Muslims Law' in *Hawwa* 9(1–2), pp. 194–214.

Abdi, Hawa, and Sarah J. Robbins (2013). *Keeping Hope Alive: One Women, 90,000 Lives Changed.* New York: Grand Central Publishing.

Abdullahi, Abdurahman M. (2011). 'The Islamic Movement in Somalia: A Historical Evolution with a Case Study of the Islah Movement (1950–2000)', Ph.D. dissertation. Montréal: McGill University.

Abdullahi, Abdurahman (2018). *Making Sense of Somali History: Volume Two.* London: Adonis and Abbey Publishers.

Adam, Hussein, and Richard Ford (1998). *Removing Barricades in Somalia: Options of For Peace and Rehabilitation.* Washington, D. C.: United States Institute for Peace.

Adjei, Maxwell (2019). 'Women's Participation in Peace Processes: A Review of Literature', *Journal of Peace Education,* 16(2), pp. 133–54.

Affi, Ladan (2004). 'Men Drink Tea While Women Gossip', in Abdi M. Kusow (ed.) *Putting the Cart Before the Horse: Contested Nationalism and the Crisis of the Nation-State in Somalia.* Trenton: The Red Sea Press.

Affi, Ladan (2020a). 'Excluding Women: The Clanization of Somali Political Institutions', Bergen: Chr. Michelsen Institute, CMI Brief No. 2020:9, available at: https://www.cmi.no/publications/7277-excluding-women-the-clanization-of-somali-political-institutions, accessed 19 March 2021.

Affi, Ladan (2020b). 'The Old Men Who Hold Us Back: Clan Elders, Elite Bargaining and Exclusionary Politics'. *Journal of Somali Studies,* 7(2), pp. 125–45.

Africa Development Bank Group (ADBG) (2018). 'The Political Economy of South Sudan', ADB/IF/2018/211–ADF/BD/IF/2018/159, available at: https://www.afdb.org/fileadmin/uploads/afdb/Documents/Generic-Documents/The_Political_Economy_of_South_Sudan.pdf, accessed 19 March 2021.

African Centre for Justice and Peace Studies (2011). 'Stemming the Tide: Arrests of Students and Youth Continue in Efforts to Curb Potential Organizing Power', available at: http://www.africancentreforjustice.org/wp-content/uploads/2012/04/StemmingtheTide_ArrestsofStudentsandYouthContinueinEffortstoCurbPotentialOrganisingPower.pdf, accessed 19 March 2021.

African Centre for Justice and Peace Studies (2013). 'Over 170 Dead, including 15 Children, and 800 Detained as Demonstrations Spread throughout Sudan', available at: https://www.acjps.org/over-170-dead-including-15-children-and-800-detained-as-demonstrations-spread-throughout-sudan, accessed 19 March 2021.

Agerholm, Harriet (2017). 'Algerian Women in their Thousands are Defying Conservative Islamists by Wearing Bikinis', *Independent,* 7 August, available at: https://www.independent.co.uk/news/world/africa/algeria-women-bikinis-conservative-islamists-muslim-cover-up-skin-beach-a7880371.html, accessed 19 March 2021.

Ahmed, Leila (1982). 'Feminism and Feminist Movements in the Middle East, A Preliminary Exploration: Turkey, Egypt, Algeria, People's Democratic Republic of Yemen', *Women's Studies International Forum,* 5(2), pp. 153–68.

Aka, Ebenezer (2000). *Regional Disparities in Nigeria's Development: Lessons and Challenges for the 21st Century.* Lanham, Maryland: University Press of America.

Al Amin, Nafisa Ahmed and Ahmed Abdel Magied (2001). 'A History of Sudanese Women Organizations and the Strive for Liberation and Empowerment', *Ahfad Journal,* 18(1), pp. 2–23.

Al Bakri, Zeinab Bashir (1995). 'The Crisis in the Sudanese Women's Movement', in Saskia Wieringa (ed.) *Subversive Women: Historical Experiences of Gender and Resistance.* London and New Jersey: Zed Books.

Al-Ali, Nadje (2012). 'Gendering the Arab Spring', *Middle East Journal of Culture and Communication,* 5(1), pp. 26–31.

Al-Gadal, F. (2016). *A Witness to the Progress of Sudanese Women Union in Half a Century,* Omdurman: Abdel Kareem Mirghani Cultural Center.

Ali, Hawo Abdullahi (2020). 'Hawo Abdullahi Ali: Illiteracy Must be Defeated by Whatever Means', UNSOM, available at: https://unsom.unmissions.org/hawo-abdallahi-ali-illiteracy-must-be-defeated-whatever-means, accessed 19 March 2021.

Alin, Fadumo Ureji Ahmed (2012). 'Arrimaha Bulshada TV Show', *Somali Channel,* 13 March, available at: https://www.youtube.com/watch?v=ui4Qn9XRAN0, accessed 19 March 2021.

Alin, Fadumo (1977). 'Somali Women's Report', *Halgan,* 1(6).

Alliance of 149 (2010). 'Sudan: "Alliance of 149" for Reform of Rape Law', 27 January, available at: http://www.wluml.org/fr/node/5900, accessed 19 March 2021.

Al-Nagar, Samia, and Liv Tønnessen (2015). 'Women and Girls Caught between Rape and Adultery in Sudan: Criminal Law Reform, 2005–2015', CMI Report R 2015:10. Bergen: Chr. Michelsen Institute, available at: https://www.cmi.no/publications/5661-women-and-girls-caught-between-rape-and-adultery, accessed 19 March 2021.

Al-Nagar, Samia, and Liv Tønnessen (2017a). 'Women's Rights and the Women's Movement in Sudan (1952–2014)', in B. Badri and A. M. Tripp (eds.) *Women's Activism in Africa: Struggles for Rights and Representation.* London: Zed Books, pp. 121–55.

Al-Nagar, Samia, and Liv Tønnessen (2017b). 'Family Law Reform in Sudan: Competing Claims for Gender Justice between Sharia and Women's Human Rights', CMI Report R 2017:5. Bergen: Chr. Michelsen Institute, available at: https://www.cmi.no/publications/6401-family-law-reform-in-sudan, accessed 19 March 2021.

Al-Nagar, Samia, and Liv Tønnessen (2019). '"I'm Against All of the Laws of This Regime": What Sudan's Women Want', *African Arguments,* 2 July, available at: https://africanarguments.org/2019/07/02/against-laws-regime-sudan-women-protesters-want, accessed 19 March 2021.

Amin, Mohammed (2020). 'Delays in Sudan's Massacre Investigation Prompt Protests from Victims' Families', *Middle East Eye,* 27 May, available at: https://www.middleeasteye.net/news/sudan-investigation-lags-families-massacre-victims-ready-seek-justice-elsewhere, accessed 19 March 2021.

Amnesty International (2015). '"Our Job Is to Shoot, Slaughter and Kill": Boko Haram's Reign of Terror in North-East Nigeria', AFR 44/1360/2015. London, available at: https://www.amnesty.org/en/documents/afr44/1360/2015/en, accessed 19 March 2021.

Amnesty International (2019). "'Sudan: Decision to Repeal Public Order Laws a Step Forward for Women's Rights', 29 November, available at: https://www.amnesty.org/en/latest/news/2019/11/sudan-decision-to-repeal-public-order-laws-a-step-forward-for-womens-rights, accessed 19 March 2021.

APS (2016). 'Algeria: President Bouteflika Calls for Reconsidering Reservations on Convention Against Discrimination Toward Women', 8 March.

Arabi, Asha (2011). 'In Power without Power: Women in Politics and Leadership Positions in South Sudan', in Frederike Bubenzer and Orly Stern (eds.) *Hope, Pain and Patience: The Lives of Women in South Sudan*. Wynberg, South Africa: The Institute for Justice and Reconciliation.

Aretxaga, Begoña (1997). *Shattering Silence: Women, Nationalism, and Political Subjectivity in Northern Ireland*. Princeton: Princeton University Press.

Aroussi, Sahla (2020). 'Strange Bedfellows: Interrogating the Unintended Consequences of Integrating Countering Violent Extremism with the UN's Women, Peace, and Security Agenda in Kenya', *Politics & Gender*, published online 6 July, available at oi:10.1017/S1743923X20000124. https://www. cambridge.org/core/journals/politics-and-gender/article/strange-bedfellows-interrogating-the-unintended-consequences-of-integrating-countering-violent-extremism-with-the-uns-women-peace-and-security-agenda-in-kenya/4867E46 CE1DF9A4AAE84B5C159BBFA52, accessed 26 May 2021.

Asante, Doris, and Laura Shepard (2020). 'Gender and Countering Violent Extremism in Women, Peace and Security National Action Plans', *European Journal of Politics and Gender*, 3(3), pp. 311–30.

Assal, Munzoul A. M (2019). 'Sudan's Popular Uprising and the Demise of Islamism', Bergen: Chr. Michelsen Institute, CMI Brief No. 2019:3, 4 pp.

Baldez, Lisa (2002). *Why Women Protest: Women's Movements in Chile*. Cambridge: Cambridge University Press.

Barre, Jaalle Mohamed Siad (1975). Speech, 11 January.

Barry, Jane (2005). *Rising up in Response: Women's Rights Activism in Conflict*. Alameda, California: Urgent Action Fund.

Bayat, Asef (2013). *Life as Politics: How Ordinary People Change the Middle East*. Stanford: Stanford University Press.

Bayat, Asef (2017). 'Foreword: Arab Revolts in Post-Islamist Times', in Are Knudsen and Basem Ezbidi (eds.) *Popular Protest in the New Middle East*. London and New York: I. B. Tauris, pp. XV–XXIV.

Bekoe, Dorina, and Parajon, Christina (2007). 'Women's role in Liberia's reconstruction,' United States Institute for Peace, available at: https://www. usip.org/publications/2007/05/womens-role-liberias-reconstruction, accessed 19 March 2021.

Belkaïd, Meryem (2019). 'Pour une véritable justice transitionnelle', *Al HuffPost Maghreb*, 15 April, available at: https://www.huffpostmaghreb.com/entry/ pour-une-veritable-justice-transitionnelle_mg_5cc18341e4b0764d31dd1c9a, accessed 19 March 2021.

Bell, Christine, Sanja Badanjak, Robert Forster, Astrid Jamar, Kevin McNicholl, Kathryn Nash, Jan Pospisil, and Laura Wise (2019) 'PA-X Codebook, Version 1', Political Settlements Research Programme. Edinburgh: University of Edinburgh, available at: www.peaceagreements.org, accessed 19 March 2021.

Ben Mansour, Latifa (2002). *Frères musulmans, frères féroces. Voyage dans l'enfer du discours islamiste* [Muslim brothers, ferocious brothers: a journey into the inferno of Islamist discourse]. Paris: Ramsay.

Benfodil, Mustapha (2018). 'Echec des garçons au bac: Pourquoi ça ne les fait plus rêver', *El Watan*, 23 July, available at: https://www.elwatan.com/ edition/actualite/echec-des-garcons-au-bac-pourquoi-ca-ne-les-fait-plus-rever-23-07-2018, accessed 19 March 2021.

Bennoune, Karima (2013). *Your Fatwa Does Not Apply Here: Untold Stories from the Fight Against Muslim Fundamentalism.* New York and London: W. W. Norton & Company.

Benrabah, Mohamed (2013). *Language Conflict in Algeria: From Colonialism to PostIndependence.* Bristol: Multilingual Matters.

Berkani, Mohamed (2018). 'Agression d'une joggeuse: 300 Algériennes ont couru à Alger pour leur liberté', *Franceinfo,* 11 June, available at: www.francetvinfo.fr/ monde/afrique/societe-africaine/agression-dune-joggeuse-300-algeriennesont-couru-a-alger-pour-leur-liberte_3054319.html, accessed 19 March 2021.

Berridge, Willow J. (2016). *Civil Uprisings in Modern Sudan: The 'Khartoum Springs' of 1964 and 1985.* London: Bloomsbury.

Berry, Marie (2017). 'Barriers to Women's Progress after Atrocity: Evidence from Rwanda and Bosnia-Herzegovina', *Gender & Society,* 31(6), pp. 830–53.

Berry, Marie (2018). *War, Women, and Power: From Violence to Mobilization in Rwanda and Bosnia-Herzegovina.* New York: Cambridge University Press.

Bindi, Idrissa Tamba, and Ozgur Tufekci (2018). 'Liberal Peacebuilding in Sierra Leone: A Critical Exploration', *Journal of Asian and African Studies,* 53(8), pp. 1158–72.

Bouzeboudjen, Kamel (2019). 'Chansons et humour au service de la contestation en Algérie', *Radio Canada,* 8 March, available at: https://ici.radio-canada.ca/ nouvelle/1157225/algerie-artistes-etudiants-humour-contestation-cinquieme-manda, accessed 19 March 2021.

Bradbury, Mark (2008). *Becoming Somaliland.* Oxford: James Currey.

Bratton, Kathleen A. (2005). 'Critical Mass Theory Revisited: The Behavior and Success of Token Women in State Legislature', *Politics and Gender,* 1(1), pp. 97–125.

Bratton, Michael, Jeremy Seekings, and Daniel Armah-Attoh (2019). 'AD290: Better but Not Good Enough? How Africans See the Delivery of Public Services', Dispatches No. 290, Afrobarometer, available at: https://afrobarometer.org/ publications/ad290-better-not-good-enough-how-africans-see-delivery-public-services, accessed 19 March 2021.

Castagno, Margaret F. (1975). *Historical Dictionary of Somalia.* Methuen: Scarecrow Press.

Center for Civilians in Conflict (2019). *Nigerian Community Militias: Towards a Solution,* Washington, D. C., available at: https://civiliansinconflict.org/ nigerian-community-militias-toward-a-solution, accessed 30 May 2021.

Charef, Abed (2017). 'La Tunisie et le Maroc entrent dans l'ère post-islamiste', *Middle East Eye,* 18 June.

Chetail, Vincent (ed.) (2009). *Post-Conflict Peacebuilding: A Lexicon.* Oxford and New York: Oxford University Press.

Chetail, Vincent, and Céline Bauloz (2014). *Research Handbook on International Law and Migration,* Research Handbooks in International Law. Cheltenham: Edward Elgar.

Childs, Sarah, and Mona Krook (2009). 'Analysing Women's Substantive Representation: From Critical Mass to Critical Actors', *Government and Opposition,* 44(2), pp. 125–45.

Choi Ahmed, Christine (1995). 'Finely Etched Chattel: The Invention of Somali Women', in Ali Jimale Ahmed (ed.) *The Invention of Somalia.* Lawrenceville: The Red Sea Press.

Coakley, Amanda (2021). 'Biden's Strategy in the Sahel Looks a Lot Like Trump's Foreign Policy', 1 April, available at: https://foreignpolicy.com/2021/04/01/

biden-sahel-strategy-burkina-faso-counterterrorism-africa-trump, accessed 18 May 2021.

Cockburn, Cynthia (1998). *The Space between Us: Negotiating Gender and National Identities in Conflict.* London: Zed Books.

Cockburn, Cynthia (2004). 'The Continuum of Violence: A Gender Perspective on War & Peace', in Wenona Giles and Jennifer Hyndman (eds.) *Sites of Violence: Gender and Conflict Zones.* Berkeley: University of California Press, pp. 24–44.

Cockburn, Cynthia (2007). *From Where We Stand: War, Women's Activism and Feminist Analysis.* London: Zed Books.

Cockburn, Cynthia (2013). 'Against the Odds: Sustaining Feminist Momentum in Post-War Bosnia-Herzegovina', *Women's Studies International Forum,* 37, pp. 26–35.

Cohn, Carol (2008). 'Mainstreaming Gender in UN Security Policy: A Path to Political Transformation?' in Shirin Rai and Georgina Waylen (eds.) *Global Governance: Feminist Perspectives.* New York: Palgrave Macmillan, pp. 185–206.

Conover, Pamela J., and Virginia Sapiro (1993). 'Gender, Feminist Consciousness, and War', *American Journal of Political Science,* 37(4), pp. 1079–99.

Coomaraswamy, Radhika, and Dilrukshi Foneska (eds.) (2004). *Peace Work: Women, Armed Conflict and Negotiation.* New Delhi: International Center of Ethnic Studies.

Copnall, James (2009). 'Lubna Hussein: "I'm Not Afraid of Being Flogged. It Doesn't Hurt. But It Is Insulting"', *The Guardian,* 2 August, available at: https://www.theguardian.com/world/2009/aug/02/sudan-women-dress-code, accessed 19 March 2021.

Council on Foreign Relations (CFR) (2020a). 'Boko Haram in Nigeria', Global Conflict Tracker, 5 August, available at: https://cfr.org/global-conflict-tracker/conflict/boko-haram-nigeria, accessed 19 March 2021.

Council on Foreign Relations (2020b). 'South Sudan: Current Peace Effort', available at: https://www.cfr.org/womens-participation-in-peace-processes/south-sudan-0, accessed 19 March 2021.

Counter-Extremism Project (2020). 'Boko Haram', available at: https://www.counterextremism.com/threat/boko-haram, accessed 19 March 2021.

Curtis, Devon, and Gwinyayi Albert Dzinesa (2012). *Peacebuilding, Power, and Politics in Africa,* Cambridge Centre of African Studies Series. Athens: Ohio University Press, available at: http://www.h-net.org/reviews/showrev.php?id=40484.

Cutter, Susan M. (2009). 'Grassroots Perspectives of Peacebuilding in Sierra Leone, 1991–2006', Coventry University, available at: https://www.semanticscholar.org/paper/Grassroots-perspectives-of-peace-building-in-Sierra-Cutter/34f5283a9c90646f534760ba09be77627bd4e49d, accessed 19 March 2021.

Dahlstrom, Ida (2012). 'Women's Recognition in Peacebuilding Implementing Security Council Resolution 1325 in South Sudan', Master of Science in Global Studies University of Gothenburg, available at: https://gupea.ub.gu.se/bitstream/2077/32550/1/gupea_2077_32550_1.pdf, accessed 19 March 2021.

Daly, Mary (1984). *Pure Lust: Elemental Feminist Philosophy.* Boston: Beacon Press.

Dapel, Zuhumnan (2018). 'Poverty in Nigeria: Understanding and Bridging the Divide between North and South', Center for Global Development, 6 April, available at: https://www.cgdev.org/blog/poverty-nigeria-understanding-and-bridging-divide-between-north-and-south, accessed 19 March 2021.

Davidson, Basil (1975). 'Notes on the Revolution in Somalia', *The Socialist Register*, 12, pp. 198–223.

Dini, Shukria (2010). *Somali Women Respond to State Collapse and Civil War: Two Decades of Collective Self-Organizing in Somaliland and Puntland*, Ph.D. dissertation. Toronto: York University.

Dini, Shukria (2014). 'Women in the Government of Somalia', *Afrikas Horn*: Horn of Africa.

Duale, Mohamed (2018). 'Somaliland: Cabinet Approves 20% Quota for Women in the Upcoming Parliament and Local Councils', *Horn Diplomat*, available at: https://www.horndiplomat.com/2018/06/07/somaliland-cabinet-approves-20-quota-for-women-in-the-upcoming-parliament-and-local-councils, accessed 19 March 2021.

Dudouet, Veronique (2017). 'Powering to Peace: Integrated Civil Resistance and Peacebuilding Strategies', International Center on Nonviolent Conflict, Special Report Series, Volume No. 1, April, available at: www.nonviolent-conflict.org/wp-content/uploads/2017/04/powering_to_peace_veronique_dudouet_icnc_special_report_series_april2017.pdf, accessed 19 March 2021.

Edward, J. K. (2019). 'Reconfiguring the South Sudan Women's Movement', *Journal of Women of the Middle East and the Islamic World*, 17, pp. 55–84.

Egge, M. A. (2019). 'Somaliland Hosts National Women Conference on Quota Representation', *Horn Diplomat*, available at: https://www.horndiplomat.com/2019/10/20/somaliland-hosts-national-women-conference-on-quota-representation, accessed 19 March 2021.

Eisenstein, Zillah (2007). *Sexual Decoys: Gender, Race and War in Imperial Democracy*. London: Zed Books.

El Haitami, Meriem (2012). 'Restructuring Female Religious Authority: State-Sponsored Women Religious Guides (Murshidat) and Scholars (Alimat) in Contemporary Morocco', *Mediterranean Studies*, 20(2), pp. 227–40.

El Jack, A. (2003). 'Gender and Armed Conflict Overview Report'. Brighton: BRIDGE, Institute of Development Studies, University of Sussex.

El-Bushra, Judy (2003). 'Fused in Combat: Gender Relations and Armed Conflict', *Development in Practice*, 13(2/3).

Elmi, Afyare Abdi (2010). *Understanding the Somalia Conflagration: Identity, Political Islam and Peacebuilding*. New York: Pluto Press.

Elmi, Maryan Xaaji (2014). 'Dilkii culumuda Somali 1975', Barnaamijka Xusuus Reeb, video, available at: https://www.youtube.com/watch?v=JuGv78k6ndg, accessed 19 March 2021.

Engeler, Miriam, Elena Braghieri, and Samira Manzur (2020). 'From White Teyab to Pink Kandakat: Gender and the 2018–2019 Sudanese Revolution', *Journal of Public and International Affairs*, available at: https://jpia.princeton.edu/news/white-teyab-pink-kandakat-gender-and-2018-2019-sudanese-revolution#Miriam%20Engeler, accessed 19 March 2021.

Enloe, Cynthia (1993). *The Morning After: Sexual Politics at the End of the Cold War*. Berkeley: University of California Press.

Enloe, Cynthia (2002). 'Masculinity as a Foreign Policy Issue', in Susan Hawthorne and Bronwyn Winter (eds.), *Feminist Perspectives*. Melbourne: Spirifex. pp. 254–59.

Enloe, Cynthia (2010). *Nimo's War, Emma's War: Making Feminist Sense of the Iraq War*. Berkeley: University of California Press.

Eriksson Baaz, M., and M. Stern (2013). *Sexual Violence as a Weapon of War? Perceptions, Prescriptions, Problems in the Congo and Beyond.* London: Zed Books.

Fabiani, Riccardo (2017). 'Algerian Islamists, Fragmented and Irrelevant'. Beirut: Carnegie Middle East Center.

Farah, Nuruddin (1996). 'Women of Kismayo'. London: *Times Literary Supplement.*

Finnoff, Kade (2012). 'Intimate Partner Violence, Female Employment, and Male Backlash in Rwanda', *The Economics of Peace and Security Journal,* 7(2), pp. 14–24.

Fluehr-Lobban, Carolyn (1994). 'A Comparison of the Development of Muslim Family Law in Tunisia, Egypt, and the Sudan', in R. Kuppe and R. Potz. Dordrecht (eds.) *International Yearbook for Legal Anthropology.* Boston and London: Martinus Nijhoff Publisher, pp. 353–70.

Gale, Julius (2016). 'Women Pray for Peace in South Sudan', *The Niles,* 28 July, available at: https://www.theniles.org/en/articles/archive/20410, accessed 19 March 2021.

Gass, Jonathan (2019). 'Trump's Africa Surprise', *Atlantic Council* (blog), 4 February, available at: https://www.atlanticcouncil.org/blogs/new-atlanticist/trump-s-africa-surprise-2, accessed 19 March 2021.

Gayoum, A. A. (2011). *149 Campaign in Sudan.* London: Women Living Under Muslim Laws.

Gbowee, Leymah (2004). 'Women and Peacebuilding in Liberia: Excerpts from a talk by Leymah Gbowee at the ELCA's Global Mission Event in Milwaukee, WI', Evangelical Lutheran Church in America, 30 July.

Gbowee, Leymah (2014). 'The Heroic Women of Nigeria Are Standing up to Boko Haram', *Los Angeles Times.*

Gerring, John (2004). 'What Is a Case Study and What Is It Good For?' *The American Political Science Review* 98, No. 2: 341–54, available at: http://www.jstor.org/stable/4145316, accessed 22 March 2021.

Ghanem, Dalia (2019). 'The Shifting Foundations of Political Islam in Algeria'. Washington, D. C.: Carnegie Endowment for International Peace.

Ghanmi, Lamine (2019). 'Burial of Islamist Leader in Algeria a Bellwether of Fading Islamism', *The Arab Weekly,* 5 May, available at: https://thearabweekly.com/burial-islamist-leader-algeria-bellwether-fading-islamism, accessed 19 March 2021.

Gouws, Amanda, and Azille Coetzee (2019). 'Women's movements and feminist activism', *Agenda,* 33(2), pp. 1–8, available at: 10.1080/10130950.2019.1619263, accessed 22 March 2021.

Grewal, Sharan, M. Tahir Kilavuz, and Robert Kubinec (2019). 'Algeria's Uprising: A Survey of Protesters and The Military', *Foreign Policy at Brookings,* July, available at: https://www.brookings.edu/wp-content/uploads/2019/07/FP_20190711_algeria.pdf, accessed 19 March 2021.

Grey, Sandra (2002). 'Does Size Matter? Critical Mass and New Zealand's Women MPs', *Parliamentary Affairs,* 55.

Haji Mukhtar, Mohamed (2003). *Historical Dictionary of Somalia.* Lanham: Scarecrow Press.

Hale, Sondra (1997). *Gender Politics in Sudan: Islamism, Socialism, and the State.* Boulder: Westview.

Hasan, Dahabo Farah, Amina H. Adan, and Amina Mohamoud Warsame (1995).

'Somalia: Poetry as Resistance against Colonialism and Patriarchy', in Saskia Wierenga (ed.) *Subversive Women: Historical Experiences of Gender and Resistance.* Atlantic Highlands: Zed Books.

Hedstrom, Jenny, and Thiyumi Senarathna (eds.) (2015). *Women in Conflict and Peace.* Stockholm: International Institute for Democracy & Electoral Assistance, available at: https://www.idea.int/publications/catalogue/women-conflict-and-peace, accessed 19 March 2021.

Higate, P., and M. Henry (2004). 'Engendering (in)Security in Peace Support Operations', *Security Dialogue*, 35(4), pp. 481–98.

Hilhorst, Dorothea, and Mathijs van Leeuwen (2005). 'Grounding Local Peace Organisations: A Case Study of Southern Sudan', *The Journal of Modern African Studies*, 43, pp. 537–63.

Houge, Anette Bringedal, and Kjersti Lohne (2017). 'End Impunity! Reducing Conflict-Related Sexual Violence to a Problem of Law', *Law and Society Review* 51(4), pp. 755–89.

Hughes, Melanie M (2009). 'Armed Conflict, International Linkages, and Women's Parliamentary Representation in Developing Nations', *Social Problems*, 56(1), pp. 174–204.

Hughes, Melanie M., and Aili Mari Tripp (2015). 'Civil War and Trajectories of Change in Women's Political Representation in Africa, 1985–2010', *Social Forces*, 93(4), pp. 1513–40.

Ibrahim, Haydar (2015). *Khamsun 'Aaman Ala Thawrat Uktubir al-Sudaniyya, 1964–2014: Nuhud al-Sudan al-Bakir.* Khartoum: Markaz al-Dirasat al-Sudaniyya.

Ibrahim, Rhoda, and Zamzam Abdi Adan (1991). *The Integration of Women into Development in Northern Somalia: Task Force Report.* London: Somali Relief.

IGAD (2017). 'Communiqué of the 31st Extra-Ordinary Summit of IGAD Assembly of Heads of State and Government on South Sudan', 12 June, available at: https://igad.int/communique/1575   -communique-of-the-31st-extra-ordinary-summit-of-igad-assembly-of-heads-of-state-and   -government-on-south-sudan, accessed 19 March 2021.

IGAD (2018). 'Revitalised Agreement on the Resolution of the Conflict in South Sudan', available at: https://www.dropbox.com/s/6dn3477q3f5472d/R-ARCSS.2018-i.pdf?dl=0, accessed 19 March 2021.

Ileka, Nekwaya, and Julia Imene-Chanduru (2020). 'How Namibia Helped Birth UN Resolution 1325 on Women, Peace and Security', *Africa Renewal*, 27 October.

Imam, Ayesha and Hauwa Biu and Maina Yahi (2020). 'Women's Informal Peacebuilding in North East Nigeria', Bergen: Chr. Michelsen Institute, CMI Brief No. 2020:09, available at: https://www.cmi.no/publications/7296-womens-informal-peacebuilding-in-north-east-nigeria, accessed 19 March 2021.

Imam, Ayesha M. T. (1994). '"If You Won't Do These Things for Me, I Won't Do Seclusion for You": Local and Regional Constructions of Seclusion Ideologies and Practices in Kano, Northern Nigeria,' Ph.D. dissertation. Brighton: University of Sussex.

Imam, Ayesha M., Mufuliat Fijabi, and Hurera Akilu-Atta (2005). *Women's Rights in Muslim Laws: A Resource Document.* Lagos: BAOBAB for Women's Human Rights: Nigeria.

Institute for Economics & Peace (2019). 'Global Terrorism Index 2019: Measuring the Impact of Terrorism'. Sydney, Australia, available at: http://visionofhumanity.org/reports, accessed 19 March 2021.

International Commission of Inquiry on Darfur (2005). *Report of the International Commission of Inquiry on Darfur to the United Nations Secretary-General,* available at: https://www.un.org/ruleoflaw/files/com_inq_darfur.pdf, accessed 19 March 2021.

International Criminal Court (ICC) (2009). *The Prosecutor v. Omar Hassan Ahmad Al Bashir,* available at: https://www.icc-cpi.int/darfur/albashir, accessed 19 March 2021.

International Development Law Organization (IDLO) (2017). *Tunisia Workshop Promotes Pathways for Women Justice Professionals.*

Inter-Parliamentary Union (IPU) (2020). Monthly ranking of women in national parliaments. Available at: https://www.ipu.org, accessed 19 March 2021.

Itto, Anne (2006). 'Guest at the Table? The Role of Women in Peace Processes,' in M. Simmons and P. Dixon (eds.) *Peace by Piece: Addressing Sudan's Conflicts. Accord: An International Review of Peace Initiatives.* London: Conciliation Resources, pp. 55–59, available at: https://rc-services-assets.s3.eu-west-1. amazonaws.com/s3fspublic/Peace_by_piece_Addressing_Sudans_conflicts_ Accord_Issue_18.pdf, accessed 19 March 2021.

Iyaa, Dominic, and Katie Smith (2018). *Women and the Future of South Sudan: Local Insights on Building Inclusive Constituencies for Peace.* Washington, D. C.: Search for Common Ground.

Iyorah, Festus (2018). *Women's Interfaith Network Builds Bridges Amid Nigeria's Violence, Muslim and Christian Mistrust.* Abuja: Global Sisters Report, available at: https://www.globalsistersreport.org/news/equality/womens- interfaith-network-builds-bridges-amid-nigerias-violence-muslim-and- christian, accessed 19 March 2021.

Jama, Faiza (2010). 'Somali Women and Peacebuilding', in M. Bradbury and D. Healy (eds.) *Whose Peace Is It Anyway? Connecting Somali and international Peacemaking.* London: Conciliation Resources, pp. 62–65.

Jama, Zainab Mohamed (1991). 'Fighting to be heard: Somalia Women's Poetry', *African Languages and Culture,* 4(1), pp. 43–54.

Jama, Zainab Mohamed (1994). 'Silent Voices: The Role of Somali Women's Poetry in Social and Political Life', *Oral Traditions,* 9(1).

Jan, Ameen (2001). 'Somalia: Building Sovereignty or Restoring Peace', in Elizabeth M. Cousens, Chetan Kumar, and Karin Wermester (eds.) *Peacebuilding as Politics: Cultivating Peace in Fragile Societies.* Boulder: Lynne Rienner Publishers.

Jansson, Maria and Maud Eduards (2016). 'The Politics of Gender in the UN Security Council Resolutions on Women, Peace and Security', *International Feminist Journal of Politics,* 18(4), pp. 590–604.

Jendia, C. (2020). 'Conspicuously Absent: Women's Role in Conflict Resolution and Peace Building in Northern Uganda In the Context of United Nations Resolution 1325', *Journal of Law and Conflict Resolution,* 11(1), pp. 1–14.

Jewkes, Rachel, Robert Morrell, Jeff Hearn, Emma Lundquist, David Blackbeard, Graham Lindegger, Michael Quayle, Yandisa Sikweyiya, and Lucas Gottzen (2015). 'Hegemonic masculinity: combining theory and practice in gender interventions', *Culture, Health and Sexuality,* 2(2), pp. 112–27.

Jibril, Fadumo (n.d.). *Puntland Development Research Center.* Video.

Jibril, Hawa (2008). *Saa Waxay Tiri: Maansadii iyo Waayihii Xaawa Jibril – And Then She Said: The Poetry and Times of Hawa Jibril.* Translated by Faduma Ahmed Alim. Toronto: Coach House Printing.

Johnson, Douglas (2018). 'South Sudan's Peace Agreement: Good News or

More Trouble Ahead?' *Deutsche Welle*, 6 August, available at: https://www.dw.com/en/south-sudans-peace-agreement-good-news-or-more-trouble-ahead/a-44971840, accessed 19 March 2021.

Kapinga, Marithe (2003). 'Africa: Women in Congo Form Common Front for Peace', *Ms. Magazine*, 3 March, pp. 25–26, available at: http://www.msmagazine.com/mar03/kapinga.asp, accessed 19 March 2021.

Kappler, Stefanie (2015). 'The Dynamic Local: Delocalisation and (Re-)Localisation in the Search for Peacebuilding Identity', *Third World Quarterly*, 36(5), pp. 875–89.

Kapteijns, Lidwien (2010). 'Making Memories of Mogadishu in Somali Poetry about the Civil War', in Lidwien Kapteijns and Annemiek Richters (eds.) *Mediations of Violence in Africa: Fashioning New Futures from Contested Pasts.* Leiden: Brill.

Karam, Azza (2000). 'Women in War and Peacebuilding: The Roads Traversed, the Challenges Ahead', *International Feminist Journal of Politics,* 3(1), pp. 2–25.

Karama (2019). 'Sudanese Women Are Right to Demand Parity in the Transition', 24 April, available at: http://www.el-karama.org/news/sudanese-women-are-right-to-demand-parity-in-the-transition, accessed 19 March 2021.

Karim, S., and M. Henry (2018). 'Gender and Peacekeeping', in *The Oxford Handbook of Gender and Conflict.* Oxford: Oxford University Press, pp. 390–409.

Karlsrud, John (2019). 'From Liberal Peacebuilding to Stabilization and Counterterrorism', *International Peacekeeping,* 26(1).

Kezie-Nwoha, Helen, and Juliet Were (2018). 'Women's Informal Peace Efforts: Grassroots Activism in South Sudan', Bergen: Chr. Michelsen Institute, CMI Brief No. 2018:07, available at: https://www.cmi.no/publications/file/6700-womens-informal-peace-efforts.pdf, accessed 19 March 2021.

Khalil, Andrea (2014). 'Tunisia's Women: Partners in Revolution', *Journal of North African Studies*, 19(2), pp. 186–99.

Khelifi, Meriem (2019). 'Pourquoi l'Algérie ne sera pas islamiste!' *El Watan*, 28 March, available at: https://www.elwatan.com/edition/contributions/pourquoi-lalgerie-ne-sera-pas-islamiste-28-03-2019, accessed 19 March 2021.

Kimani, Mary (2008). 'Women in North Africa secure more rights', *Africa Renewal,* July, available at: https://www.un.org/africarenewal/magazine/july-2008/women-north-africa-secure-more-rights, accessed 19 March 2021.

Kinsella, Helen M. (2004). 'Securing the Civilian: Sex and Gender in the Laws of War', in Michael Barnett and Raymond Duvall (eds.) *Power and Global Governance.* Cambridge: Cambridge University Press, pp. 249–72.

Kirk, Jackie (2004). 'Promoting a Gender-Just Peace: The Roles of Women Teachers in Peacebuilding and Reconstruction', *Gender and Development* 12, No. 3: 50–59.

Knudsen, Are (2017). 'Introduction', in Are Knudsen and Basem Ezbidi (eds.) *Popular Protest in the New Middle East.* London and New York: I. B. Tauris.

Koontz, Claudia (1997). 'Motherhood and Politics on the Far Right', in Alexis Jetter, Annelise Orleck, and Diana Taylor (eds.) *The Politics of Motherhood: Activist Voices from Left to Right.* Hanover: University Press of New England for Dartmouth College, pp. 229–46.

Koshin, Sahro Ahmed (2016). '2016 Elections in Somalia: The Rise of Somali Women's New Political Movements'. Garowe, Somalia: SIDRA.

Krause, J., W. Krause and P. Bränfors (2018). 'Women's Participation in Peace Negotiations and the Durability of Peace', *International Interactions,* 44(6), pp. 985–1016.

Kreft, Ann Kathrin (2018). 'Responding to sexual violence: Women's mobilization in war', *Journal of Peace Research*, 56(2), pp. 220–33.

Kuol, Luka (2018). 'Navigating the Competing Interests of Regional Actors in South Sudan', African Centre for Strategic Studies, available at: https://reliefweb. int/report/south-sudan/navigating-competing-interests-regional-actors-south-sudan, accessed 19 March 2021.

Kyari, Mohammed (2014). 'Boko Haram Message and Method', in Marc-Antoine Pérouse de Montclos (ed.) *Boko Haram: Islamism, Politics, Security, and the State in Nigeria.* Leiden: African Studies Centre and Institut Français de Recherche en Afrique, pp. 9–33.

Lalami, Feriel (2014). 'Algérie, pause dans les mobilisations féministes?' *Nouvelles Questions Féministes,* 33(2), pp. 34–42.

Landman, Maeve (2006). 'Getting Quality in Qualitative Research: A Short Introduction to Feminist Methodology and Methods', *The Proceedings of the Nutrition Society,* 65(4), pp. 429–33, available at: https://pubmed.ncbi.nlm.nih. gov/17181910, accessed 19 March 2021.

Lavrilleux, Ariane (2019). 'Awadeya Mahmoud Koko: From Tea Seller to Union Leader to "Mother of the Revolution"', *Mada,* 21 May, available at: https:// madamasr.com/en/2019/05/21/feature/politics/awadeya-mahmoud-koko-from-tea-seller-to-union-leader-to-mother-of-the-revolution, accessed 19 March 2021.

Lee, Sung Yong, and Alpaslan Özerdem (eds.) (2015). *Local Ownership in International Peacebuilding: Key Theoretical and Practical Issues.* London: Routledge.

Legal Action Worldwide (2014). 'Women's Rights in the New Somalia: Best Practices and Guidelines of MPs and CSOs', *IIDA Women's Development Organization Project,* available at: https://land.igad.int/index.php/documents-1/countries/ somalia/gender-4/900-women-s-rights-in-the-new-somalia/file, accessed 19 March 2021.

Leithead, Alastair (2016). 'Torment of a Freed Boko Haram "Bride"', *BBC News,* 14 April, sec. Africa, available at: https://www.bbc.com/news/world-africa-36041860, accessed 19 March 2021.

Leonardsson, Hanna, and Gustav Rudd (2015). 'The "Local Turn" in Peacebuilding: A Literature Review of Effective and Emancipatory Local Peacebuilding', *Third World Quarterly,* 36(5), pp. 825–39.

Life and Peace Institute (2018). 'Women, Conflict and Peace: Learning from Kismayo', *Life and Peace Institute, Peace Direct and Somali Women's Solidarity Organization,* available at: https://www.peacedirect.org/wp-content/ uploads/2018/04/Kismayo_Report_WEB2-April-2018.pdf, accessed 19 March 2021.

London School of Economics and Political Science (1995). *A Study of Decentralised Structures for Somalia: A Menu of Options.* London.

Luckham, Robin (2017). 'Whose Violence, Whose Security? Can Violence Reduction and Security Work for Poor, Excluded and Vulnerable People?' *Peacebuilding,* 5(2): 99–117.

Mac Ginty, Roger, and Oliver Richmond (2013). 'The Local Turn in Peace Building: A Critical Agenda for Peace', *Third World Quarterly,* 34(5), pp. 763–83.

Mac Ginty, Roger, and Pamina Firchow (2016). 'Top-Down and Bottom-up Narratives of Peace and Conflict', *Politics,* 36(3), pp. 308–23.

Mahamat, Moussa Fako (2017). Twitter post, 21 December, 1:39pm, available at: https://twitter.com/AUC_MoussaFaki/status/943928984349429762, accessed 19 March 2021.

Mahdi, Hauwa (2008). 'The hijab in Nigeria, the woman's body and the feminist private/public Discourse', unpublished paper, available at https://www.ascleiden.nl/pdf/papermahdi.pdf, accessed 19 March 2021.

Mahmood, Omar S. (2018). 'Women Claim Their Place in Somalia's politics', *ISS Today*, 14 September, available at: https://issafrica.org/iss-today/women-claim-their-place-in-Somalias-politics, accessed 19 March 2021.

Malik, Nesrine (2019). 'She's an Icon of Sudan's Revolution. But the Woman in White Obscures Vital Truths', *The Guardian*, 24 April, available at: https://www.theguardian.com/commentisfree/2019/apr/24/icon-sudan-revolution-woman-in-white, accessed 19 March 2021.

Marzouki, Nadia (2010). 'Algeria', in Sanja Kelly and Julia Breslin (eds.) *Women's Rights in the Middle East and North Africa: Progress Amid Resistance*. New York and Lanham: Freedom House and Rowman & Littlefield.

Mayah, Emmanuel, Chiara Mariotti, Evelyn Mere, and Celestine Okwudili Odo (2017). 'Inequality in Nigeria: Exploring the Drivers', Oxfam International, available at: https://www.oxfam.org/en/research/inequality-nigeria-exploring-drivers, accessed 19 March 2021.

Mayen, Apuk Ayuel (2013). 'Women in Peace Making Processes in South Sudan'. Juba: Sudd Institute, 18 April, available at: https://www.jstor.org/stable/resrep11056, accessed 19 March 2021.

Mazurana, Dyan, and Susan McKay (2002). *Raising Women's Voices for Peacebuilding: Vision, Impact and Limitations of Media Technologies.* London: International Alert.

Mazurana, Dyan E., Susan A. McKay, Khristopher C. Carlson and Janel C. Kasper (2002). 'Girls in Fighting Forces and Groups: Their Recruitment, Participation, Demobilization, and Reintegration', *Peace and Conflict: Journal of Peace Psychology*, 8(2), pp. 97–123, available at: 10.1207/S15327949PAC0802_01, accessed 19 March 2021.

Mbabazi, Donah, and Joan Mbabazi (2018). 'Hashtag Activism: Powerful or Pointless?' *The New Times*, 27 September, available at: https://www.newtimes.co.rw/society/hashtag-activism-powerful-or-pointless, accessed 19 March 2021.

Medar-Gould, Sindi, Chibogu Obinwa, Ngozi Nwosu-Juba, Bunmi Dipo-Salami, Rose Musa, and Monica Ighorodje (2014). *Women's Human Rights in Christian Belief Systems*. Lagos: BAOBAB for Women's Human Rights Nigeria.

Meintjes, Sheila (2001). 'War and Post-War Shifts in Gender Relations', in Sheila Meintjes, Anu Pillay, and Meredith Turshen (eds.) *The Aftermath: Women in PostConflict Transformation*. London: Zed Books, pp. 63–77.

Mesbah, Salim (2019). 'Trois questions à Melissa Ziad, danseuse classique et model: "cette photographie représente l'Algérie d'aujourd'hui"', *Al Huffpost Maghreb*, 3 March, available at: https://www.huffpostmaghreb.com/entry/trois-questions-a-melissa-ziad-danseuse-classique-et-model-cette-photographie-represente-l-algerie-d-aujourd-hui_mg_5c80f8cbe4b0e62f69ea1abe, accessed 19 March 2021.

Messaoudi, Khalida, and Elisabeth Schemla (1995). *Une algérienne debout: entretiens avec Elisabeth Schemla*. Paris: Flammarion.

Ministry of Gender, Child and Social Welfare (MOGCSW) (2012). 'South Sudan National Gender Policy'.

Modi, Roger Alfred (2018). 'South Sudan Revised Governance Deal', *Sudan Tribune*, 27 June, available at: http://www.sudantribune.com/spip.php?article65741, accessed 19 March 2021.

Moghadam, Valentine M. (2018). 'Explaining Divergent Outcomes of the Arab Spring: The Significance of Gender and Women's Mobilizations', *Politics, Groups, and Identities,* 6(4), pp. 668–81.

Mohamud, Maimuna (2015). 'The Politics and Civic Engagement of Somali women', The Heritage Institute for Policy Studies, Mogadishu, available at: http://www.heritageinstitute.org/the-political-and-civic-engagement-of-somali-women, accessed 19 March 2021.

Mohiedeen, Naba (2019). 'Sudan's Ruling Council Appoints 1st Woman Chief Justice', *VOA News,* 16 September, available at: https://www.voanews.com/africa/sudans-ruling-council-appoints-1st-woman-chief-justice, accessed 19 March 2021.

Molyneux Maxine (1998). 'Analysing Women's Movement', *Development and Change,* 29(2), pp. 219–45.

Mueller-Hirth, Natascha (2018). 'Women's Experiences of Peacebuilding in Violence-Affected Communities in Kenya', *Third World Quarterly,* 40(1), pp. 163–79.

Muggah, Robert, and José Luengo Cabrera (2019). 'The Sahel Is Engulfed by Violence. Climate Change, Food Insecurity and Extremists Are Largely to Blame'. Geneva: World Economic Forum, available at: https://www.weforum.org/agenda/2019/01/all-the-warning-signs-are-showing-in-the-sahel-we-must-act-now, accessed 19 March 2021.

Murdie, Amanda, and Dursun Peksen (2014). 'Women and Contentious Politics: A Global Event-Data Approach to Understanding Women's Protest', *Political Research Quarterly* 68(1), pp. 180–92.

Mustapha, Abdul Raufu (ed.) (2017). *Sects & Social Disorder: Muslim Identities & Conflict in Northern Nigeria.* Reprint edition. Suffolk: James Currey.

Mustapha, Abdul Raufu, and David Ehrhardt (eds.) (2018). *Creed & Grievance: Muslim-Christian Relations & Conflict Resolution in Northern Nigeria.* Suffolk: James Currey.

Mustapha, Abdul Raufu, and Kate Meagher (eds.) (2020). *Overcoming Boko Haram: Faith, Society & Islamic Radicalization in Northern Nigeria.* Suffolk: James Currey.

Mutawinaat (1997). 'Review of Sudanese Legislation Discriminating against Women', unpublished report, Khartoum (on file with author).

Na'im, Abdullahi A. (2002). *Islamic Family Law in a Changing World: A Global Resource Book.* New York: Zed Books.

Nabukeera-Musoke, H. (2009). 'Transitional Justice and Gender in Uganda: Making Peace, Failing Women During the Peace Negotiation Process', in *Views from the Field: Transitional Justice and Gender in Uganda,* AJCR 2009/2, available at: https://www.accord.org.za/ajcr-issues/transitional-justice-and-gender-in-uganda, accessed 19 March 2021.

Nagarajan, Chitra (2017). 'Gender Assessment of Northeast Nigeria', Managing Conflict in North East Nigeria (MCN), available at: https://chitrasudhanagarajan.files.wordpress.com/2018/03/gender-assessment-of-northeast-nigeria.pdf, accessed 19 March 2021.

Nageeb, Salma Ahmed (2004). *New Spaces and Old Frontiers: Women, Social Space, and Islamization in Sudan.* Lanham: Lexington Books.

Naples, Nancy A. (1998). *Grassroots Warriors: Activist Mothering, Community Work, and the War on Poverty.* Perspectives on Gender. New York: Routledge.

Nazneen, Sohela, and Sam Hickey (2019). 'Beyond the Inclusion-to-Influence Debate: The Politics of Negotiating Gender Equity', in Sohela Nazneen, Sam

Hickey and Elini Sifaki (eds.) *Negotiating Gender Equity in the Global South: The Politics of Domestic Violence Policy.* London and New York: Routledge.

Newman, Roland Paris, and Oliver P. Richmond (eds.) (2009). *New Perspectives on Liberal Peacebuilding.* New York: United Nations University Press.

Ní Aoláin, Fionnuala, Dina Francesca Haynes, and Naomi Cahn (2012). 'Women in the Post-Conflict Process: Reviewing the Impact of Recent UN Actions in Achieving Gender Centrality', *Santa Clara Law Review,* 11(1), pp. 189–217.

Nilsson, Desirée (2012). 'Anchoring the Peace: Civil Society Actors in Peace Accords and Durable Peace', *International Interactions,* 38(2), pp. 243–66.

Nugdalla, Sarah O. (2020). 'The Revolution Continues: Sudanese Women's Activism', in Okech A (ed.) *Gender, Protests and Political Change in Africa.* Gender, Development and Social Change book series. London: Palgrave Macmillan, Cham.

Nwangwu, Chikodiri, and Christian Ezeibe (2019). 'Femininity is Not Inferiority: Women-Led Civil Society Organizations and "Countering Violent Extremism" in Nigeria,' *International Feminist Journal of Politics* 21(2), pp. 168–93.

Nyathon, J. H. M. (2015). 'The Role of Women in Peacebuilding in South Sudan', SUDD Institute, available at: https://reliefweb.int/report/south-sudan/role-women-peace-building-south-sudan, accessed 19 March 2021.

Ogunmade, Omololu (2019). 'Nigeria: Leah Sharibu's Freedom Hindered by Boko Haram's Fear of "Heavy Military Presence", Says Buhari', *This Day, All Africa,* 13 April, available at: https://allafrica.com/stories/201904130364.html, accessed 19 March 2021.

OHCHR (2007). *Consideration of Reports Submitted by States Parties under Article 40 of the Covenant: Concluding Observations of the Human Rights Committee.* CCPR/C/SDN/CO/3/CRP.1, Geneva, 26 July, available at: https://www.securitycouncilreport.org/atf/cf/%7B65BFCF9B-6D27-4E9C-8CD3-CF6E4FF96FF9%7D/Sudan%20CCPR.C.SDN.CO.3.CRP.1.pdf, accessed 19 March 2021.

Okoli, Al Chukwuma, and Stephen Nnaemeka Azom (2019). 'Boko Haram Insurgency and Gendered Victimhood: Women as Corporal Victims and Objects Of War', *Small Wars & Insurgencies,* published online September, available at: https://www.tandfonline.com/doi/abs/10.1080/09592318.2019.1650473?journalCode=fswi20 and https://doi.org/10.1080/09592318.2019.1650473, accessed 19 March 2021.

Olidort, Jacob (2015). 'The Politics of "Quietist" Salafism', Brookings Institution, Brookings Project on US Relations with the Islamic World, No. 18, February.

Otto, Dianne (2006). 'A sign of "weakness"? Disrupting gender uncertainties in the implementation of Security Council Resolution 1325', *Michigan Journal of International Law,* 13, pp. 113–75.

Oulahbib, Lucien-Samir (2016). 'Nationalisme arabe et islamisme, les deux faces d'une même médaille', Mondesfrancophone.com, available at https://mondesfrancophones.com/espaces/politiques/nationalisme-arabe-et-islamisme-les-deux-faces-d'une-meme-medaille, accessed 19 March 2021.

Paffenholz, Thania, Nick Ross, Steven Dixon, Anna-Lena Schluchter, and Jacqui True (2016). *Making Women Count – Not Just Counting Women: Assessing Women's Inclusion and Influence on Peace Negotiations,* Inclusive Peace and Transition Initiative. Geneva: The Graduate Institute of International and Development Studies and UN Women.

Pankhurst, Donna (2008). 'Post-War Backlash Violence against Women: What Can

"Masculinity" Explain?' in Donna Pankhurst (ed.) *Gendered Peace Women's Struggles for Post-War Justice and Reconciliation.* New York: Routledge.

Parke, A., S. Stevens, M. Walls, S. Ali, S. Butterfield, C. Elder, D. Le Deaut (2017). *Somali Women's Political Participation and Leadership: Evidence and Opportunities,* U. K. Department of International Development. London: Social Development Direct and Forcier Consulting.

Partners in Development Services (PDS) (2009). 'Mapping and Capacity Assessment of Civil Society Organizations (CSOs) In Darfur', UNDP: Sudan Office.

Patinkin, Jason (2017). 'Somali Rape Law Gets First Test', *Voice of America,* 25 January, available at: https://www.voanews.com/africa/somali-rape-law-gets-first-test, accessed 19 March 2021.

Paulson-Smith, Kaden, and Aili Mari Tripp (forthcoming). 'Women's Rights and Critical Junctures in Constitutional Reform in Africa (1951–2019)'.

Paxton, Pamela, and Melanie M. Hughes (2017). *Women, Politics and Power: A Global Perspective,* 2nd ed. Thousand Oaks: Sage Publications.

Pedersen, Jennifer (2008). 'In the Rain and in the Sun: Women in Peacebuilding in Liberia', paper presented at the annual meeting of the ISA's 49th Annual Convention, 'Bridging Multiple Divides', Hilton San Francisco, San Francisco, CA, USA, 26 March.

Pepper, Mollie (2018). 'Ethnic Minority Women, Diversity, and Informal Participation in Peacebuilding in Myanmar', *Journal of Peacebuilding & Development,* 13(2), pp. 61–75.

Peterson, V. Spike (1992). 'Security and Sovereign States: What is at Stake in Taking Feminism Seriously?' in V. Spike Peterson (ed.) *Gendered States: (Re)Visions of Feminist International Relations Theory.* Boulder: Lynne Rienner, pp. 31–64.

Peterson, V. Spike, and Anne Sisson Runyan (1999). *Global Gender Issues.* Boulder: Westview Publishers.

Pew Research Center (2013). 'Muslim Publics Share Concerns about Extremist Groups', *Pew Research Center's Global Attitudes Project* (blog), 10 September, available at: https://www.pewresearch.org/global/2013/09/10/muslim-publics-share-concerns-about-extremist-groups, accessed 19 March 2021.

Pitkin, Hanna Fenichel (1967). *The Concept of Representation.* Berkeley: University of California Press.

Porter, Elisabeth (2007). *Peacebuilding: Women in International Perspective.* New York: Routledge.

Pratt, Nicola, and Sophie Richter-Devroe (2011). 'Critically Examining UNSCR 1325 on Women, Peace and Security', *International Feminist Journal of Politics,* 13(4), pp. 489–503.

Pring, Coralie, and Jon Vrushi (2019). *Global Corruption Barometer Africa 2019: Citizens' Views and Experiences of Corruption.* Berlin, Germany: Transparency International, available at: https://www.afrobarometer.org/publications/global-corruption-barometer-africa-2019-citizens-views-and-experiences-corruption, accessed 19 March 2021.

Puig, Larrauri, H. and A. Kahl, (2013). 'Technology for Peacebuilding', *Stability: International Journal of Security and Development,* 2(3), p. 61.

Qasim, Maryam Arif (2000). 'IRIN Interview with Maryam Arif Qasim, Member of Somalia's Transitional Parliament', 4 September, available at: https://www.thenewhumanitarian.org/news/2000/09/04/irin-interview-maryam-arif-qasim-member-somalia%E2%80%99s, accessed 19 March 2021.

Rachidi, Ilhem (2007). 'New Law Leaves Divorced Algerian Women Homeless',

Women's E-News, 7 November, available at: https://womensenews.org/2007/03/new-law-leaves-divorced-algerian-women-homeless, accessed 19 March 2021.

Rahmouni, Zahra (2018). 'Algérie: elle voulait faire son footing, il la frappe et lui dit que "sa place est dans une cuisine"', *Jeune Afrique*, 11 June.

Randazzo, Elisa (2016). 'The Paradoxes of the "Everyday": Scrutinising the Local Turn in Peace Building', *Third World Quarterly*, 37(8), pp. 1351–70.

Rayale, Siham, Ed Pomfret, and Deborah Wright (2015). *Somali Solutions, Creating Conditions for a Gender-Just Peace.* Oxford: Oxfam.

Redress and KCHRED (Khartoum Center for Human Rights and Environmental Development) (2020). 'Sudan Legal amendments: Explanatory Table', Redress, available at: https://redress.org/wp-content/uploads/2020/07/3-REDRESS-Sudan-Legal-Amendments-July-2020-Explanatory-Table.pdf, accessed 19 March 2021.

Reilly, Niamh (2018). 'How Ending Impunity for Conflict-Related Sexual Violence Overwhelmed the UN Women, Peace, and Security Agenda: A Discursive Genealogy', *Violence Against Women*, 24(6), pp. 631–49.

Reis, Chen, and Marie E. Berry (2019). 'How Do You Reduce Sexual and Gender Violence in Conflict? Consider These Five Key Issues', *Washington Post (Monkey Cage)*, 22 May.

Republic of South Sudan (2015). 'South Sudan National Action Plan 2015–2020 on UNSCR1325 on Women, Peace and Security and Related Resolutions', available at: https://gnwp.org/wp-content/uploads/SS-NAP-.pdf, accessed 19 March 2021.

Rigual, Christelle (2018). 'Rethinking the Ontology of Peacebuilding. Gender, Spaces and the Limits of the Local Turn', *Peacebuilding*, 6(2), pp. 144–69.

Ruddick, Sara (1995). *Maternal Thinking: Toward a Politics of Peace; with a New Preface.* Boston: Beacon Press.

Rupp, Leila J. (1997). *Worlds of Women: The Making of an International Women's Movement.* Princeton: Princeton University Press.

Sabra, Martina (2012). 'Interview with the Algerian Women's Rights Activist Nadia Ait Zai: "We need to completely change the system of government"', *Qantara. de*, 14 June, available at: http://en.qantara.de/We-need-to-completely-change-the-system-of-government/19321c20433i1p497, accessed 19 March 2021.

Sada, Ibrahim Naiya, Fatima L. Adamu, and Ali Ahmad (2005). 'Promoting Women's Rights through Sharia in Northern Nigeria', The British Council and UK Department for International Development, available at: http://www.ungei.org/resources/files/dfid_promoting_womens_rights.pdf, accessed 19 March 2021.

Sadiqi, Fatima (ed.) (2016). *Women's Movements in Post-'Arab Spring' North Africa.* Comparative Feminist Studies Series, New York: Palgrave Macmillan/Springer.

Salah, Alaa (2019). 'Statement to the UN Security Council Open Debate on Women, Peace and Security', *UN Women*, 29 October, available at: https://www.unwomen.org/en/news/stories/2019/10/speech--alaa-salah-at-the-open-debate-on-wps, accessed 19 March 2021.

Salah, Walaa (2015). 'Amendments to Sudanese Criminal Law', *Open Democracy*, 30 April, available at: https://www.opendemocracy.net/arab-awakening/walaa-salah/new-amendments-to-sudanese-criminal-law, accessed 19 March 2021.

Salhi, Zahia Smail (2010). 'The Algerian feminist movement between nationalism, patriarchy and Islamism', *Women's Studies International Forum*, 33, pp. 113–24.

Salhi, Zahia Smail (2011). 'Gender and Violence in Algeria Women's Resistance against the Islamist Femicide', University of Leeds public lecture, 31 January.

Salih, Zeinab Mohammed (2019). '"I was raised to love our home": Sudan's singing protester speaks out', *The Guardian*, 10 April, available at: https://www.theguardian.com/global-development/2019/apr/10/alaa-salah-sudanese-woman-talks-about-protest-photo-that-went-viral, accessed 19 March 2021.

Sharkey, Heather J. (2014). 'Review: Language Conflict in Algeria: From Colonialism to Post-Independence', *Journal of French Language Studies*, 24(2), pp. 317–18.

Sharoni, Simona (2001). 'Rethinking Women's Struggles in Israel–Palestine', in Caroline Moser and Fiona Clark (eds.) *Victims, Perpetrators or Actors: Gender, Armed Conflict and Political Violence*. Oxford: Zed Books, pp. 85–98.

Sheikh-Abdi, Abdi (1993). *Divine Madness: Mohammed Abdulle Hassan (1856–1920)*. London: Zed Books.

Shepherd, Laura (2008). *Gender, Violence and Security: Discourse as Practice*. New York: Zed Books.

Shepherd, Laura (2011). 'Sex, Security and Superhero(in)es: From 1325 to 1820 and Beyond', *International Feminist Journal of Politics*, 13(4), pp. 504–21.

Singerman, Diane (2013). 'Youth, Gender, and Dignity in the Egyptian Uprising', *Journal of Middle East Women's Studies*, 9(3), pp. 1–27.

Sisk, Timothy D., and Anna K. Jarstad (eds.) (2010). *From War to Democracy: Dilemmas of Peacebuilding*. New York: Cambridge University Press.

Skjelsbæk, Inger (2001). 'Is Femininity Inherently Peaceful? The Construction of Femininity', in Inger Skjelsbæk and Dan Smith (eds.) *Gender, Peace and Conflict*. London: Sage, pp. 47–67.

Smail, Philippe (2019). 'Cannes 2019. Papicha de la réalisatrice Mounia Meddour: Ces belles et rebelles Algériennes', *El Watan*, 21 May, available at: https://www.elwatan.com/edition/culture/cannes-2019-papicha-de-la-realisatrice-mounia-meddour-ces-belles-et-rebelles-algeriennes-21-05-2019, accessed 19 March 2021.

Southern African Liaison Office (SALO) (2018). 'SawaSouthSudan virtual summit connecting women activists in South Sudan to leaders from around the world', 25 May, available at: https://www.salo.org.za/sawasouthsudan-virtual-summit-connecting-women-activists-in-south-sudan-to-leaders-from-around-the-world, accessed 19 March 2021.

Strategic Initiative for Women in the Horn of Africa (SIHA) (2009). 'Beyond Trousers: The Public Order Regime and the Human Rights of Women and Girls in Sudan. Submission to the 46th Ordinary Session of the African Commission on Human and Peoples' Rights, Banjul, the Gambia', available at: https://www.peacewomen.org/sites/default/files/vaw_publicorderrecs_siha_nov2009.pdf, accessed 19 March 2021.

Sudan (2019). 'Draft Constitutional Charter for the 2019 Transitional Period', 4 August, available at: https://www.docdroid.net/GifnnTU/sudan-constitutional-declaration-2019-english.pdf, accessed 19 March 2021.

Sudanese Organization for Research and Development (SORD) (2012). 'Towards Gender Justice in Sudan: Proposed Family Law 2012'. Khartoum: SORD.

Sudanese Organization for Research and Development (SORD) (2020). *Her Resistance. A Book of Documentation for Stories and Experiences of Girls and Women in 2018 Revolution*. Khartoum: SORD and Urgent Action Fund Africa.

Swerdlow, Amy (1993). *Women Strike for Peace: Traditional Motherhood and Radical Politics in the 1960s*. Women in Culture and Society. Chicago: University of Chicago Press.

Tamir, Christine (2019). 'As Elections near, Nigerians View Their Country's Economy and Political System Negatively', *Pew Research Center* (blog), 12 February, available at: https://www.pewresearch.org/fact-tank/2019/02/12/as-elections-near-nigerians-view-their-countrys-economy-and-political-system-negatively, accessed 19 March 2021.

Taylor, Diana (1997). 'Making a Spectacle: The Mothers of the Plaza de Mayo', in Alexis Jetter, Annelise Orleck, and Diana Taylor (eds.) *The Politics of Motherhood: Activist Voices from Left to Right*. Hanover: University Press of New England for Dartmouth College, pp. 182–97.

The Federal Republic of Somalia (2012). *Provisional Constitution,* available at: http://hrlibrary.umn.edu/research/Somalia-Constitution2012.pdf, accessed 19 March 2021.

Tickner, Ann J. (1992). *Gender in International Relations: Feminist Perspectives on Achieving Global Security*. New York: Columbia University Press.

Tier, Akolda M., and Balghis Badri (eds.) (2008). *Law Reform in Sudan: Collection of Workshop papers*. Omdurman: Ahfad University for Women.

Tilly, Charles (1978). *From Mobilization to Revolution*. New York: Addison-Wesley.

Timmons, Debra M. (2004). *The Sixth Clan – Women Organize for Peace in Somalia: A Review of Published Literature*. Switzerland: University of Peace.

Tønnessen, Liv, (2011). 'The Many Faces of Political Islam in Sudan: Muslim Women's Activism for and against the State', PhD dissertation. Bergen: University of Bergen.

Tønnessen, Liv (2013). 'Between Sharia and CEDAW in Sudan: Islamist women negotiating gender equity', in Rachel Sieder and John McNeish (eds.) *Gender Justice and Legal Pluralities: Latin American and African Perspectives*. New York: Routledge-Cavendish.

Tønnessen, Liv (2014). 'When Rape becomes Politics: Negotiating Islamic Law Reform in Sudan', *Women's Studies International Forum*, 44, pp. 145–53.

Tønnessen, Liv (2017). 'Enemies of the State: Curbing Women Activists Advocating Rape Reform in Sudan', *Journal of International Women's Studies*, 18(2), pp. 143–55, available at: https://www.cmi.no/publications/5974-enemies-of-the-state, accessed 19 March 2021.

Tønnessen, Liv (2018). 'An Increasing Number of Muslim Women in Politics: A Step towards Complementarity, Not Equality', CMI Brief No. 2018: 3. Bergen: Chr. Michelsen Institute, available at: https://www.cmi.no/publications/6534-increasing-number-of-muslim-women-in-politics, accessed: March 19, 2021.

Tønnessen, Liv (2019). 'Women at Work in Sudan: Marital Privilege or Constitutional Right', *Social Politics: International Studies in Gender, State and Society*, 26(2), pp. 223–44.

Tønnessen, Liv, and Samia al-Nagar (2013). 'The Women's Quota in Conflict Ridden Sudan: Ideological Battles for and against Gender Equality', *Women's Studies International Forum*, 41(2), pp. 122–131.

Tønnessen, Liv, and Samia al-Nagar (2019). 'Sexual Violence Does Not Stop Sudan's Women from Speaking Up', *Sudan Blog*, Chr. Michelsen Institute, 4 September, available at: https://www.cmi.no/publications/6999-sexual-violence-does-not-stop-sudans-women-from-speaking-up, accessed 19 March 2021.

Tønnessen, Liv, and Samia al-Nagar (2020). 'Patriarchy, Politics and Women's Activism in Post-Revolution Sudan', Bergen: Chr. Michelsen Institute, Sudan Brief 2020:02, available at: https://www.cmi.no/publications/7267-patriarchy-politics-and-womens-activism-in-post-revolution-sudan, accessed 19 March 2021.

Tripp, Aili Mari (2010). 'Legislating Gender-Based Violence in Post-Conflict Africa', *Journal of Peacebuilding & Development,* 5(3), pp. 7–20.

Tripp, Aili Mari. (2015). *Women and Power in Postconflict Africa.* Cambridge Studies in Gender and Politics. New York: Cambridge University Press.

Tripp, Aili Mari. (2019). 'Beyond Islamist Extremism: Women and the Algerian Uprisings of 2019'. Bergen: Chr. Michelsen Institute, CMI Brief No. 2019:09, available at: https://www.cmi.no/publications/6983-beyond-islamist-extremism-women-and-the-algerian-uprisings-of-2019, accessed 19 March 2021.

Tripp, Aili Mari. (2019). *Seeking Legitimacy.* Cambridge: Cambridge University Press.

Tripp, Aili Mari, Isabel Casimiro, Joy Kwesiga, and Alice Mungwa (2009). *African Women's Movements: Transforming Political Landscapes.* New York: Cambridge University Press.

Turshen, Meredeth. (2001). 'Engendering Relations of States to Societies in the Aftermath – Meredeth Turshen', in Sheila Meintjes, Anu Pillay, and Meredeth Turshen (eds.) *The Aftermath: Women in Post-Conflict Transformation.* London: Zed Books, pp. 63–77.

UNICEF and International Alert (2016). *'Bad Blood': Perceptions of Children Born of Conflict-Related Sexual Violence and Women and Girls Associated with Boko Haram in Northeast Nigeria,* available at: https://www.international-alert.org/sites/default/files/Nigeria_BadBlood_EN_2016.pdf, accessed 19 March 2021.

UN Office of the High Commissioner for Human Rights (2015). 'Access to Justice for Victims of Sexual Violence', United Nations High Commissioner for Human Rights, available at: https://www.refworld.org/docid/46cc4a650.html, accessed 19 March 2021.

UN Women (2015). *Africa – South Sudan,* available at: http://africa.unwomen.org/en/where-we-are/eastern-and-southern-africa/south-sudan, accessed 19 March 2021.

UN Women (2019). *Global Gender Equality Constitutional Database,* available at: https://constitutions.unwomen.org, accessed 19 March 2021.

UN Women (*n.d.*). '16 Days of Activism against Gender-Based Violence', available at: https://www.unwomen.org/en/what-we-do/ending-violence-against-women/take-action/16-days-of-activism, accessed 19 March 2021.

United Nations (2002). *Women, Peace and Security: Study Submitted by the Secretary-General Pursuant to Security Council Resolution 1325 (2000),* available at: https://www.un.org/womenwatch/daw/public/eWPS.pdf, accessed 19 March 2021.

United Nations (2003). *Intercongolese Negotiations: The Final Act (Sun City Agreement),* UN Peacemaker, available at: https://peacemaker.un.org/drc-suncity-agreement2003, accessed 19 March 2021.

United Nations (*n.d.*). *Women in Peacekeeping: A Key to Peace,* available at: https://Peacekeeping.Un.Org/En/Women-Peacekeeping, accessed 19 March 2021.

UNOCHA (2016). *2016 South Sudan Humanitarian Needs Overview,* available at: https://reliefweb.int/report/south-sudan/2016-south-sudan-humanitarian-needs-overview, accessed 19 March 2021.

Verduzier, Pauline (2015). 'En Algérie, une campagne incite les hommes à voiler leur femme pour être plus virils', *Le Figaro,* 26 May, available at: http://madame.lefigaro.fr/societe/sois-un-homme-la-campagne-anti-jupe-qui-agace-lalgerie-260515-96699, accessed 19 March 2021.

Verjee, Aly (2017). *South Sudan's High Level Revitalization Forum: Identifying conditions for success*, US Institute for Peace, Peacebrief, available at: https://www.usip.org/sites/default/files/PB228-South-Sudan-s-High-Level-Revitalization-Forum.pdf, accessed 19 March 2021.

Wahba, Dina (2016). 'Gendering the Egyptian Revolution', in Sadiqi, Fatima (ed.) *Women's Movements in Post-'Arab Spring' North Africa*, Comparative Feminist Studies Series. New York: Palgrave Macmillan/Springer, pp. 61–76.

Waller, Marguerite, and Jennifer Rycenga (eds.) (2001). *Frontline Feminisms: Women, War, and Resistance.* New York: Routledge.

Webster, Kaitlyn, Chong Chen, and Kyle Beardsley (2019). 'Conflict, Peace, and the Evolution of Women's Empowerment', *International Organization, 73*, pp. 255–89.

Wesely, Marissa, and Dina Dublon (2015). 'Empowering women at the Grassroots', available at: https://ssir.org/articles/entry/empowering_women_at_the_grassroots, accessed 19 March 2021.

Westendorf, Jasmine Kim (2018). 'Peace Negotiations in the Political Marketplace: The Implications of Women's Exclusion in the Sudan–South Sudan Peace Process', *Australian Journal of International Affairs*, 72(5), p: 433–54.

Willis, Michael (1996). *The Islamist Challenge in Algeria: A Political History.* Ithaca: Ithaca Press.

Willis, Michael J. 1999. 'Between alternance and the Makhzen: At-Tawhid wa Al-Islah's entry into Moroccan politics', in *The Journal of North African Studies*, 4(3): 45–80.

Willis, Michael J. (2012). *Politics and power in the Maghreb: Algeria, Tunisia and Morocco from independence to the Arab spring.* New York: Columbia University Press.

World Bank (2015). *Morocco – Mind the Gap: Empowering Women for a More Open, Inclusive and Prosperous Society.* Washington: World Bank.

World Health Organization and World Bank (eds.) (2011). *World Report on Disability.* Geneva, Switzerland: World Health Organization, available at: https://www.who.int/disabilities/world_report/2011/report.pdf, accessed 19 March 2021.

Zanaz, Hamid (2019). 'After Protests, Algerian Women Reconquer the Public Space', *The Arab Weekly*, 28 April, available at: https://thearabweekly.com/after-protests-algerian-women-reconquer-public-space, accessed 19 March 2021.

INDEX

maternal peace, 7
Mauritania, 20, 57, 144–5
Mbagathi Reconciliation Conference
  2004 (Somalia), 80
militarism, 5, 7, 36
military, 5–7, 9, 14, 23–4, 26, 54, 56,
  62, 65, 68, 73–4, 82, 90, 103, 105–7
military, women in, 9
Ministry of Gender, Child, and Social
  Welfare (South Sudan), 35
Monthly Women's Forum, 51
Mother's Union (South Sudan), 39, 40
motherhood, 7, 19, 27, 34, 154–55
mothering, 7, 150
Movement of Society for Peace (MSP),
  136–7
Mozambique, 15
MSP *see* Movement of Society for
  Peace
Muslim Brotherhood
  Algeria, 136
  Egypt ,131
  Somalia, 87
Muslim Family Law (Sudan), 111

Nagaad Network (Somalia), 96
Nasser, President Gamal Abdul, 131
National Assembly representation
  of women *see* parliamentary
  representation of women
National Dialogue, 32, 39
National Liberation Front (FLN), 21,
  28–9, 33
National Rally for Democracy (RND),
  33
National Reconciliation Conference in
  Addis Ababa, 14
National Umma Party, 21
nationalism, 7, 19, 26, 73
Nazi Germany, 7
Niger, 20, 24, 53, 57, 76
Nigeria, 2, 3, 15, 16, 17, 20, 25, 26, 48,
  53–78
nonconforming gender and sexuality,
  6
Noon movement, 109, 24
Norwegian Refugee Council, 64
Nuer, 18, 29, 42, 50, 56

Obama, President Barack, 23
Organisation for Economic Co-
  operation and Development
  (OECD), 23, 25
Osman, Amira, 18
Overseas Development Assistance, 23
  see also donors

parliament, representation of women,
  2, 11–5, 17, 20, 22, 25
  Algeria, 134–6, 141–2, 144, 145, 151–2
  Nigeria, 65–6
  South Sudan, 14, 29–31, 33, 45–6,
    50
  Somalia, 80, 84, 86–7, 90, 97–101
  Sudan, 104, 107, 109–10, 117, 127
pastoralists, 19
patronage networks, 16
peace accords *see* peace agreements
peace agreements, 3, 4, 5, 9, 10, 11, 12,
  14, 19 38, 48, 76, 96
  women as advisers, 26
  women as mediators, 11–2, 33, 58,
    63
  women as signatories, peace
    agreements, 11, 12, 33
  women as observers, peace
    agreements, 4, 9, 13, 14, 26, 33, 97
peacebuilding, exclusion of women,
  2–4, 12–3, 15, 19, 23–4, 30, 34,
  53, 65–6, 80–8, 98, 105, 124–26,
  149–58
peacebuilding, as gendered, 4, 6, 8, 26
Peace Building Committee, Wau
  (South Sudan), 51
Peace negotiations, 1- 4, 8–9, 11–19,
  26,
  observer status, women, 13
  Somalia, 85, 96,
  South Sudan, 29–30, 34, 36–37, 42,
    44–5, 48–9, 76,
  Sudan, 105
peace talks *see* peace negotiations
peacekeeping, 1, 2, 3, 6, 7, 9, 22, 24
Personal Status Code *see* Family Law
police force, women in, 9
polygamy *see* polygyny
polygyny, 54, 132, 134, 143
power-sharing system, 80, 82, 97
prayer vigils, 19, 35, 38–9, 41–2
Preventing and Countering Violent
  Extremism, 23
protests, 3, 7, 17, 20, 30, 35, 37, 38, 43,
  50, 56, 63, 94, 103–9
psychosocial support, 16, 55, 64–5, 75
Public Order Laws, 15, 17, 25, 59, 111
Puntland, 80, 95–100

quotas, 9, 10, 20, 26, 41

reserved seats for women, 126–7, 144,
rape, 42, 55, 59, 61, 77, 93, 95, 12, 13,
  14, 16, 42, 59, 72